Praise for Thomas
7 Kinds of S

"Armstrong's book is a rich dish of ideas for
exploring those other ways of becoming more
intelligent . . . ways that are so often neglected in
our culture. Every reader should dip in with gusto."
—Betty Edwards, author of
Drawing on the Right Side of the Brain

"*7 Kinds of Smart* makes a major contribution to
our understanding of the wide scope of intelligence.
I'm going to tell my friends and clients to run,
not walk, to the bookstore to get this book."
—Muriel James, co-author of
Born to Win and *Passion for Life*

"Armstrong issues us a lifetime pass for honoring
the intelligence we possess, and he also offers
advice on how to add breadth and richness to
experience. So long to boredom and living in ruts.
We have permission to be free."
—Robert Samples, author of
The Metaphoric Mind

THOMAS ARMSTRONG, PH.D., is the author of seven books,
including *The Myth of the A.D.D. Child, In Their Own
Way,* and *Awakening Your Child's Natural Genius.* A former special education teacher, he has written frequently
on parenting and education issues for publications such
as *Ladies' Home Journal* and *Family Circle.* He lives in
Sonoma County, California.

ALSO BY THOMAS ARMSTRONG

The Myth of the A.D.D. Child
The Radiant Child
In Their Own Way
Awakening Your Child's Natural Genius

THOMAS ARMSTRONG, Ph.D.

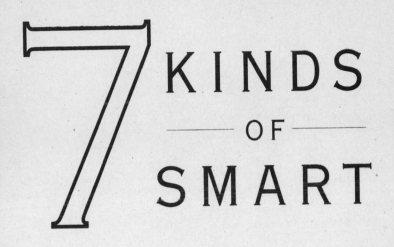

7 KINDS OF SMART

IDENTIFYING AND DEVELOPING YOUR MULTIPLE INTELLIGENCES

Revised and Updated with Information on 2 New Kinds of Smart

A PLUME BOOK

PLUME
Published by New American Library, a division of
Penguin Putnam Inc., 375 Hudson Street,
New York, New York 10014, U.S.A.
Penguin Books Ltd, 27 Wrights Lane,
London W8 5TZ, England
Penguin Books Australia Ltd, Ringwood,
Victoria, Australia
Penguin Books Canada Ltd, 10 Alcorn Avenue,
Toronto, Ontario, Canada M4V 3B2
Penguin Books (N.Z.) Ltd, 182–190 Wairau Road,
Auckland 10, New Zealand

Penguin Books Ltd, Registered Offices:
Harmondsworth, Middlesex, England

First published by Plume, an imprint of New American Library,
a division of Penguin Putnam Inc.

First Printing, March, 1993
First Printing (Revised and Updated Edition), October, 1999
10   9   8   7

 REGISTERED TRADEMARK—MARCA REGISTRADA

LIBRARY OF CONGRESS CATALOGING-IN-PUBLICATION DATA:

Armstrong, Thomas.
    7 kinds of smart : identifying and developing your multiple intelligences
Thomas Armstrong.—Rev. and updated ed.
        p. cm.
    Includes bibliographical references and index.
    ISBN 0-452-28137-7
    1. Ability.   2. Intellect.   3. Tyupology (Psychology)   I. Title.   II. Title: Seven
kinds of smart
    BF431 .A579 1999
    153.9—dc21   99-34423
                                                                        CIP
Printed in the United States of America
Set in Copperplate, Futura and Garamond Light
Designed by Steven N. Stathakis

BOOKS ARE AVAILABLE AT QUANTITY DISCOUNTS WHEN USED TO PROMOTE PRODUCTS OR SER-
VICES. FOR INFORMATION PLEASE WRITE TO PREMIUM MARKETING DIVISION, PENGUIN PUTNAM
INC., 375 HUDSON STREET, NEW YORK, NEW YORK 10014.

For my wife, Brahmi

CONTENTS

ACKNOWLEDGMENTS

My thanks go out in particular to three people who were instrumental in the creation of this book. First, my agent, Linda Allen, who patiently led me through the publishing labyrinth to find the right house for this book. Second, my editor, Rachel Klayman, whose intellectual curiosity and linguistic acumen contributed significantly to the final product. Third, and most important, Dr. Howard Gardner, who quietly supported me for several years, sharing bibliographies, unpublished papers, and working drafts, as well as his words of wisdom on the phone in letters, and via e-mail. Thanks also to Deb Brody and John Paine for their invaluable assistance in preparing the updated version of this book. I also want to thank several individuals who influenced me or supported me in one way or another during the incubation, research, and writing of this book, a period that spanned many years. They include: DeLee Lantz, Robert McKim, Mert Hanley, Sue Teele, Sally

Smith, Dee Dickinson, Roger Peters, Kurt Meyer, Frank Barr, Lawrence Greene, David Thornburg, Richard Bolles, Maggie Strong, and Coby Schasfoort. Thanks also to the thousands of participants in my MI workshops over the years whose questions and comments helped me articulate MI theory and make it practical and useful to all learners.

PREFACE

How intelligent are you? Chances are your answer to this question centers on tests and school-related skills. Maybe you've taken a ten-minute quiz in a popular magazine that involved solving problems like "x is to y as b is to_____" or that asked you to provide the definitions to words such as *curmudgeon* and *mutafacient*. Perhaps you took an intelligence test in school or as a part of a job application. The concepts of IQ and intelligence exert a powerful hold on the imaginations of millions of Americans. To have a low IQ or to lack smarts in our society is to risk being labeled *retarded* or worse. In fact, many of our culture's grimiest epithets, including *moron, idiot,* and *imbecile,* were at one time regarded as scientifically correct ways of describing individuals who scored at the low end of the intelligence-testing curve. On the other hand, to be considered *gifted* or a *genius* (achieving an IQ score of 140 or more) is to enjoy the accolades of a society that provides perks for the best and brightest among us: Ivy League schools, advanced degrees, high incomes, and more. It's no wonder, then, that many of us still lie awake at night wondering what our IQ scores really are.

This book won't help you raise your IQ score. Nor will it assist you in preparing for the SAT, LSAT, ACT, or any of a host of other socially valued tests. Although a few items in this book do mimic those on intelligence and academic tests, there are plenty of books already on the market that will do a much better job of teaching you the skills you need in order to survive a typical IQ test or college entrance exam.

Nor is this a speed-learning book. In fact, one of the implicit messages of this book is that intelligent behavior may take a long time to unfold. Remember that it took Michelangelo years to paint the Sistine Chapel and that Goethe spent almost sixty years writing his masterwork *Faust*. Good things take time.

Finally, *Seven Kinds of Smart* is not a "boost your brainpower" book. I don't really feel your brainpower needs boosting. If anything, it needs celebrating, for you already have enough active brain cells inside you to accomplish many great things in your life.

I'd like you to think of *Seven Kinds of Smart* as your own personal cognitive self-renewal kit. In it you'll find validation for the fact that you're a highly gifted person, even if everyone else in your life has been telling you for years that you're not. I hope this book will convince you that you're nothing short of a genius. In ancient times, *everyone* was considered to possess inner genius. It was a kind of guardian spirit that accompanied a person through life and helped one overcome odds and achieve personal heights. We've lost touch with this original meaning of *genius* (related etymologically to the fabled genie in the lamp) in all our concern over IQ testing and similar nonsense. It's time we brought it back. That's what this book intends to do, by showing you the many ways there are to be smart. *Seven Kinds of Smart* includes:

◆ background information on how your many intelligences operate;
◆ checklists for determining your strongest and weakest intelligences;
◆ exercises for exploring the many ways of being smart;
◆ practical tips and suggestions for developing each intelligence; and
◆ ideas and resources for applying the theory of multiple intelligences directly to your life.

In addition the book provides concrete examples of intelligent behavior from scores of occupations in numerous cultures around the world. You'll have the opportunity to practice the observational skills of a Kalahari Bushman, the interpersonal intelligence of a Manhattan socialite, the meditative discipline of a Theravadan Buddhist monk, the musical image-making capabilities of a European composer, and more. After finishing this book I guarantee you'll have a newfound appreciation for the many ways of knowing that have been practiced in all quarters of the globe for thousands of years.

The book begins with a basic introduction to the theory of multiple intelligences. Chapter 1 presents an overview of the Harvard-based research suggesting the presence of at least *seven* primary intelligences in the human mind. Chapters 2 through 8 deal in turn with each of the seven intelligences: linguistic (chapter 2), spatial (chapter 3), musical (chapter 4), bodily-kinesthetic (chapter 5), logical-mathematical (chapter 6), interpersonal (chapter 7), and intrapersonal (chapter 8). The final four

chapters give you the opportunity to apply your understanding of the seven intelligences to the development of
late-blooming potentials (chapter 9), the overcoming of
learning difficulties (chapter 10), the enhancement of your
work life (chapter 11), and the nurturing of personal relationships (chapter 12). A concluding section explores how
the value placed on different intelligences may change in
the future. *Seven Kinds of Smart* ends with a comprehensive
resource section of books, organizations, computer software
programs, and games that you can use to help you develop
your abilities in each of the seven intelligences.

This book is for you if you really want to expand your
natural abilities in life. It will be particularly useful to you
if you fit one or more of the following descriptions:

- ◆ You've taken intelligence tests, or other standardized tests, and feel that the results don't describe
  the real you.
- ◆ You need information about your interests and ap-
  titudes to help prepare for a new career or for a
  new role in your current career.
- ◆ You're interested in exploring creative potentials
  that will enhance your personal growth.
- ◆ You want to discover how you most naturally think
  and learn.
- ◆ You want to understand how your thinking style
  affects the way you relate to a spouse, son or
  daughter, friend, relative, or colleague.
- ◆ You're an artist, athlete, musician, or other creative
  individual who's looking for a model of intelligence that honors and esteems what you do for a
  living.
- ◆ You think you have a learning disability and want
  to gain some insight into your condition.
- ◆ You teach or counsel individuals who require in-

telligence assessment, self-esteem building, and/or practical life skills.

My interest in exploring the seven kinds of smart began after I had worked for several years as an elementary school teacher and become disenchanted with the way parents and teachers all too often plucked the learning potential from blossoming children by focusing too much attention on words and numbers at the expense of other gifts and talents. Perhaps you were like one of those children: an individual who displayed a musical, artistic, intuitive, social, mechanical, physical, or even spiritual capability that withered for lack of attention at home or in school. This book will help you reclaim that intelligence and assist you in finding ways to realize your many other gifts as well. As Ben Franklin once said, "Hide not your talents. They for use were made. What's a sundial in the shade?" Get ready to move out into the sun, then, and learn how brilliant you *really* are!

MANY KINDS OF MINDS: THE THEORY OF MULTIPLE INTELLIGENCES

Imagine for a moment that you're living in prehistoric times. You've been awakened in the middle of the night by the thundering noise of a herd of mastodons moving toward your encampment. Now, let's say for the sake of argument that you're able to bring any individual from the twentieth century into your primitive setting to help you out of this jam. Who's it going to be? Will it be Albert Einstein? Nope, too puny. How about James Joyce? Sorry, too nearsighted. What about Franklin Delano Roosevelt? Not in a wheelchair. The most "brilliant" men of the twentieth century would be of little use to you in your hour of need. In fact, many of them would be at risk for early extinction in such an environment. On the other hand, if I suggested you summon someone like Michael Jordan or Arnold Schwarzenegger, I'd be closer to bailing you out of your predicament. The truth is that intelligence in that environment had more to do with quick reflexes, acute spatial orientation, speed, strength, and agility than with $E = MC^2$, *Finnegans Wake,* or the New Deal.

We've grown accustomed in the twentieth century to associating high intelligence with the bookworm, the egghead, and the academic. Yet by definition intelligence is the ability to respond successfully to new situations and the capacity to learn from one's past experiences. If your car breaks down on the highway, who's the most intelligent person for the job? Is it someone with a Ph.D. from a major university or a car mechanic with a junior high school education? If you become lost in a large city, who's likely to be of greatest help to you? An absentminded professor or a little boy with a great sense of direction? Intelligence depends on the context, the tasks, and the demands that life presents to us and not on an IQ score, a college degree, or a prestigious reputation.

Research on the predictive value of IQ tests bears this out. For although intelligence tests consistently predict school success, they fail to indicate how students will do after they get out into the real world. One study of highly successful professional people indicated that fully a third of them had low IQ scores. The message is clear: IQ tests have been measuring something that might be more properly called *schoolhouse giftedness,* while real intelligence takes in a much broader range of skills.

This book is about the many different ways of being intelligent. Rather than talking about *intelligence* as if it were some magical cerebral substance that could be measured by an IQ test or as if it were a golden chromosome given at birth to a few lucky individuals, we'll be referring instead to *multiple intelligences* that can be found in every walk of life. We'll look at the intelligences of the athlete, artist, musician, executive, theologian, counselor, salesperson, elementary school teacher, welder, mechanic, architect, and others. Crossing the globe, we'll also examine intelligences used in numerous cultures, including the navigational abilities of Polynesian peoples, the storytelling capacities of Yugoslavian epic singers, and the social acumen of Japanese executives.

In this book you'll learn about a revolutionary idea that is gaining increasing respect from both the scientific community and the public at large. Developed over the past fifteen years by psychologist Howard Gardner, the theory of multiple intelligences challenges old beliefs about what it means to be smart. Gardner believes that our culture has focused too much attention on verbal and logical thinking—the abilities typically assessed on an intelligence test—and neglected other ways of knowing. He suggests that there are at least *seven* intelligences worthy of being taken seriously as important modes of thought.

◆ THE SEVEN INTELLIGENCES

The first kind of smart, *linguistic intelligence,* is the intelligence of *words.* This is the intelligence of the journalist, storyteller, poet, and lawyer. It's the kind of thinking that brought us Shakespeare's *King Lear,* Homer's *Odyssey,* and the tales of the Arabian nights. People who are particularly smart in this area can argue, persuade, entertain, or instruct effectively through the spoken word. They often love to play around with the sounds of language through puns, word games, and tongue twisters. Sometimes they're also trivia experts because of their ability to retain facts in their mind. Or alternatively, they're masters of literacy. They read voraciously, can write clearly, and can gain meaning in other ways from the medium of print.

The second kind of smart, *logical-mathematical,* is the intelligence of *numbers* and *logic.* This is the intelligence of the scientist, accountant, and computer programmer.

Newton tapped into it when he invented the calculus. So did Einstein when he developed his theory of relativity. Traits of a logical-mathematically–inclined individual include the ability to reason, sequence, think in terms of cause-and-effect, create hypotheses, look for conceptual regularities or numerical patterns, and enjoy a generally rational outlook on life.

Spatial intelligence is the third kind of smart and involves thinking in *pictures* and *images* and the ability to perceive, transform, and re-create different aspects of the visual-spatial world. As such it's the playground of architects, photographers, artists, pilots, and mechanical engineers. Whoever designed the Pyramids in Egypt had a lot of this intelligence. So too did individuals like Thomas Edison, Pablo Picasso, and Ansel Adams. Highly spatial individuals often have an acute sensitivity to visual details and can visualize vividly, draw or sketch their ideas graphically, and orient themselves in three-dimensional space with ease.

Musical intelligence is the fourth kind of smart. Key features of this intelligence are the capacity to perceive, appreciate, and produce rhythms and melodies. It's the intelligence of a Bach, Beethoven, or Brahms, and also that of a Balinese gamelan player or a Yugoslavian epic singer. Yet musical intelligence also resides in the mind of any individual who has a good ear, can sing in tune, keep time to music, and listen to different musical selections with some degree of discernment.

The fifth intelligence, *bodily-kinesthetic,* is the intelligence of the *physical* self. It includes talent in controlling one's body movements and also in handling objects skillfully. Athletes, craftspeople, mechanics, and surgeons possess a great measure of this kind of thinking. So too did Charlie Chaplin, who drew upon it in order to perform his many ingenious routines as the "Little Tramp." Body-smart individuals can be skilled at sewing, carpentry, or model-building. Or they may enjoy physical pursuits like hiking, dancing, jogging, camping, swimming, or boating. They're hands-on people who have good tactile sensitivity, need to move their bodies frequently, and get "gut reactions" to things.

The sixth intelligence is *interpersonal*. This is the ability to understand and work with other people. In particular, it requires a capacity to perceive and be responsive to the moods, temperaments, intentions, and desires of others. A social director on a cruise ship needs to have this intelligence. So does an administrator of a large corporation. An interpersonally intelligent individual may be very compassionate and socially responsible like Mahatma Gandhi, or manipulative and cunning like Machiavelli. But they all have the ability to get inside the skin of another person and view the world from that individual's perspective. As such they make wonderful networkers, negotiators, and teachers.

The final intelligence is *intrapersonal* or the intelligence of the inner self. A person strong in this kind of smart can easily access her own feelings, discriminate between many different kinds of inner emotional states, and use her self-understanding to enrich and guide her life. Examples of individuals intelligent in this way include counselors, theologians, and self-employed businesspeople. They can be very introspective and enjoy meditation, contemplation, or other forms of deep soul-searching. On the other hand they might be fiercely independent, highly goal-directed, and intensely self-disciplined. But in any case they're in a class by themselves and prefer to work on their own rather than with others.

Remember that although you may strongly identify with one or two of the above descriptions, you actually possess all seven intelligences. Moreover, virtually any normal person can develop every one of the seven kinds of minds to a reasonable level of mastery. We're each unique in the way that the seven intelligences express themselves in our lives. It's the rare person who achieves high levels of competence in six or seven of the intelligences. Early-twentieth-century German thinker Rudolf Steiner may have been one example. He was a philosopher, writer, and scientist. He also created a system of dance, a theory of color, and a system of gardening, and was a sculptor, social theorist, and architect as well.

On the other hand there are a few people who seem to have developed only one intelligence to a high level, while their other intelligences lagged far behind. These are the savants of society. People like Raymond in the Oscar-winning movie *Rainman,* who could calculate numbers with lightning speed but couldn't take care of himself. Or individuals who can sculpt brilliantly but can't read, or who have perfect pitch but need help tying their shoes.

Most of us fall somewhere between the self-actualized human being and the savant. We have a few intelligences that stand out, some that seem average, and others that we've had considerable difficulty with in our lives. The important thing to understand, however, is that there's room for everyone to shine in this new model of intelligence. The farmer, the parent, the painter, the mechanic, and the merchant have as much right to the term *intelligent* as do the psychiatrist, the brain surgeon, and the law professor. The theory of multiple intelligences incorporates the broad spectrum of human abilities into a sevenfold system that can make any person a winner in life.

◆ EVIDENCE FOR THE THEORY ————————————

The theory of multiple intelligences isn't the first model to suggest that there are different ways to be smart. In the past two hundred years there have been a wide range of theories touting anywhere from 1 to 150 different kinds of intelligence. What makes Gardner's model particularly powerful, however, is that he backs it up with research from a wide range of fields, including anthropology, cognitive psychology, developmental psychology, psychometrics, biographical studies, animal physiology, and neuroanatomy. Gardner established specific requirements that each intelligence had to meet in order to be included in his theory. Here are four of these criteria:

Each intelligence is capable of being symbolized. The theory of multiple intelligences suggests that the ability to symbolize—or depict ideas and experiences through representations like pictures, numbers, or words—is a hallmark of human intelligence. When Vanna White points to the empty space in "pr——gram" on the TV game show "Wheel of Fortune," most television viewers can supply the missing vowel because they share a common symbol system: the English language. This is an example of a linguistic symbol system. The theory of multiple intelligences says that there are different ways that each intelligence can be symbolized. Logical-mathematical thinkers use numbers and Greek letters, among other symbols, to serve their rational needs. Musicians, on the other hand, typically use notes of the bass and treble clef to symbolize melodies and rhythms. Marcel Marceau uses complex gestures and expressions as bodily-kinesthetic symbols to represent concepts like freedom and loneliness. There are also social symbols, such as waving goodbye, and symbols of the self, as found, for example, in early-morning dream images.

Each intelligence has its own developmental history. Intelligence isn't some absolute trait fixed at birth that remains stable throughout the life span as some conservative adherents of the IQ myth still hold. According to the theory of multiple intelligences, each intelligence emerges at a certain point in childhood, has periods of potential blossoming during the life span, and contains its own unique pattern of either gradual or rapid decline as a person ages. Musical genius reveals itself earliest among the seven intelligences. Mozart was composing simple tunes at three and writing symphonies by the age of nine. And musical talent remains relatively robust into old age, as witnessed in the lives of creative personalities like Pablo Casals, Igor Stravinsky, and George Friedrich Handel.

Logical-mathematical thinking, on the other hand, has a different developmental pattern. It arises somewhat later in childhood, peaks in adolescence or early adulthood, and then declines in later life. A look at the history of mathematical thought reveals that few major discoveries were made by people after the age of forty. Indeed, many important discoveries came from teenagers like Blaise Pascal and Evariste Galois. Even Albert Einstein received the initial insights into his theory of relativity at the tender age of sixteen. Similarly, each of the other intelligences has its own patterns of waxing and waning during the human life cycle.

Each intelligence is vulnerable to impairment through insult or injury to specific areas of the brain. Multiple-intelligence (MI) theory predicts that intelligences can actually be isolated through brain damage. Gardner suggests that in order to be viable, any theory of intelligence must be *biologically based*—that is, rooted in the physiology of brain structure. As a neuropsychologist at the Boston Veterans Administration, he worked with victims of brain injury who had selective impairments in each of the seven intelligences: for example, a person suffering damage to the frontal lobe of his left hemisphere who wasn't able to speak or write easily yet could sing, draw, and dance without difficulty. In this case, it was his linguistic intelligence that had been selectively impaired. On the other hand, individuals possessing brain lesions in the right temporal lobe might experience difficulty with musical tasks but be able to speak, read, and write with ease. Patients with damage in the occipital lobe of the right hemisphere might have their ability to recognize faces, visualize, or notice visual details significantly curtailed.

The theory of intelligences argues for the existence of seven relatively autonomous brain systems. Linguistic intelligence appears to function primarily in the left hemisphere in most people, while musical, spatial, and interpersonal intelligences tend to be more right-hemispheric functions. Bodily-kinesthetic intelligence involves the motor cortex, the basal ganglia, and the cerebellum. The frontal lobes are particularly important for the personal intelligences. Although the brain is incredibly complex and can't be mapped out in seven clearly delineated sectors, MI theory nevertheless synthesizes in a remarkable way much of what has been discovered over the past twenty-five years in the area of neuropsychology.

Each intelligence has its own culturally valued end-states. The theory of multiple intelligences declares that intelligent behavior can best be viewed by looking at civilization's highest accomplishments—and not by scoring responses to standardized test items. Typical IQ test skills, such as the ability to repeat random digits backward and forward or the capacity to solve analogy problems, have limited cultural value. When was the last time you heard a grandparent take a grandchild up on her knee and say, "I want to share something with you that's meant a lot to me, I hope it's meaningful to you: 23, 16, 94, 3, 12 . . ."

On the other hand, what *does* get passed along from generation to generation are myths, legends, literature, music, great art, scientific discoveries, and physical skills.

The theory of multiple intelligences says that we can best learn what it means to be intelligent by studying examples of culture's most accomplished work in each of the seven areas: *Moby Dick* by Herman Melville rather than nonsense syllables in a psychometrician's manual; *Guernica* by Pablo Piccaso rather than geometric designs in a test of spatial reasoning; the Magna Carta or the Sermon on the Mount rather than the Vineland Scale of Social Maturity.

Further, MI theory celebrates the diversity of ways in which different cultures show intelligent behaviors. Rather than regarding the verbal and logical discoveries of white Europeans as the apex of intelligence (again, something promoted and sustained by IQ testing), it provides a more broadly conceived spectrum of human intelligence. Honored equally in this schema are the tracking abilities of Himalayan Sherpas, the intricate classification methods of Kalahari Bushmen, the musical genius of the Anang culture in Nigeria, the unique mapping systems of Polynesian navigators, and the special abilities of many other peoples around the world.

In addition to the above characteristics, the theory suggests that each intelligence has its own separate cognitive processes in the areas of memory, attention, perception, and problem solving. You may not have the same memory for melodies, for example, that you have for faces or numbers. Similarly, you can have acute perception for musical pitch yet be unable to distinguish the difference between "th" and "sh" as verbal sounds. The seven intelligences even have their own evolutionary histories. Musical intelligence evolved in part from bird song, while bodily-kinesthetic intelligence emerged from the hunting activities of earlier life-forms. For those who want quantifiable data, there's even support for the seven intelligences from psychological testing and experimental research. The theory of multiple intelligences is more than just an idea. It constitutes the most up-to-date synthesis of research on the topic of intelligence currently available.

◆ DISCOVERING YOUR SEVEN INTELLIGENCES

Now that you know something about the scientific basis for the theory, let's take a look at how you fit into it. During the workshops and lectures I give around the country, people often ask, "Is there a test I can take to tell me what my intelligences are?" I certainly hope not. This book is based on the belief that intelligence is far too rich and diverse a concept to be squeezed into a ninety-minute test. Although there are many individual tests that assess different aspects of the seven intelligences, the best way to discover your own multiple intelligences profile is through an honest appraisal of how you function in the course of everyday life.

Consider something that you do every day: use the telephone. What's your technique for remembering a telephone number? Do you repeat the number semiaudibly to yourself before dialing? If so, then you're using a linguistic strategy. Or do you visualize the pattern of buttons you need to press mapped out against the three-by-four grid of a telephone? That would suggest a spatial mind-style at work. I've even heard people say that they remember phone numbers by the characteristic melodies made by touch-tone phones. These must be musically intelligent people. The point is that knowledge of one's intelligences comes from everyday activities such as making a telephone call and not from artificially contrived problems and tasks such as one finds on an IQ test.

There is no set group of skills that will ultimately define your profile of intelligences. You can, however, come closer to an understanding of your thinking styles by surveying a healthy sample of events from your own life. The following seventy-item checklist will help you do this. There's room at the end of each category for writing about other abilities not specifically mentioned in the checklist. Don't regard this checklist as the last word on your seven kinds of smart. There will be many other exercises and activities in this book that will add to your understanding of how you learn most effectively. Think of this checklist simply as a way to get started in your quest to discover your *true* intelligence quotient.

MULTIPLE INTELLIGENCES CHECKLIST

Check those statements that apply in each intelligence category:

LINGUISTIC INTELLIGENCE
_____ Books are very important to me.
_____ I can hear words in my head before I read, speak, or write them down.
_____ I get more out of listening to the radio or a spoken-word cassette than I do from television or films.
_____ I show an aptitude for word games like Scrabble, Anagrams, or Password.
_____ I enjoy entertaining myself or others with tongue twisters, nonsense rhymes, or puns.
_____ Other people sometimes have to stop and ask me to explain the meaning of the words I use in my writing and speaking.

_____ English, social studies, and history were easier for me in school than math and science.

_____ When I drive down a freeway, I pay more attention to the words written on billboards than to the scenery.

_____ My conversation includes frequent references to things that I've read or heard.

_____ I've written something recently that I was particularly proud of or that earned me recognition from others.

Other Linguistic Strengths:

LOGICAL-MATHEMATICAL INTELLIGENCE

_____ I can easily compute numbers in my head.

_____ Math and/or science were among my favorite subjects in school.

_____ I enjoy playing games or solving brainteasers that require logical thinking.

_____ I like to set up little "what if" experiments (for example, "What if I double the amount of water I give to my rosebush each week?")

_____ My mind searches for patterns, regularities, or logical sequences in things.

_____ I'm interested in new developments in science.

_____ I believe that almost everything has a rational explanation.

_____ I sometimes think in clear, abstract, wordless, imageless concepts.

_____ I like finding logical flaws in things that people say and do at home and work.

_____ I feel more comfortable when something has been measured, categorized, analyzed, or quantified in some way.

Other Logical-Mathematical Strengths:

SPATIAL INTELLIGENCE
_____ I often see clear visual images when I close my eyes.
_____ I'm sensitive to color.
_____ I frequently use a camera or camcorder to record what I see around me.
_____ I enjoy doing jigsaw puzzles, mazes, and other visual puzzles.
_____ I have vivid dreams at night.
_____ I can generally find my way around unfamiliar territory.
_____ I like to draw or doodle.
_____ Geometry was easier for me than algebra in school.
_____ I can comfortably imagine how something might appear if it were looked down upon from directly above in a bird's-eye view.
_____ I prefer looking at reading material that is heavily illustrated.

Other Spatial Strengths:

BODILY-KINESTHETIC INTELLIGENCE
_____ I engage in at least one sport or physical activity on a regular basis.
_____ I find it difficult to sit still for long periods of time.
_____ I like working with my hands at concrete activities such as sewing, weaving, carving, carpentry, or model-building.
_____ My best ideas often come to me when I'm out for a long walk or a jog, or when I'm engaged in some other kind of physical activity.
_____ I often like to spend my free time outdoors.
_____ I frequently use hand gestures or other forms of body language when conversing with someone.

_____ I need to touch things in order to learn more about them.

_____ I enjoy daredevil amusement rides or similar thrilling physical experiences.

_____ I would describe myself as well coordinated.

_____ I need to practice a new skill rather than simply reading about it or seeing a video that describes it.

Other Bodily-Kinesthetic Strengths:

MUSICAL INTELLIGENCE

_____ I have a pleasant singing voice.

_____ I can tell when a musical note is off-key.

_____ I frequently listen to music on radio, records, cassettes, or compact discs.

_____ I play a musical instrument.

_____ My life would be poorer if there were no music in it.

_____ I sometimes catch myself walking down the street with a television jingle or other tune running through my mind.

_____ I can easily keep time to a piece of music with a simple percussion instrument.

_____ I know the tunes to many different songs or musical pieces.

_____ If I hear a musical selection once or twice, I am usually able to sing it back fairly accurately.

_____ I often make tapping sounds or sing little melodies while working, studying, or learning something new.

Other Musical Strengths:

INTERPERSONAL INTELLIGENCE

_____ I'm the sort of person that people come to for advice and counsel at work or in my neighborhood.

_____ I prefer group sports like badminton, volleyball, or softball to solo sports such as swimming and jogging.

_____ When I have a problem, I'm more likely to seek out another person for help than attempt to work it out on my own.

_____ I have at least three close friends.

_____ I favor social pastimes such as Monopoly or bridge over individual recreations such as video games and solitaire.

_____ I enjoy the challenge of teaching another person, or groups of people, what I know how to do.

_____ I consider myself a leader (or others have called me that).

_____ I feel comfortable in the midst of a crowd.

_____ I like to get involved in social activities connected with my work, church, or community.

_____ I would rather spend my evenings at a lively social gathering than stay at home alone.

Other Interpersonal Strengths:

INTRAPERSONAL INTELLIGENCE

_____ I regularly spend time alone meditating, reflecting, or thinking about important life questions.

_____ I have attended counseling sessions or personal growth seminars to learn more about myself.

_____ I have opinions that set me apart from the crowd.

_____ I have a special hobby or interest that I keep pretty much to myself.

_____ I have some important goals for my life that I think about on a regular basis.

_____ I have a realistic view of my strengths and weaknesses (borne out by feedback from other sources).

_____ I would prefer to spend a weekend alone in a cabin

in the woods rather than at a fancy resort with lots
of people around.

_____ I consider myself to be strong willed or independent minded.

_____ I keep a personal diary or journal to record the
events of my inner life.

_____ I am self-employed or have at least thought seriously
about starting my own business.

Other Intrapersonal Strengths:

◆ HOW TO USE THIS BOOK ──────────────

Completing the above checklist probably told you things
about yourself that you already knew. In one sense this
book serves as a way of validating your beliefs about how
you think and learn most effectively. You may be pleased
to learn that many of the talents you possess qualify as
full-fledged intelligent behaviors. This may be particularly
refreshing if you happen to think in a way that's different
from the verbal or logical modes esteemed by our culture.
You probably also discovered at least a few surprises in
the above assessment and may be eager to discover more
about your many intelligences. Before continuing with the
rest of this book, however, keep in mind the following
suggestions:

Look at the total picture. You may be a math genius, a
decent athlete, a good reader, a poor visualizer, a party
animal, and a musical klutz—all wrapped up in one mag-
nificently unique package. That's why it's important for you
to read through the material for each intelligence in the
book, so that you can get a full-spectrum video of your
total abilities as a learner and not just a black-and-white
snapshot that tags you with a meaningless label.

Celebrate your strengths. One of the greatest contributions of the theory of multiple intelligences is that it provides everyone with a chance to shine in something. In my role as a learning specialist I've talked with too many people who've gone through their entire lives thinking of themselves as losers because they weren't able to be the logical or verbal people that society expected them to be. This book provides these individuals with an opportunity to experience themselves as highly intelligent people in one or more of the other intelligences.

Pay attention to your hidden intelligences. While doing the exercises in this book, you may discover abilities you once had—possibly in childhood—that you've neglected over the years. These intelligences represent your untapped potentials. Maybe you shut them out at an early age because of a negative experience at home or school. Or perhaps you simply never had anybody to help you develop them. Whatever the reason for their neglect, you can use this book to reawaken dormant abilities and extend your intelligences in directions you never dreamed possible. Chapter 9 shows you how to dig into the past to retrieve neglected intelligences that you can start putting into action today.

Be optimistic about your weaknesses. Don't despair if you're physically awkward, whistle Dixie poorly enough to start another Civil War, can't balance your checkbook, or have other weaknesses that haunt you. There are a number of things you can do to help cope with your learning difficulties. Chapter 10 describes several productive ways of working with your weakest intelligences. And remember: everyone has learning disabilities in something. Picasso could never remember the alphabet. Beethoven was notoriously clumsy. Moses had a stutter. You're in good company.

Whether you're interested in bolstering your strengths

or shoring up your weaknesses, *Seven Kinds of Smart* provides hundreds of ideas and resources for developing your seven intelligences. More than than, it will give you a new attitude about yourself. On one level, this is a book about expanding your intelligence. But in a broader sense, you've already increased your intelligence. Because now you know the answer to the question asked at the beginning of the preface. How intelligent *are* you? Far more intelligent than you realized. You know much more than you think because you think in more ways than you know.

2

WORD SMART: EXPRESSING YOUR VERBAL INTELLIGENCE

I was a radio addict as a child. I'd spend hours dialing my way from one end of the AM band to the other, sampling bits of music, news, and entertainment. But there was always one place on the dial I'd linger around and listen to a bit more intently than the rest. It was a show called "The World Tomorrow," produced by the evangelist Herbert W. Armstrong. I'm sure the fact that Armstrong had the same last name as I do added to my interest. But what fascinated me was the sound of his voice, the words he used, and the *way* he used them. I was entranced by his oratory and often had a hard time pulling myself away from the show.

This early experience initiated me into the power of words to bamboozle (I'd soon come to separate the evangelist's message from his eloquence). But it also showed me how language can inspire, entertain, and instruct. It revealed to me the effect that language has on consciousness—how it ultimately represents one of humanity's most *intelligent* forms of behavior. This chapter will explore the power of language in your life. It will show you how to marshal the linguistic intelligence you already have to derive more satisfaction from life and to gain a greater sense of competence from the many words that you speak, read, and write every day.

◆ A WAY WITH WORDS

Linguistic intelligence is perhaps the most universal of the seven intelligences in MI theory. While accomplished orators are few and far between, virtually everyone learns to speak, and in many cultures the majority of citizens can also read and write adequately. In our culture language ability ranks among the most highly regarded intelligences, along with logical-mathematical thinking. We're impressed by the individual who has a large vocabulary (witness the popularity of books like *Word Power Made Easy* and *30 Days to a More Powerful Vocabulary*). We esteem the individual who can express himself fluently in front of an audience—the master of ceremonies, the stand-up comedian, the elder statesman, the dynamic executive. We exalt our writers (though not necessarily the better ones) to celebrity status. Similarly, we regard scholars and other well-read individuals with a sense of awe

The ultimate arbiter of intelligence in our culture—the IQ test—draws heavily upon verbal elements for its construction. True linguistic intelligence, however, is much more complex than the simple ability to parrot back answers on a standardized test. It consists of several components, including *phonology, syntax, semantics,* and *pragmatics.*

The highly linguistic individual has an acute sensitivity to the sounds or *phonology* of language, often using puns, rhymes, tongue twisters, alliteration, onomatopoeia, and other tantalizing tintinnabulations. James Joyce, for example, created thousands of multilingual puns and delightfully expressive Irish word-stews in his brilliant novels *Ulysses* and *Finnegans Wake.*

The linguistic thinker is also often adept at manipulating the structure or *syntax* of language. Like Marcel Proust, he may be capable of stringing clause after clause together in paragraph-sized sentences to achieve a dazzling impact. Proust's teachers, scarcely able to keep up with him, often criticized the boy for writing run-on sentences! Or such a highly verbal thinker may be the ultimate grammarian—constantly on the lookout for the occasional oral or written blunder in his own life or the lives of others.

The linguistic genius may also show his sensitivity to language through a deep appreciation of its meaning or *semantics.* The poet Robert Lowell was reputed to be able to take any word discussed in his poetry-writing classes at Harvard and examine the different ways it was used historically throughout English literature. Similarly, William Safire, who writes a weekly column for *The New York Times,* has made a career out of examining neologisms and subtle shades of meaning in the continually evolving English language.

But perhaps the most important component of linguistic intelligence is the capacity to *use* language to achieve practical goals (*pragmatics*). This is the intelligence of a Herbert W. Armstrong (to proselytize), a Joan Rivers (to entertain), an Isaac Asimov (to instruct), a Winston Churchill (to inspire), or a Clarence Darrow (to persuade). The language itself may not be dazzling or first-rate, but the purpose to which language is bent serves to enhance, or at the very least, to change lives in some tangible way.

◆ THE ROOTS OF DISCOURSE ──────────

The printed word has been around for only about 6,000 years. Oral communication, by contrast, goes back as far as Neanderthal man—30,000 to 100,000 years ago, and even further if you consider the meaningful grunting of apes to be the beginnings of linguistic intelligence. Over these many thousands of years, cultures have evolved richly complex oral traditions, from elaborate clan histories to myths, yarns, riddles, fables, and tales designed to teach the basic truths of God, humankind, and nature. These oral traditions continue to operate strongly in many parts of the globe. In certain African cultures the chief derives his power largely from an ability to debate his opponents effectively. One native language in Mexico features more than 400 terms referring to language use. And in the Middle East individuals are celebrated for their capacity to recite poetry in public places and to memorize the holy Koran—a feat that entitles one to the honorable title of "Hafiz."

In our own culture oral traditions seem to have declined significantly over the past few decades. The art of rhetoric—once a highly valued craft —has been relegated to the level of an insult ("That's mere rhetoric!"). We have only the dim memory of great orators from our nation's past ringing in our ears: Lincoln's Gettysburg Address, the stirring speeches of William Jennings Bryan (who once called eloquence "thought on fire"), and the fireside chats of Franklin Delano Roosevelt. One commentator has suggested that Americans may have to go back two decades to Martin Luther King's "I Have a Dream" speech or JFK's inaugural address for examples of true verbal eloquence in our society.

Up until the 1920s or 1930s, according to poet and critic Donald Hall, we lived in an "out-loud" culture. Families read regularly from the Bible, told stories together, attended public readings and debates, and recited their lessons orally in school. Today, however, passive reading and television watching seem to have supplanted storytelling and oratory as preferred sources of information. I remember several years ago being with a group of people in India who were sharing stories, poems, and other contributions around the circle. When it came time for me to speak, I was surprised to begin reciting a poem I had memorized in sixth grade: *Abou ben Adhem* by Leigh Hunt. It meant a great deal to me to know that I had this poem securely stowed away in my private storehouse of memories. The following exercise will help you begin to reconnect to your own oral tradition and assist you in developing ways of bringing the "out-loud" culture back to your personal circle of family and friends.

TAPPING YOUR ORAL ROOTS

Do this activity with a group of three or more people. Begin by asking participants to think about what they'd be able to contribute verbally to the group if they were stranded together without paper and pencil or books in a bomb shelter after a nuclear war and had to start an oral tradition from scratch. What folk and fairy tales, animal fables, ghost stories, mountain yarns, riddles, humorous offerings, jokes, or tongue twisters could they contribute? What poetry selections, famous sayings, proverbs, or other literary passages have they committed to memory that they could share? Go around the circle and take turns reciting a special oral memory that might become part of this new tradition. If you wish, keep a tape recorder handy to preserve your contributions. You can also do this activity on your own by recording or writing down oral memories as they occur to you.

The experience of mining this inner treasury of cultural riches may stimulate you to want to develop your oral language capacities even more. Here are some suggestions: Allot a few minutes every week to commit to memory a few phrases from your favorite literary works, or use reference works such as *Bartlett's Familiar Quotations* or anthologies as sources of material to memorize. Read favorite fairy tales or myths several times over so that you'll be familiar with them, and then practice telling the stories to friends and family. Radio humorist Garrison Keillor says that it usually takes about ten to twelve tellings to get a story told right. Go to storytelling festivals, poetry readings, and other places where oral traditions still flourish. Obtain recordings by accomplished storytellers (often available at a public library), and learn both the content and the method of storytelling from them. As you watch your verbal memory grow, you'll find that you can incorporate this newly acquired skill into speeches and talks in your professional life, conversations and discussions in your social life, and letters, reports, and other writings that you do.

◆ THE WRITER'S VOICE

Surrounded as we are by oral language from infancy onward, most of us learn to internalize verbal sounds to form an "inner speech" that becomes a primary instrument of our thought. Some people refer to this faculty of mind as *self-talk* or *mind-chatter*—the interior monologue that's always going on below the surface of consciousness. James Joyce illustrated how this process works in the minds of his characters in the novel *Ulysses,* especially in the final section of the novel, in which we are shown the private thoughts of Molly Bloom as she drifts off to sleep ("and then he asked me would I yes to say yes my mountain flower . . .").

Writers sometimes refer to this stream of conscious-ness as if there were someone in the room actually talking to them. Nobel laureate Saul Bellow reflected: "I suppose that all of us have a primitive prompter or commentator within, who from earliest years has been advising us, tell-ing us what the real world is. There is such a commentator in me. . . . From this source come words, phrases, syllables; sometimes . . . whole paragraphs fully punctuated." English poet Stephen Spender revealed a similar experience: "Sometimes, when I lie in a state of half-waking, half-sleep-ing, I am conscious of a stream of words which seem to pass through my mind, without their having a meaning, but they have a sound, a sound of passion, or a sound recalling poetry that I know." The next exercise will help you become aware of some of these sounds from your own linguistic world.

VERBAL IMAGES

Read each of the following items, and for each one, practice "hearing" in your mind's ear the speech sounds requested:

- a friend speaking your name
- your mother reading from a book or newspaper
- a speech given by the president of the United States
- a classroom of children reciting the Pledge of Allegiance
- your own inner voice describing what you plan to do for the rest of the day
- a ninety-year-old man telling you the story of his life
- a five-year-old child explaining how he built a sand castle
- a teacher that you had in school delivering a lecture
- a radio or television announcer doing a commercial

Don't worry if you fail to get clear linguistic images in this exercise. Many writers make use of data from other intelligences in their writing, including kinesthetic and visual images. Still others access words but in a silent way. For example, poet Amy Lowell reported: "I do not hear a voice, but I do hear words pronounced, only the pronouncing is toneless." Whatever your experience, this exercise should heighten your capacity to hear words in your mind—an ability that can have practical significance to you in developing fluency as a writer. The next exercise will use this interior word-producing capacity as a means of overcoming writer's block and developing your writer's voice.

WORD RIVERS

Sit at a desk or table with several sheets of paper and two or three pencils nearby. Close your eyes and listen to the undercurrent of words flowing through your mind. Notice whether they come in single drops (individual words), in rivulets (sentence fragments), in torrents (streams of commentary), or in some other way. After two or three minutes of inner listening, take up a pencil, still with eyes half-closed, and begin writing exactly what you hear in your mind's ear. Even if you don't hear anything, write what you *think* you'd hear if you *could* hear something. Write like this for at least fifteen minutes.

After completing the exercise you should have a healthy collection of words on the page. Use this "priming-the-pump" technique whenever you're sitting at your desk with a poem, speech, story, report, essay, letter, or paper to write and you can't get started. This approach can also sensitize you to the internal sounds that shape and solidify your emerging writer's voice and help you create dialogue for different characters in your work if you're writing fiction.

This process of generating verbal "trains of thought" is an ongoing activity for the linguistically inclined individual. Writers traditionally tap this underground stream using record-keeping devices of many shapes and varieties. Isaac Bashevis Singer carried a little notebook around wherever he went for recording story ideas. Joyce Carol Oates keeps a journal that "resembles a sort of ongoing letter to myself." Joseph Heller stores a small sheaf of 3 x 5 cards in his billfold for note taking. Jack London wrote in bed and had a system of clotheslines and pulleys crisscrossing the room upon which he fastened index cards with ideas for stories. The writer/comedian Steve Allen has a number of tape recorders scattered around his house so that one is always available whenever a brilliant idea hits. Each of these individuals has devised a means of tapping the word rivers flowing within them.

Choose a notebook format that works best for you and use it regularly to collect the runoff from your own mind storms (the Russian psychologist Lev Vygotsky once said that a "thought may be compared to a cloud shedding a shower of words"). Should you encounter a dry spell, you might try writing about some of the following topics suggested by Natalie Goldberg, author of *Writing Down the Bones*:

- ◆ your first memory
- ◆ people you've loved
- ◆ people you've lost
- ◆ the most frightened you've ever been
- ◆ the closest you ever felt to God or nature
- ◆ a teacher you had
- ◆ memories of a grandparent

- your first sexual experience
- a time of great physical endurance

While writers are usually experts at diving into their internal worlds, most writers also keep their eyes and ears open to the external environment for sources of inspiration. So, some objective data to put into a writer's notebook might include:

- captivating words, phrases, or passages you come across in your reading;
- interesting things you hear other people say (including special dialects);
- curious phrases you see on billboards, signs, and posters; and
- snippets from radio, television, or movies that catch your ear.

Your writer's notebook can become the cauldron within which you brew new ideas, plans, and projects. It can also serve as an incubator for poems, stories, essays, reports, and books. In a sense, a writer's notebook represents a kind of halfway house between your mind and the outside world and can provide you with a practical tool for externalizing what goes on inside your verbal mind.

◆ THE ART OF READING ─────────────────

A great deal has been reported during the past twenty years about the problem of illiteracy in this country. More than 20 million adults can't read menus, signs, or other simple printed matter. Another 40 million can function only at a fourth-grade reading level. But while these statistics represent a national tragedy with sweeping political and social implications, there is an even more widespread reading problem in our country that is not even being addressed. This is the problem of *aliteracy*, which is knowing how to read but choosing not to do so. According to a recent Gallup poll, each day Americans watch television an average of two hours and thirty-eight minutes, listen to radio an hour and fifty-six minutes, and read for only twenty-three minutes. And the literature Americans read is often not of the highest caliber. A study conducted by the National Endowment for the Arts indicated that only 7 to 12 percent of the population reads serious literature (Hemingway, Joyce, Updike, Dickens, and others) in the course of a year.

These figures suggest something about the low value our culture places on personal reading, which may be even more devastating than the presence of nonreaders in our society. Since the invention of the printing press in 1457, books have made knowledge accessible to large numbers of people in ways scarcely imaginable in preliterate days. The capacity of books to extend our world beyond the immediacy of the five senses has never been stated with as much authenticity as in the writings of Helen Keller: "Literature is my Utopia. Here I am not disenfranchised. No barrier of the senses shuts me out from the sweet, gracious discourse of my book friends. They talk to me without embarrassment or awkwardness."

Books have the power to change lives—to change the very fabric of civilization. Martin Luther was moved to reform the Catholic Church after reading Paul's *Epistle to the Romans*. Charles Darwin developed his theory of evolution upon reading Malthus's work on population. Freud credited Goethe's essay *Fragment Upon Nature* with stimulating him to pursue medicine (and ultimately psychiatry) as a career. Writer Harold Brodkey points out that in Europe, "reading is known to be dangerous. Reading always leads to personal metamorphosis, sometimes irreversible." In our country,

however, fewer than half of all Americans have even *heard*
of such authors as James Joyce, Herman Melville, Virginia
Woolf, or Gustave Flaubert. The next exercise will reveal
your own level of *bibliophilia,* or love of books.

THE BOOKS IN YOUR LIFE

Divide a sheet of paper into four vertical columns. In the first
column list important books from your childhood (including
both those that were read to you and those you read yourself). In the second column write down four or five of the
most influential books in your life—books that made you see
the world in a different way and/or books that helped trigger
significant changes in your life. In the third column include
books that, if you died tomorrow, you'd regret not having
read. In the final column list all the books you've read in the
past twelve months. Have a friend also do this exercise and
then talk together about your experiences with books. Use
the exercise as a basis for thinking about how you'd like to
shape your future reading habits.

Strangely enough, when it comes to developing one's
literacy skills, the emphasis in our culture has often been
on *speed reading.* It's almost as if Americans, anxious to
cope with the information overload of the past few decades, want to get their reading over with as quickly and
painlessly as possible. However, the term *speed reading* is
actually a misnomer. Research indicates that the human
eye can read a maximum of 800 to 900 words per minute
(wpm) because of neuromuscular limitations on eye
movement and that most accomplished readers lose full
comprehension around 500 to 600 wpm. This contrasts
with the claims of speed-reading specialists that students

will learn to read tens of thousands (or even hundreds of thousands) of words per minute in their programs. In reality what speed-reading instructors teach is the ability to scan and skim key words, topic sentences, flap material, and other book features to distill key points. Author and educator Mortimer Adler calls this form of perusal *inspectional* reading: a process whereby the reader develops skill in systematic skimming of a book to determine its essential message. According to Adler, 99 percent of books don't even have to be read thoroughly. Skimming will serve the purpose just as well.

Inspectional reading contrasts sharply with another— probably more important—method of reading that allows one time to dawdle over delicious words, reread favorite passages, and savor the meaning of ideas and images without pressure or pain. In this type of reading, as author William Gass puts it, "every page is a pasture, and we are let out to graze like hungry herds." Lip-reading or subvocalization (at one time considered by remedial reading teachers to be a linguistic "no-no") and full vocalization are an important part of this type of reading. These practices reconnect the reader to the *sounds* of language and ultimately to the roots of language itself in an oral tradition like that of medieval times when books were usually read out loud. The following exercise serves to reawaken a sense of play and delight while reading at one's own pace—a process some have called *ludic* reading (from the Latin *ludere*—"to play").

LUDIC READING

Select a book that you've enjoyed in the past or one that you'd really like to spend some "quality time" with now. As you read note words or phrases that particularly delight you.

Say these to yourself under your breath or out loud. If a passage is unclear, take time to reread it slowly, and refer back to previous pages if necessary to clarify it. Allow yourself to access other intelligences as you read—visualizing scenes, feeling physical sensations, hearing nonverbal sounds or music referred to in the book, feeling and expressing emotions, and so forth. If you feel like using a marker to underline favorite passages do so. Take as much time as you need.

Ludic readers typically allow themselves to become absorbed by books for their own sake, not to achieve some external goal. Nothing is more appealing to them than curling up with a good book and getting lost in its pages. Ludic readers aren't led to books based on structured reading lists (though for those who want them, Clifton Fadiman's *Lifetime Reading Plan* is an excellent place to begin). Rather, they are drawn to books instinctively. Alan Bloom, author of *The Closing of the American Mind,* pointed out in this regard: "One needn't set up a canon of books to read. In fact, I think such lists are rather silly. The important thing is to find one book and follow where it leads. ..."

◆ THE JOY OF LEX

The process of ludic reading can lead to another form of linguistic passion where one revels in encounters with single words. It's worthwhile to note that children—who are constantly playing with words and word sounds from the earliest stages of babbling —learn around 5,000 new words per year between the ages of six and ten. The average adult, on the other hand, masters only about fifty new words a year. I would suggest that this poverty of new learning occurs because adults have lost touch with the mystery and magic of words. In a sense each word in the English language rides upon the waves of history. It represents the outcome of an evolutionary process that has its origins in archaic languages and at each step in history underwent a refining process in its spelling, pronunciation, and meaning until it reached its present status in the dictionary (which is still "in progress"). The following exercise will help you appreciate this multilayered substratum of words and assist you in developing a richer vocabulary.

WORD ARCHAEOLOGY

Write down unfamiliar words from your reading on a sheet of paper (or keep them in a special section of your writer's notebook). Select a word that is particularly interesting to you for your archaeological expedition. Go to a library and look up the word in the *Oxford English Dictionary*. This multivolume work traces the origins of words and provides examples throughout the history of English literature, showing how a word has evolved over time. On a blank sheet of paper draw several horizontal lines, evenly spaced on the page, to represent geological layers. At the top of the page provide the current, commonly accepted definitions and spelling of the word. In each subsequent layer (or horizontal column) moving down the page, indicate how the word was used in an earlier time (include examples and dates, with altered spelling if applicable). In the bottom layer give the origins of the word in other languages.

In addition to the serious work of digging into the history of words, you might also approach unfamiliar words with a whimsical spirit. As Willard Espy, author of *The Game of Words,* puts it: "Housebreak your words while they are still too young to know better. Teach them to do tricks, and reward them for behaving properly.... The instant you shrink back, they will rush at you and take a piece out of your trouser leg." Look for ways to incorporate new words into your writing and conversation. Have fun repeating new words to yourself and discover rhyming words, alliterative words (words that have the same initial sound), words hidden inside of larger words, synonyms, antonyms, and humorous definitions for these newfound friends.

Word games are probably the best way of learning new words and developing greater flexibility with familiar words. An estimated 30 million Americans do crossword puzzles in more than 1,700 newspapers every day. Scrabble sets are found in 27 percent of American households, and 100 million of them have been sold worldwide since 1931. A wide variety of other word games are available in toy stores throughout the country, with scores of new games coming on the market every year. (See page 250 for a list of some of the best commercially made word games.) But there are also many open-ended word games that you can play without boards or magazines that will enrich your linguistic intelligence. Here are three to start with (others can be found in word-game books listed in the Resources section):

◆ *Word Tic-Tac-Toe.* Play a normal game of tic-tac-toe, but substitute letters for *x*'s and *o*'s; players who make words receive 1 point for each letter in the word

◆ *Word Ladders.* Select two words of equal length; players attempt to transform the first word into the second by changing one letter at a time in the fewest number of steps; each step must make a meaningful word (e.g., saw—but: saw, sat, bat, but)

◆ *Dictionary Bluff.* One player picks an unfamiliar word from the dictionary and provides either the correct definition or a "bluff" definition he makes up on the spot. Other players must decide if the definition is true or false.

Language can provide us with unlimited hours of exploration as we experiment with it, manipulate it, interpret it, produce it, transform it, distort it, expand it, and in other ways modify it to suit whatever dimensions we choose. In the process we may find that our own minds have expanded, for language is ultimately a tool of thought. By using it consciously in this way to enhance our intelligence, we can experience its richness and diversity in a pragmatic, but also thoroughly entertaining way.

25 WAYS TO DEVELOP YOUR LINGUISTIC INTELLIGENCE

◆ Join a Great Books seminar.
◆ Hold Trivial Pursuit parties.
◆ Play word games (e.g., anagrams, Scrabble, crosswords).
◆ Join a book club.
◆ Attend a writer's conference or a class or workshop on writing through a local college.
◆ Attend book signings or other events featuring accomplished writers.
◆ Record yourself speaking into a tape recorder and listen to the playback.
◆ Go regularly to the library and/or bookstores.
◆ Subscribe to a high-quality newspaper (e.g., *The New York Times, The Washington Post*) and/or to

a literary magazine (e.g., *The New Yorker, Grand Street*) and read them regularly.

◆ Read a book a week and develop a personal library.

◆ Join a speaker's club (e.g., Toastmasters International) or prepare an informal ten-minute talk for a business or community event.

◆ Learn to use a word processor.

◆ Listen to recordings of famous orators, poets, storytellers, and other speakers (check them out from a library).

◆ Keep a daily diary or write 250 words a day about anything on your mind.

◆ Pay attention to the different verbal styles (dialects, slang expressions, intonations, vocabularies, and so forth) of the various people you meet during an average day.

◆ Have a regular storytelling time with family or friends.

◆ Make up your own jokes, riddles, or puns.

◆ Attend a speed-reading seminar.

◆ Teach an illiterate person to read through a volunteer organization.

◆ Memorize favorite poetry or prose passages.

◆ Rent, borrow, or buy audio recordings of great literature and listen to them as you commute to work or during other times of the day.

◆ Circle unfamiliar words you encounter during your reading and look them up in the dictionary.

◆ Buy a thesaurus, a rhyming dictionary, a book of word origins, and a style manual and use them regularly in your writing.

◆ Go to a storytellers' festival and learn about the art of storytelling.

◆ Use one new word in your conversation every day.

3

PICTURE SMART:
THINKING
WITH YOUR
MIND'S EYE

American scientist Louis Agassiz was a man who valued detail. One day a new assistant reported for duty and Agassiz set the man to work studying an unusual specimen of fish. Having given his instructions, Agassiz stepped out of the lab for what the assistant thought would be a few minutes. After half an hour of observation, the student felt he had discovered everything there was to know about the fish. But Agassiz did not return. Several more hours went by, during which time the student alternately felt bored, frustrated, and angry at this apparent abandonment. To pass the time he counted scales and fins and began to diagram the fish. He discovered things he had missed in his initial viewing, including the fact that the fish had no eyelids. Eventually, the master returned, to the relief of the novice researcher. Agassiz, however, was not satisfied with what the young scientist had discovered and kept the apprentice looking at the fish for another two days. Many

years later, the man—who had by then risen to promi-
nence in his field—recalled those three days as the most
valuable training he had ever received.

This incident suggests something about the power of
focused perception to reveal what is present—though hidden to the casual observer—in all things visible. It touches
on an intelligence of seeing that Howard Gardner refers
to as *spatial intelligence*. The core components of this intelligence include the ability to perceive the visual-spatial
world accurately and the capacity to perform transformations on one's initial perceptions. This is the intelligence
of the architect and the Sherpa, the inventor and the mechanic, the engineer and the land surveyor. The spatially
intelligent person sees things—whether in the "real"
world or in the mind—that others are likely to miss. She
also has the capacity to mold and shape these images,
either through physical means such as drawing, sculpting,
building, and inventing, or through mental rotations and
transformations of subjective images. This chapter will describe the varieties of spatial intelligence and explore ways
in which you—like Agassiz's apprentice— can develop your
visual-spatial powers through patient and consistent
practice.

◆ SEEING IS BELIEVING —————————————————

The direct perception of the visual world is the central
feature of spatial intelligence. Although those without sight
do possess spatial intelligence (even three-year-old blind
children can understand trajectories of objects and interpret maps), the capacity to actually *see* the world is, in
most cases, an important first step for working with spatial
information. Such visual acuity occurs in varied degrees in
all sighted persons, with 20/20 vision being considered

normal. There are, however, people who have a sort of hawk-eyed ability that allows them to see at distances far beyond this optical standard. German student Veronica Seider, for example, could identify individuals seen at a distance of more than a mile. And one of the nation's astronauts reportedly located specific houses from one hundred miles above the earth's surface during one of his orbital missions. These individuals have what scientists call *hypereidesis*—or super visual acuity.

Other spatially intelligent people seem to possess remarkable observation skills for objects seen at closer range. The Gikwe bushmen of the Kalahari can look at the track marks of an antelope and determine the animal's size, sex, build, and mood. And Eskimo hunters carefully attend to small details in the shaping of the ice and snow under their feet, since any mistake could lead them onto an ice floe that might break off and leave them stranded. In our own culture the ability to notice spatial features in the environment is less important since we have signs, maps, and other forms of verbal and numerical information to orient us. Yet we still may be missing a great deal of what goes on in front of our eyes when we rely too heavily on linguistic and logical-mathematical intelligence. The following exercise is designed to help you recover observational skills that may have lain dormant since early childhood:

SEEING WITH A HUNTER'S EYES

Find a place outdoors where you will be relatively undisturbed: your backyard, a park, or some other natural location. Spend an hour in one spot, simply looking around at the visible environment. Notice as much as you can about your surroundings. Try to go beyond the obvious and look at what is "hidden" in the fabric of nature. See if you can begin to approach the observational powers of the Kalahari bushman or the Eskimo hunter in perceiving subtle detail in the scenery. Look at the scenery with "soft" eyes—that is, don't look at any one thing in particular but rather at the whole visual field simultaneously. Be aware of what's present in your peripheral vision. See if you can even notice what is behind you. Come back to the same location on several different occasions. Notice how your perceptions of the place change as you spend more time observing what is around you.

◆ THE INNOCENT EYE ─────────

The kind of viewing experience described above can lead to another form of direct observation that is more consciously aesthetic. This is the spatial intelligence of the interior decorator, the landscape architect, the artist, the sculptor, or the art critic. Such visual perception involves a sensitivity to key elements in an artistic work, including line, shape, volume, space, balance, light and shade, harmony, pattern, and color. Artists in particular seem to thrive on these elements. Picasso, for example, revealed an intense sensibility to *color* when he recounted in an interview: "I take a walk in the forest of Fontainebleau. There I get an indigestion of greenness. I must empty this sensation into a picture." Similarly, Russian painter Wassily Kandinsky, remembering an experience he had with his first art materials, wrote:

> *As a thirteen- or fourteen-year-old boy I bought a box of oil-colors with pennies slowly and painfully saved. To this very day I can still see these*

colors coming out of the tubes. One press of my fingers and jubilantly, festively, or grave and dreamy, or turned thoughtfully within themselves, the colors came forth. Or wild with sportiveness, with a deep sigh of liberation, with the deep tone of sorrow, with splendid strength and fortitude, with yielding softness and resignation, with stubborn self-mastery, with a delicate uncertainty of mood—out they came, these curious, lovely things that are called colors.

Having expressed himself in this way, the artist leaves a legacy to the rest of us. He invites us to awaken a similar mode of perception in ourselves so that we might truly see the work as intended by its creator. British art historian Kenneth Clark relates his own first encounter with art on this level as a youth visiting an exhibition of Japanese art in London:

At the end of the gallery was a small flight of steps. We ascended rather wearily, entered another gallery and immediately I was transported. On either side were screens with paintings of flowers of such ravishing beauty that I was not only struck dumb with delight, I felt that I had entered a new world. In the relationship of the shapes and colours a new order had been revealed to me, a new certainty established.

This childhood experience is all the more remarkable after hearing Clark relate how fifty-five years later he was visiting a temple near Kyoto, Japan, and recognized those same paintings (they had been part of a traveling exhibition that came to London in 1910 when he was a child). The creative vision leaves its ecstatic trace on those who possess the aesthetic sensitivity to receive it. The next exercise will help you cultivate your own ability to see with the eyes of an artist or art critic.

GALLERY GLANCES

Visit an art museum or private gallery in your area. (If one isn't accessible to you, then obtain a well-illustrated art history book such as Jansen's History of Art and let that be your portable gallery.) Walk through the museum until you come to an object of art (painting, drawing, sculpture, collage, assemblage, photo) or a set of objects that interests you in some way. Avoid focusing on the subject matter. Instead, pay attention to your own direct perception of the work. Keep an open mind and let yourself be surprised by the unexpected. Notice where your eye falls and how it is drawn from one area of the work to the next. What sticks out for you in examining the piece? Is it the colors? The use of space? The way elements combine? Or is it something undefinable? Don't try to analyze what you see immediately, but notice the presence of delight, disgust, or other feelings that may be present. Limit your time in the museum to an hour. Afterwards you may want to write about your experience or talk to someone familiar with the art you have seen. Return to the museum in a month or two and notice how your experience of the work has changed or stayed the same (and take time to explore other works as well).

In some cases visiting a museum and directly encountering original art can have unexpected consequences. Among certain sensitive individuals, classic masterpieces of painting, sculpture, or architecture have been known to cause rapid heart beat, emotional upheaval, fainting, and even hallucinations. This condition is known as *Stendhal syndrome,* after the nineteenth-century French writer who wrote about his experience of being overwhelmed by the frescoes of Florence. Though relatively rare, it is indicative of the tremendous power that art can have on the human psyche. More typically, your own museum experiences will simply leave you with an awakened eye and a deepened aesthetic sensibility.

◆ DEVELOPING YOUR INNER ARTIST ──────

It's not enough for many of us simply to appreciate other people's art. We want to become artists ourselves. However, most people stop drawing and painting after the age of eight or nine because of their frustrations in making their pictures look realistic. According to Betty Edwards, author of *Drawing on the Right Side of the Brain,* adults who still draw at the stick-figure level do so because they're trying to portray a mental representation of a person (two arms, two legs, a head, and so forth) instead of drawing what they actually see in front of their eyes. Through a number of structured exercises, Edwards helps potential artists use their perceptual abilities to draw more clearly and accurately. The following activity is adapted from her work.

DRAWING UPSIDE DOWN

Obtain a straight-line black-and-white cartoon from a newspaper or magazine that includes one or two human figures. Turn the cartoon upside down. On a separate sheet of paper, draw what you see in the cartoon. Pick any point on the drawing as a starting place. Then copy on your sheet exactly what you see, line by line. Avoid focusing on the conceptual content of the cartoon. Instead, see the lines, angles, shapes, connections, and other purely perceptual features. Don't turn either the cartoon or your drawing right-side up until you've finished. At times it may seem as if you are simply drawing disconnected lines and angles. But after you're finished, turn your own drawing and the cartoon right-side up and compare them. Notice how accurate your drawing is in replicating the original cartoon.

Edwards suggests employing a similar process of looking directly at perceptual features in drawing house-hold items, landscapes, human portraits, and other three-dimensional objects and figures. "People need to be taught to set aside the symbol systems and to see what is really in front of their eyes," she says. To assist in this effort, she advises that aspiring artists notice the relationships be-tween the elements of an object, pay attention to the nega-tive or empty spaces around things, and close one eye from time to time to flatten images as they draw. The goal is to shift into a mode of perceiving controlled by the right hemisphere (which is largely responsible for spatial intelligence). In this *R-mode,* as she calls it, things are seen directly, completely, spontaneously, and immediately. While Edwards's approach is only one of several drawing methods available (see pages 229–31 for other books on the subject), it does result in dramatic changes for many people in their ability to draw realistically. Later on in this chapter we'll look at a totally different kind of drawing experience, one that helps externalize the inner images we all unconsciously produce on a regular basis.

◆ THE INNER PICTURE ──────────────────────

While spatial intelligence begins by looking outwardly at the visible world, it's in the turning inward and trans-forming of such perceptions that we really begin to ap-preciate the wisdom of the eye. The ability to create subjective visual images is still little understood by scientists. But it represents an important way for individuals to create, remember, and process information. Scientists call the clearest of these pictures *eidetic* images (from the Greek *eidetikos,* meaning "pertaining to images"). These have nearly the quality of photographic prints. Individuals who possess the capacity to produce eidetic imagery report that they can look at a picture, form an internal image of what they see, and then with eyes still closed, scan that image for additional details not seen in the original viewing of the picture. In one experiment a young girl with eidetic imagery was shown the left half of a stereoscopic picture (e.g., in "3-D"), not sufficient in itself to create the illusion of depth. The next day she was presented with the right half of the picture and, by calling up her mental image of the previous day's viewing, was able to combine the two to achieve the experience of depth.

Individual reports of eidetic imagery illustrate how remarkable this talent can be in assisting a person with memory-related or problem-solving tasks. One man related how this ability worked for him as a youngster in school: "I was fifteen. During an exam, I 'saw' my chemistry book. I mentally opened it, turned over the pages, and 'copied' the nitric acid diagram onto my exam paper." Even more remarkable are stories attributed to Nikola Tesla, the inventor of the fluorescent light bulb and the AC generator. Reflecting on Tesla's capacity to visualize the creation of a new invention, one observer noted: "Telsa could project before his eyes a picture, complete in every detail, of every part of the machine. These pictures were more vivid than any blueprint." Tesla's co-workers claimed he was able to visualize his mechanisms' dimensions down to the ten-thousandth of an inch and test the imaginary devices in his mind's eye by having them run for weeks—"after which time he would examine them thoroughly for signs of wear."

Most normal adults are not able to visualize at this level of clarity. Studies suggest that eidetic imagery occurs only rarely after the onset of puberty (although it is fairly common among young children). According to British neurophysiologist W. Gray Walter, approximately one-sixth of a normal population sees vivid inner imagery, another sixth generally does not use visual images in their thinking unless required to do so, and the remaining two-thirds "can evoke satisfactory visual patterns when necessary." The following exercise will help you decide which particular group you happen to fall into.

MENTAL POSTCARDS

Sit in a comfortable chair or lie on the floor to do this exercise. Close your eyes, breathe normally for a minute or two, and then read through the list of items below (or have a friend read each item to you). Allow enough time to form a clear visual image of each scene before going on to the next item.

- ◆ your bedroom
- ◆ a pair of scissors
- ◆ a yellow hippopotamus with orange spots in a pink tutu
- ◆ your mother on the ceiling
- ◆ the skyline of a large metropolitan city
- ◆ the bottom of a lake or ocean
- ◆ a photograph of Albert Einstein
- ◆ a map of the world
- ◆ how you looked as a seven-year-old
- ◆ a green square, red circle, and blue triangle

Rate each image on a scale from 0 to 6 (0 = no image; 1 = very faint image; 2 = faint image; 3 = fairly clear image; 4 = clear image; 5 = very clear image; 6 = as clear as actual perception).

You might have found it difficult to image some of these scenes and yet still be a good visualizer. Some individuals have better visualizing capacities when they can invent their own scenarios. According to research conducted by Jerome Singer, professor of psychology at Yale University, practically everyone daydreams. Such daydreams serve to help people cope with stress, explore future possibilities, and overcome boredom. In one experiment subjects who managed to sneak in some daydreaming while engaged in a rote task involving counting skills reported less drowsiness and managed to perform more effectively. The next exercise provides you with an opportunity to do a little daydreaming of your own.

DAYDREAM SMORGASBORD

Close your eyes and let your mind wander. Notice any visual images that pass across your mind's eye. Become aware of your inner fantasies. Notice the visual quality of the images as you daydream. How would you rate them on the scale listed above? What other intelligences do you use during your daydreams (kinesthetic, musical, linguistic and so forth)? Daydream as much as you'd like before continuing with your reading. In the future pay attention to times when you begin to drop into daydreaming during work and leisure.

Still others can visualize better when they're thinking about some concrete object or problem. The mechanic often visualizes while working on a car engine. The surgeon uses visualization abilities as he goes in to repair a ruptured aorta. The following exercise will give you an opportunity to exercise your own three-dimensional mind in relation to your daily surroundings.

THE SEEING EYE

Imagine that you have a "roving eyeball" that can leave your body at will and examine everyday objects from all points of view. Select a common object such as a chair, a desk, a sofa, or an appliance to observe. Then, while seated a few feet away from the object of viewing, use your "third eye" to inspect it from every conceivable point of view: from the top looking down, from the bottom looking up, from each side, at weird angles, close up, far away, inside out, and so forth. If you wish, quickly sketch these different viewpoints on a sheet of paper. After you've completed your examination, get up and position your body in different ways so that you can actually see the object from some of these perspectives. Compare your imagined viewing with your real perceptions. How accurate are you? Do this for a number of other objects.

◆ VISUAL THINKING

One of the most profound results of intelligent visualization is the stimulation of creative potentials and the cultivation of higher-order thinking processes. According to Rudolf Arnheim, professor emeritus of the psychology of art at Harvard University, practically *all* thinking—even the most theoretical and abstract—is visual in nature. As an example he points to the thought processes of nineteenth-century psychologist E. B. Titchener, who once reported visualizing the concept of "meaning" as "the blue-grey tip of a kind of scoop, which has a bit of yellow above it (probably a part of the handle), and which is just digging into a dark mass of what appears to be plastic material."

Far more practical are the mental pictures of eminent thinkers who used visual imagery to help give birth to their life's work. The three individuals who had perhaps the greatest impact on twentieth-century thought—Albert Einstein, Charles Darwin, and Sigmund Freud—all used visual images in developing their revolutionary theories. Darwin's notebooks reflect an ongoing fascination with the image of the tree. This symbol appeared to be important in helping him conceptualize the theory of evolution. In one of his notebooks (alongside a sketch of a tree), Darwin wrote: "Organized beings represent a tree, irregularly branched ... as many terminal buds dying as new ones generated." Similarly, Albert Einstein received one of the original inspirations for his theory of relativity at the age of sixteen, when he visualized what it might be like to ride on a beam of light. And Sigmund Freud supported his theories of personality in part by relying on the image of an island rising up out of the sea—a metaphor for the relationship of the ego to the unconscious.

These images represent cognitive schemas or "mental maps" that helped guide the development of thought in these geniuses over a period of years. Psychologist Howard Gruber calls these internal pictures "images of wide scope" and suggests that great thinkers may have perhaps four or five of these in their lifetime, compared to the roughly six hundred concrete images that a good visualizer will produce in an hour of serious daydreaming. Most of us carry around visual mental maps of considerably narrower scope that nevertheless are personally important in helping orient us to the world. These internalized visual schemas tell us how to get from our homes to our workplaces, which knob to twist when the plumbing needs fixing, and how to play simple games like chess and checkers.

The visual schemas we carry around in our minds are often quite sketchy, much like the medieval maps that depicted dragons lurking at the edge of the known world. Saul Steinberg's famous drawing showing a New Yorker's view of the world, with Manhattan taking up most of the picture and the rest of the world sparsely illustrated, indicates how cognitive maps frequently reflect our egocentric point of view. The following exercise will help you examine some of the visual-spatial maps you may be carrying around in your mind without even knowing it.

MENTAL MAPS

Create a sketch for each of the following items. Don't be concerned about neatness or making something to show to others. But do include as much detail as possible in your drawing (avoid looking at reference works until after you're finished):

- a map of your immediate neighborhood (within a three-block radius)
- a floor plan of your house or apartment
- a picture of the concept of democracy
- a diagram of the inside of the human body
- a map of the world with all the continents drawn in
- a diagram of the inside of a washing machine

You can check your visual ideas out by looking at a map of your town, a globe, a floor plan of your house, an anatomy book, the book *Visual Thinking,* which includes others' renditions of "democracy," and/or a book such as *The Way Things Work,* which describes the inner workings of machines. What do your drawings tell you about your knowledge of the world? What do they tell you about how your mind works? Ask friends to do this exercise and compare drawings.

◆ BRAIN-SKETCHING ─────────────

The kind of drawings you did above are essentially schematic drawings—quick sketches that reveal your inner picture of things. Many creative thinkers, including Leonardo da Vinci, Thomas Edison, and Henry Ford, kept notebooks or sketch diaries of their visual thinking. Leonardo's "rough-draft" notebooks are now considered fine art, but for him they were simply the means by which he could work out visual problems encountered in designing or inventing something new.

Former Stanford design professor Robert McKim recommends that all aspiring visual thinkers keep some kind of sketch journal or idea log to record their spatial thoughts. He offers these guidelines in describing what highly spatially intelligent individuals often do in recording their thoughts: "Visual thinkers who use drawings to explore and develop ideas make *many drawings;* idea-finding and formation is not a static, 'one-picture' procedure. They also *draw quickly* (ideas rarely hold still; they readily change form and even disappear). In both the exploratory and the developmental mode, graphic ideators also use *many graphic idioms.*" McKim recommends using some of the following visual forms in a graphic notebook: charts, diagrams, flowcharts, graphs, orthographic projections, cartoons, decision trees, maps, doodles, designs, and photos. Such a journal can be kept in a standard diary or looseleaf notebook or be stored on index cards or even on long rolls of wrapping paper to encourage the flow of ideas.

Spatial thinkers should also consider working with their ideas in three dimensions. James Watson and Francis Crick stunned the world and won a Nobel Prize in 1962 when they discovered the double-helix structure of the DNA molecule by using a large three-dimensional model as a thinking tool. Designers at General Motors and NASA regularly create elaborate cardboard mock-ups of cars and space modules that save them millions of dollars in development costs. You can create your own visual thinking lab at home with inexpensive materials such as Styrofoam or Foamcore (a laminated paper-and-Styrofoam sandwich) for mock-ups and miniature models; soda straws and paper clips or commercially made sticks and connectors for geometrical shapes; and a box of miscellaneous odds and ends (string, tape, blocks, toothpicks, clay, wire, wood scraps, rubber bands, tinfoil, paper scraps, and so forth). In addition, consider the power of modern technology in aiding visual thought. The computer industry has opened up a wide range of options for visual thinkers through CAD (Computer Aided Design) programs, "paint and draw" software, interactive video, and other emerging technologies (see page 248 for a list of some current visual-spatial softwares).

◆ CULTURE'S MYOPIC VISION ———————

Despite the emergence of high-tech visual-spatial tools, our culture still may be devoting too much attention to linguistic and logical-mathematical intelligences in the development of new products. Eugene S. Ferguson, professor of history at the University of Delaware, points out that engineering programs in our universities are becoming increasingly numerical and analytical, losing sight of the education of the mind's eye. As a result, he says, "we can expect to witness an increasing number of silly but costly errors that occur in advanced engineering systems today." One example of this devaluation of spatial intelligence may have occurred in the space-shuttle disaster. Apparently, the Challenger's poorly designed O-rings failed to remain flexible in cold weather and thus allowed a leakage of fuel that led to the explosion that destroyed the spacecraft. This flaw was spotted by spatially intelligent technicians but overruled by analytically oriented and politically motivated supervisors who were perhaps less able to visualize the consequences of the problem.

If you're a spatially intelligent individual, then you've probably felt this cultural bias in your own life. You may have spent years languishing in schools where teachers placed little emphasis on the things you did best. Rarely did you get an opportunity to describe your mental images and draw or diagram your visual thoughts. Daydreamers typically have been thought of as lazy and unfocused. Yet it may be the daydreamers and other visual-spatial thinkers in our society who will envision the creative possibilities of life as we move into the twenty-first century.

25 THINGS YOU CAN DO TO DEVELOP YOUR SPATIAL INTELLIGENCE

- ◆ Play Pictionary, three-dimensional tic-tac-toe, or other visual thinking games.
- ◆ Work on jigsaw puzzles, Rubik's cube, mazes, or other visual puzzles.
- ◆ Purchase a graphics software program and create designs, drawings, and images on the computer.
- ◆ Learn photography and use a camera to record your visual impressions.
- ◆ Purchase a camcorder and create video presentations.
- ◆ Watch films and television shows with attention to the use of light, camera movement, color, and other cinematic elements.
- ◆ Redecorate the interior of your house or landscape the exterior.
- ◆ Create a picture library of favorite images from magazines and newspapers.
- ◆ Learn orienteering skills for hiking in nature.
- ◆ Study geometry.
- ◆ Take a class in drawing, sculpting, painting, photography, video, graphic design, or some other visual art at a local college or community center.

- Learn an ideographically-based language such as Chinese.
- Make three-dimensional models of ideas you have for inventions or other projects.
- Learn how to use and interpret flowcharts, decision trees, diagrams, and other forms of visual representation.
- Purchase a visual dictionary and study how common machines and other objects work.
- Explore the space around you by putting on a blindfold and letting a friend guide you through your house or yard.
- Practice looking for images and pictures in clouds, cracks in the wall, or other natural or man-made phenomena.
- Develop your own visual symbols for note taking (use arrows, circles, stars, spirals, color-coding, pictures, and other visual forms).
- Visit a mechanical engineer, architect, artist, or designer to see how he uses spatial abilities in his work.
- Spend time engaged in art activities with family or friends.
- Study maps of your town and state, floor plans of your home, and other visual representational systems.
- Build structures with Legos, D-stix, hexaflexagons, blocks, or other three-dimensional building materials.
- Study optical illusions (e.g., in puzzle books, at science museums, via optical illusion toys, etc.)
- Rent, borrow, or purchase "how-to" videotapes on specific areas of interest.
- Incorporate drawings, photos, and diagrams into letters, projects, and presentations.

MUSIC SMART:
MAKING THE MOST
OF YOUR
MELODIC MIND

The most baffling mysteries were elementary to Sir Arthur
Conan Doyle's legendary sleuth Sherlock Holmes. Yet even
Holmes sometimes encountered intractable cases that required a special effort. At such times he would get out his
violin and play. Music seemed to unlock the gates to new
avenues of inquiry for Holmes, allowing him to see solutions where previously there had been only confusion.
This fictional detective can offer us important clues in
using music to become more effective thinkers. It has
often been said that music has charms to soothe the savage
breast; it also appears to be true that music can stimulate
the modern mind.

The role that music has in ordinary thinking processes
became clear to me one day when a carpenter put a heat-
ing vent into my dining room ceiling. He walked into the
room, looked up at the projected site of the installation,
and started to make little rhythmic humming noises. "Uh-

huh-uh-*huh*-uh-*huh*!" he crooned under his breath as he surveyed the project thoughtfully. He seemed to be thinking about how large the hole would have to be and reviewing other requirements of the job. Then he raised his hands toward the ceiling like a symphony conductor and made funny clicking sounds as if to emphasize that certain technical points were being ironed out ("click-*clack*!"). Finally, almost to suggest that the entire project was resolved in his own mind, he finished with a loud sigh and launched into a cheery popular song to celebrate. Later I discovered that he'd been a jazz musician before taking up work as a freelance carpenter. But while he left his saxophone behind, he continued to use his musical intelligence in his new career.

You don't have to be a professional musician to think musically. Most of us use our musical minds in the course of everyday life. We're surrounded by music from dusk to dawn. We wake up to musical alarm clocks, listen to songs on the radio while commuting to work, work in office buildings serenaded by Muzak, and relax at home at the end of the day listening to our CDs and MTV. We celebrate our most important rites of passage—weddings and funerals—with music. We exercise to music, worship to music, and shop to music. This informal musical education can't help but influence the way we think in powerful ways. This chapter will help you explore the impact music has on several components of your mind, including memory, imagery, and creativity.

◆ THEY'RE PLAYING OUR SONG ─────────

Advertisers have known for years an important fact that cognitive psychologists are just beginning to appreciate: putting a slogan or phrase to music can make it almost impossible to forget. If you were around during the 1950s, you'll probably be able to fill in the missing word for the musical phrase: "See the USA in your_____." Younger readers might do better with a more recent jingle: "At_____, we do it all for you." Neither of these musical statements has been broadcast for years, yet it's likely that the missing words popped into your mind more quickly than the memory of what you ate for dinner yesterday. Somewhere in our brains we have thousands of these musical phrases drifting around like flotsam and jetsam, each fragment just waiting for a signal to be activated. The following exercise will help you become aware of how much music you actually have floating around inside of you.

THE MUSICAL STREAM

Do this exercise with one or two friends. Sing the musical parts of commercials that you've recently heard on the radio or television. If necessary, spend time actually listening to some examples to get started. Write down these musical phrases or, better yet, sing them into a tape recorder. As you share commercials, further jingles should occur to you. If your memory falters, think of categories of items commonly advertised, such as cars, hamburgers, drinks, toys, and clothes. For every current commercial you remember, think of a jingle on the same subject that hasn't been broadcast for months or years. Generate as many different musical jingles as possible. You can also follow the same procedure using top-40 songs or movie and television themes of the past twenty-five years.

Advertisers have done an excellent job of filling up our minds with useless information. You can use some of the same tricks, however, to program your mind with knowledge that *you* choose to put into it. Before the invention of written language, societies had to devise ways to transmit knowledge from one generation to another. Usually it was a matter of handing down information important for the perpetuation of the tribe. Elders needed to tell younger members of the culture about their genealogical histories, navigational data, or which local plants were poisonous and which could be eaten, so that this lore would still be available after the older generation passed away. Music represented one important way for tribal elders to commit this information to memory. Information was broken down into small chunks and chanted or set to musical phrases. Even today primitive cultures transmit knowledge in this way. An educated Iatmul in New Guinea, for instance, knows between 10,000 and 20,000 clan names without the benefit of written records. Part of the secret to his success is that he chants the names in a rhythmic way. The next exercise will show you how to use rhythm and music to remember somewhat smaller chunks of information.

MUSICAL SHOPPING LISTS

Select a short list of items that you would like to commit to memory. Some possibilities: a shopping list, things to do today, procedures for a do-it-yourself job around the house, or names you need to remember. Write the items on a sheet of paper and begin saying them to yourself slowly. Gradually pick up speed and try to find a rhythm in your repetition (*Mar*-tha, *Bet*-ty, *Pe*-ter, *John*). Keep the rhythm going until you no longer need the paper in front of you.

During the Middle Ages monasteries used music to help monks memorize scripture. In the same way educators recently started using classical music to stimulate the mind to absorb knowledge. One approach, based on the work of Bulgarian psychiatrist Georgi Lozanov, involves listening to a piece of music with a consistent musical beat (4/4 time is considered optimal) while reciting material to be learned in rhythm to the music. Alternatively, learners listen passively with eyes closed while another person rhythmically repeats the information in time to the music. One study commissioned by the U.S. Army and conducted by the National Academy of Sciences suggested that the use of background music shows promise as an effective learning tool when used in conjunction with conventional learning methods. Other research indicates that this approach can be useful in mastering foreign languages, math algorithms, science concepts, and other academic material. The next exercise illustrates how to adapt this method to your own learning needs.

SUPERMUSIC SESSION

Choose a musical passage by Mozart, Beethoven, Bach, Vivaldi, Pachelbel, Handel, or Haydn that has a relatively consistent tempo (see page 244 for a list of organizations that sell specially designed superlearning music tapes). Select academic material that you would like to learn, such as mathematical formulas, historical facts, foreign-language vocabulary, literary passages, or science concepts. Read the material out loud in rhythm to the recorded music. Then have a friend read the material to you in rhythm to the recorded music while you sit or lie in a comfortable position with eyes closed in a relaxed state. The more spirit you and your friend put into the reading process, the more effective this exercise will be. Vary your intonation, reading at first loudly, then softly, then with moderate intensity, and repeating this sequence until the music ends.

◆ THE MIND'S EAR ─────────────────

When Wolfgang Amadeus Mozart was a boy, he visited the Sistine Chapel in Rome and was entranced by a piece of music he heard there. Unfortunately, the Vatican decreed that this musical work, the *Miserere* by Gregorio Allegri, could be performed only inside the Sistine Chapel and could not be copied under any circumstances. Mozart responded to this dilemma in a remarkable way. He attended one more performance of the piece and then returned to his lodgings and copied the entire score from memory. Mozart was able to accomplish this aural feat because he had a capacity to create in his mind's ear a perfect replica of the complex musical sounds that made up Allegri's sacred composition. In a sense his ability was similar to the eidetic imagery capabilities of visually skilled artists. He later said that when he composed music he could hear all of the notes of his composition simultaneously. Other composers had similar auditory imaginations. Schumann could listen to piano music and mentally fill in the tones of other instruments as if an entire orchestra were playing. And when Tchaikovsky wrote a symphonic work, he could imagine how it would sound performed in a specific concert hall in Moscow.

The ability to hear musical tones in one's head is an important trait of a musically intelligent person. In one of the very few scientific studies of auditory imagery ever conducted, more than 50 percent of the professional musicians surveyed reported that they mentally heard the song "America" on the piano as clearly as if it were actually being played. Less than 5 percent of the psychologists involved in the study could say the same thing. One psychologist wrote: "I had a very clear and distinct ... auditory image of my own voice *singing* "America," but I could not get an auditory image of this air as played on a piano." It may be, however, that this ability can be cultivated. Late Stanford psychology professor Paul R. Farnsworth, observed that "[auditory] eidetic images are known to be far more common among children than among adults, many of the latter having lost their eidetic potentialities through lack of practice." The following exercise provides an opportunity for you to recapture this lost ability by conjuring up some musical moments from your own inner "tone bank."

PHONOGRAPHIC MEMORIES

Sit in a comfortable chair with your eyes closed. Breathe easily and deeply for one or two minutes. Clear your mind of stray thoughts and feelings. Then produce the following auditory images in your mind's ear (have a friend read the items to you one by one if possible):

- ◆ the sound of rain falling on the roof
- ◆ the theme song from your favorite television show
- ◆ any piece of classical music
- ◆ the sound of your own voice singing
- ◆ some organ music
- ◆ the sound of crickets chirping
- ◆ a group of people singing "Happy Birthday"
- ◆ the sound of wind chimes
- ◆ any song you loved as a child
- ◆ a popular song that you heard recently on the radio
- ◆ an original melody of your own creation
- ◆ "Twinkle Twinkle Little Star" played on a violin

Rate each auditory image on a scale from 0 to 6 (0 = no image; 1 = very faint image; 2 = faint image; 3 = fairly clear image; 4 = clear image; 5 = very clear image; 6 =

as clear as the actual hearing). Notice which images seem clearest and whether repeated mental hearings help to develop this skill. Create other inner musical experiences not listed above.

You can cultivate your musical imagery so that you essentially have your own "inner Walkman." Think of all the times you've been stuck in a line at the grocery store, or on a bench waiting for a bus or plane, and there's been nothing for you to listen to for relaxation. Now you have your own portable melody machine wired into your musical brain with thousands of selections potentially available. The only limit is your musical imagination.

◆ EINSTEIN WITH A BEAT ────── ───────

Twentieth-century American poet Hart Crane would sometimes spend months or even years carrying around ideas for a new work before sitting down to put all the pieces of his literary puzzle together. At such times music often played an important role in his creative process. He would put on a Cuban rumba, a torch song, or perhaps a recording of Ravel's *Bolero* and begin typing furiously, stopping only to change records. He would soon emerge from this musical orgy with a new poem in his hands. Music proved to be fundamental in activating his fertile imagination to produce a completed work. Other creative individuals have used music in a similar fashion to coax their genius into action. During the development of the atomic bomb, nuclear physicist Edward Teller kept colleagues at the Los Alamos Laboratory awake at night by playing Beethoven sonatas on a piano in his thin-walled barracks quarters. Albert Einstein played the violin and Albert

Schweitzer played the organ, even as they nurtured their scientific and humanitarian pursuits.

The role of music in stimulating the creative unconscious is supported by several research studies. In one experiment adults scored higher on a test of pictorial creativity when they were exposed to background music. In two other studies subjects who were allowed to listen to music told more fanciful stories and wrote more creative compositions than individuals working in silence. It appears that music has unique properties that unlock the floodgates to new thoughts and insights. So-called primitive cultures recognize the power of music and use ritual drumming, chanting, and singing to put tribal members into trancelike states that radically alter their thinking processes. The following exercise will help you gain access through music to new avenues of thought, solve difficult problems, gain greater awareness of your own creative process, and envision new possibilities in your life.

MUSICAL INCUBATION

Before starting this exercise select one or more musical pieces to help activate your creative unconscious. They should be musical selections that you've found uplifting or inspiring in the past. Prepare the music so that it will be ready to play at the flick of a switch. Then, write down on a sheet of paper a question that you would like to have answered. It might be a specific problem that has puzzled you at work, a situation in your personal life you need to have clarified, or some other important question that you've tried to answer in other ways. Spend at least a half an hour writing about possible solutions that have occurred to you, obstacles that stand in the way, and any other associations that emerge. Then put your pencil and paper away, lie or sit in a relaxed position, and breathe deeply and easily for two or three minutes. Finally, turn on (or have a friend turn on) the tape player and listen to the music. Avoid focusing on your question during this time. Instead, simply let your mind be moved by the piece. Notice any ideas, images, or associations that arise. After the session record these experiences, and look for information in them that may suggest an answer to your question.

Music can serve as a stimulant whenever you need a creative lift in your life. If you have a learning block or find yourself getting stressed at work, consider music as a way out of your impasse. Music acts as a balance to the many linguistic and logical tasks we do during the day. It represents a refreshing shift into a different domain and provides a way of opening up to new perspectives in life.

Pay special attention to music that bubbles to the surface of awareness from the depths of your psyche. You might find yourself unconsciously whistling a tune that holds special meaning. Recently I was walking down the street in a dejected mood when I discovered that I was humming Billy Joel's "I Love You Just the Way You Are." The tune let me know that there was a deeper part of me that did not participate in my depressed mood. In a sense the musical part of my mind represented an inner voice assuring me that I was okay. The next time a song pops into your head (it may even come in a dream), examine its theme, its title, the lyrics, and its musical meaning for clues to your current life situation.

◆ THEY LAUGHED WHEN I SAT AT THE PIANO ──

When I was eight I really thought I was going to be the next Chopin. As a six-year-old I'd shown some interest in playing an old upright piano at my grandparents' home. I loved climbing onto the long wooden bench and banging out tunes I'd heard or making up little melodies of my own. Then my father sent my sisters and me to a music teacher and stocked our house with an impressive array of keyboard instruments: a Steinway grand, a harpsichord, a clavichord, and a smaller organ and piano. It turned out to be overkill. After six years of lessons I stopped playing and now as an adult only rarely sit down at the piano to improvise a tune.

Although I had access to an unusual number of musical instruments as a child, my story is not dissimilar to those of many Americans. A lot of us entered the world of music lessons bright with enthusiasm yet failed to carry this promise into adulthood as practicing virtuosos. Some of us still wonder: is it too late to learn an instrument? The answer, of course, is *no*. The educator John Holt made a point of emphasizing in his book *Never Too Late: My Musical Life Story* that learning, musical or otherwise, is lifelong affair. In that book he shared his own musical odyssey, a process that involved taking up the cello at the age of fifty and practicing intensely enough that he was able to play competently with a chamber orchestra and a string quartet. Holt comments: "... teachers say that if we don't learn to play musical instruments as children we will never be able to learn as adults ... not so. Of course it is nice, if we come freely to music, to come to it young, but if we don't come to it then, we can later. It is never too late."

Maybe you'd like to learn how to play an instrument but feel you have no ear for music. Perhaps you had a traumatic experience as a child with a music teacher or a parent who ridiculed or shamed you for singing off-key or playing an instrument poorly (or too loudly!). "For most children," says Frank Wilson, assistant clinical professor of neurology at San Francisco's University of California Medical Center, "a diagnosis of tone deafness becomes the basis of a lifelong conviction that music is out for them." Wilson declares: "I am convinced that all of us have a biologic guarantee of musicianship. This is true regardless of our age, formal experience with music, or the size and shape of our fingers, lips or ears.... We all have music inside us, and can learn how to get it out, one way or another."

The reason so many adults failed to learn how to master an instrument in childhood, and failed again during abortive attempts in adulthood, according to Wilson, is that there has been too much emphasis on readying oneself to perform pieces before an audience. Not enough importance has been placed on music making for its own sake, as a form of play or recreation. He offers these tips for the musical late-bloomer:

- Decide what sort of instrument you want to play and what kind of music you'd like to be able to perform.
- Interview several music teachers before selecting a particular instructor.
- Contact the teacher's students to learn about their experiences with the instructor.
- Choose a teacher whose musical techniques and philosophies match your own interests.
- Take your first few lessons on a trial basis; after five or ten lessons, sit down with your instructor and evaluate your experience.
- Make sure you and your teacher have a collaborative relationship; don't be afraid to ask questions; don't hide problems you may be having.

◆ THE EAR OF THE BEHOLDER

Music isn't just the province of an elite group of performers. It belongs to everybody. The evidence for this lies in the number of cultures around the world that train a large percentage of their members to become musically literate. In Hungary, due to the pioneering influence of early-twentieth-century composer Zoltán Kodály, almost every child takes music instruction in school every day. Among the Dagombas of northern Ghana, it is said that their children are as involved with active music making as American children are with passive television viewing. And even in a technologically advanced country like Japan, the existence of the Suzuki Talent Education Program is making the violin and piano accessible to wider numbers of children and adults.

Remember, though, that you don't have to take formal music lessons to develop your musical intelligence. Samuel Taylor Coleridge once remarked, "I have no ear whatever [for music]; I could not sing an air to save my life; but I have the intensest delight in music and can detect good from bad." Many people express their musical selves simply through appreciating recorded and live music and through listening to the natural rhythms that occur in everyday life. George Gershwin once said, "I frequently hear music in the heart of noise." American composer Aaron Copland suggested that there are three different levels to listening to music:

◆ The *sensuous* plane—listening for the sheer pleasure of the sounds emitted
◆ The *expressive* plane—paying attention to mood and meaning in a piece; for example, distinguishing a serene work from an exuberant one; listening for the underlying message of the composer
◆ The *musical* plane—attending to the different components of musical structure: melody, harmony, rhythm, timbre or tone color, and texture; also, understanding the musical form (being able to distinguish a sonata from a symphony, for example, or a rondo from a fugue)

Copland pointed out that an individual actually listens in all three ways simultaneously but that becoming an educated music listener requires "a firm resolve to hear a great deal more music than you have in the past." It's most important, according to Copland, to take an *active* role in music appreciation: "You can deepen your understanding of music only by being a more conscious and aware listener—not someone who is just listening, but someone who is listening *for* something." By exposing yourself to a more varied selection of musical pieces, cultivating a critical ear, and experimenting with some of the other suggestion provided in this chapter, you can learn to flex your musical muscles every day without ever practicing a single scale. Even Chopin never had it so good.

---

25 WAYS TO DEVELOP YOUR MUSICAL INTELLIGENCE

- ◆ Sing in the shower or while commuting.
- ◆ Play "Name That Tune" or other musical games with friends.
- ◆ Go to concerts or musicals.
- ◆ Develop a collection of favorite musical recordings and listen to them regularly.
- ◆ Join a church or community choir.
- ◆ Take formal music lessons in a specific instrument.
- ◆ Work with a music therapist.
- ◆ Spend one hour a week listening to an unfamiliar style of music (jazz, country western, classical, folk, international, or other genres).
- ◆ Establish a regular family sing-along time.
- ◆ Buy an electronic keyboard and learn simple melodies and chords.

- Purchase percussion instruments at a toy store and play them in rhythm to background music.
- Take a course in music appreciation or music theory at a local college.
- Read music criticism in newspapers and magazines.
- Volunteer to sing at a retirement home, hospital, or day care center.
- Put on background music while studying, working, or eating, or at some other time during the day that is normally quiet.
- Have discussions with friends about music.
- Read about the lives of famous composers and performers.
- Listen for naturally occurring melodies or rhythms in such phenomena as footsteps, bird song, and washing-machine noise.
- Re-discover the music you loved as a child.
- Make up your own tunes.
- Create your musical autobiography by collecting recordings that were popular at different stages of your life.
- Make a list of all the music you hear in the course of a day, from Muzak in the supermarket to radio and TV music.
- Purchase high-tech equipment (MIDI interface, computer software) that will allow you to teach yourself music theory or to play a musical instrument on the computer.
- Sing all of your communications to your family or friends for an hour or two.
- Learn about specific musical training programs such as the Suzuki, Kodály, Orff-Schulwerk, and Dalcroze systems. (Addresses for organizations sponsoring these methods are listed on page 244.)

BODY SMART: USING YOUR KINESTHETIC INTELLIGENCE

In James Joyce's classic short-story collection, *Dubliners*, there's a wonderful portrait of a reclusive bank cashier named Mr. James Duffy who lives next door to a distillery in a Dublin suburb. In the course of the story, he meets a woman, has an intense intellectual affair with her, and then breaks off the relationship when she presses her hand against his cheek. As part of his description of Mr. Duffy, Joyce includes this rather curious line: *"He lived a little distance from his body."* By this Joyce meant that the man lived in a mental prison divorced from any real contact with the sensory world. In a larger sense Joyce's character is a modern-day Everymind, an example of the split that has occurred in contemporary society between mental and physical faculties.

In ancient times the body and mind were seen as one. The Greeks prized the art of gymnastics as an important means of cultivating the powers of the mind. So too did the Romans, who gave us the expression *mens sana in corpore sano* ("a sound mind in a sound body"). Eastern cultures pursued the development of the mind for thousands of years through bodily activities such as yoga, tai chi, and aikido. In our own culture, however, Christians in the Middle Ages sought to mortify the body as a way of serving the spirit, and thinkers during the later Enlightenment ignored the body and located the source of a person's identity securely in the mind. As French philosopher René Descartes put it almost 400 years ago: "I think, therefore, I am."

Through his declaration Descartes made Mr. Duffys of us all. Intellectual activity came to be identified almost exclusively with logical-mathematical and linguistic abilities. Physical activity was assigned a lower-class status and restricted to the bedroom, the shipyard, and the playing field. Even today, with many Americans experiencing a kind of Renaissance in physical fitness, bodily culture is associated more often with Nautilus machines, weight-training programs, and racquetball courts than with anything having to do with the mind. Athletes are all too often seen as "dumb jocks," and working with the hands in manual arts is assigned a second-class status in comparison to the "higher" world of the humanities and sciences.

The theory of multiple intelligences seeks to heal this rift between body and mind by regarding purposeful physical activity as an intelligence in its own right. The core components of bodily-kinesthetic intelligence are the ability to control one's body movements with expertise (the intelligence of the athlete, dancer, mime, and actor) and the capacity to handle objects skillfully (the intelligence of the sculptor, furniture maker, plumber, and seamstress). This chapter describes several different aspects of bodily-kinesthetic intelligence and explores ways in which you can tap its possibilities, not just to become more physically capable but also to become a more effective thinker.

◆ BEYOND AEROBICS ─────────────────

Can you wiggle your ears? A lot of us haven't even tried since we were kids. Can you do a cartwheel? Most of us wouldn't even dare to attempt one. It seems that if we exercise our bodies at all, we're often too wrapped up with more "important" physical activities like jogging and Jazzercize to waste much time in such idle pursuits. Yet it may be through these kinds of tricks and feats that you can get a better overall sense of your kinesthetic intelligence than through the number of sit-ups or push-ups that you can do in one minute. Fitness experts suggest that there are actually a number of skills involved in physical competence, including strength, endurance, flexibility, balance, dexterity, expressiveness, coordination, and good reflexes. Only the first two of these bodily-kinesthetic capacities get much attention in our culture.

Nonwestern cultures, however, spend a great deal of time developing several of these other abilities. The Japanese place great importance on the development of poise and grace in such arts as the Japanese tea ceremony and aikido. Balinese children spend a lot of their free time playing with the joints of their fingers to achieve the kind of flexibility and dexterity required to participate in their culture's intricate dances. New Guinea youngsters, by the age of five or six, learn to paddle a canoe under a wide range of circumstances, balancing, steering, and punting with a keen physical skill. The following exercises will help you experiment with these kinds of talents and allow you to gauge your own bodily-kinesthetic intelligence in terms of this broader spectrum of abilities. (Primary skills required for each task are included in parentheses.)

BODY TESTS

◆ Stand on one foot like a stork with your eyes closed. How long can you stay like this? (Balance)

◆ Throw a crumpled-up piece of paper into a wastebasket at a distance of ten feet. Increase or decrease the distance to adjust the difficulty level. (Coordination)

◆ Write your name with a pencil stuck between your toes. Find out whether you're right- or left-footed. (Dexterity)

◆ See if you can scratch every square inch of your back with your fingers. (Flexibility)

◆ Do a cartwheel. (Coordination)

◆ Build a five-story miniature house with a deck of playing cards. (Dexterity)

◆ Walk the distance of a city block along the length of a curb. (Balance)

◆ Use some tweezers to transfer one hundred grains of rice from one bowl into another as quickly as you can. (Dexterity)

◆ Play the card game of slap-jack (players take turns flipping one card at a time into the center of play—when a jack appears, the first one to slap it gets all the cards in the pile). (Reflexes)

◆ Arm-wrestle someone who's about your own size. (Strength)

◆ Communicate the concept of "equality" using only your body. (Expressiveness)

◆ Go on a weekend backpacking trip, walking at least

five miles a day. (Those with medical problems should get a doctor's okay first.) (Endurance)

If you found yourself lacking in certain of these exercises, don't worry. Practice makes perfect (see "25 Things You Can Do to Enhance Your Bodily-Kinesthetic Intelligence"). The rest of this chapter will explore how you can develop your mind by acknowledging and using your body as an instrument of self-knowledge.

◆ THE WISDOM OF THE BODY

The body appears to be a regular barometer of cognitive events in certain individuals. Many people commonly speak of having a "gut reaction" to an answer on a test or getting a "feeling in their bones" about a certain person, place, idea, or event. British poet A. E. Housman, for example, wrote about how his body manifested certain physical symptoms whenever a particularly creative idea took hold of him:

> *Experience has taught me, when I am shaving of a morning, to keep watch over my thoughts, because if a line of poetry strays into my memory, my skin bristles so that the razor ceases to act. The particular symptom is accompanied by a shiver down the spine. There is another which consists in a constriction of the throat and a precipitation of water to the eyes; and there is a third which I can only describe by borrowing a phrase from one of Keats's last letters, where he says, speaking of Fanny Brawne, "everything that re-*

minds me of her goes through me like a spear."
The seat of this sensation is the pit of the stomach.

Art educator Viktor Lowenfeld referred to the "haptic" personality (from the Greek *haptos,* "to lay ahold of") as someone who receives information primarily from kinesthetic sources. Says Lowenfeld: "The haptic type utilizes muscular sensations, kinesthetic experiences, touch impressions, and all the experiences of the self to establish his relationship to the outside world." According to Lowenfeld's research, approximately one-fourth of the population shows a clear preference for haptic (as opposed to visual-spatial) perception, while another third appears to have at least some access to its kinesthetic sensibilities. The following exercise will help you recognize and utilize this important source of information in solving problems and making decisions in your everyday life.

GUT REACTIONS

Focus on a personal or professional issue that you're struggling with right now. Write down the nature of the problem at the top of a piece of paper (the more specific you make it the better). Then list as many potential solutions to the problem as you can. After doing this put the paper aside for a few moments and concentrate on your body. Become aware of the connection your body makes with the floor and chair. Feel the contact your skin makes with your clothes. Sense any muscular tension or other sensations in your body. Then, turn your attention to the solutions listed on the paper. Read each potential solution to the problem, pausing after each item to note any changes in your body awareness. Pay particular attention to the relaxing or tightening of muscles in your stomach, abdomen, neck, shoulders, or chest, as these reactions can give you clues as to the "rightness" or "wrongness" of a particular solution. Also look for other physical responses such as tingling or burning sensations in the skin, bristling of hairs, muscle tics, and physical pains or experiences of heat or warmth in specific areas of the body. Cross out the solutions that stimulate the most negative reactions. Circle the solution or solutions that provides the most positive physical reaction or "gut feeling."

Although the above exercise certainly does not provide a fail-safe method of problem solving, it can begin to open the doors of perception to a realm of proprioceptive experiences (e. g., sensations originating in the muscles or tendons) that you may not have considered before as an appropriate thinking tool. You can also use your "body knowing" while taking tests (go with the answers that *feel* right), while reading (note your gut reactions to specific ideas, characters, and phrases), to help you with spelling and writing, and in many other everyday tasks. Even when choosing a friend or a business partner, you're often well advised to stay away from those who give you a pain in the neck!

◆ POSTURE PERFECT

We've observed how the body expresses what the mind harbors. But the reverse is also true: subtle bodily changes can have a powerful effect on mental events. French writer Marcel Proust used his own highly refined haptic sensibilities to explore the body's impact on the mind in his masterpiece *Remembrance of Things Past*. One day, as he related it, he was walking along the cobblestone courtyard of a friend's townhouse when he felt in his body a familiar sensation that he could not readily identify. After a period of introspection he eventually traced the sensation back to an experience he'd had several years earlier when he'd been on a trip to Italy and had experienced the unevenness of the pavement there. Somewhere locked in his body was the memory of that event, needing only a specific posture to bring it to the surface of his mind.

Proust's epiphany underscores the importance that physical posture has in thinking. Nonwestern cultures have known about psychophysical phenomena for thousands of years. In India, for example, different *asanas* or yoga postures, are believed to produce specific states of consciousness in practitioners. Here in the West we've traditionally used the word *posturing* to indicate physical expressions that reveal underlying attitudes or beliefs in an individual.

Recently, educators have begun to discover that posture also seems to be a critical element in either promoting or inhibiting academic achievement in young students. While teaching in the British school system, educator Michael Gelb observed children engaged in difficult math or reading problems who would tighten up their bodies and restrict their postures in search of the right answers. When Gelb helped these students become aware of how they sat and showed them ways of opening up their posture and breathing patterns, the answers often seemed to pop right up. Some scientists have suggested that poor posture inhibits the natural flow of oxygen-bearing blood to the brain and that keeping the head in alignment with the body while sitting, standing, and walking can improve one's overall cognitive functioning. The following exercise will help raise your own awareness of habitual physical patterns that may restrict your thinking abilities.

SITTING SMART

Become aware of your posture as you're reading this book right now. Is your spine straight or crooked? Is your head in alignment with the rest of your body? Is there tension in your arms, legs, neck, face, stomach, thighs, or other areas? Is your breathing restricted in any way? Before you decide to move your body, simply be aware of the posture that you do have. Then, make a conscious and willful decision to change your posture to one that allows more freedom and poise in the alignment of your torso, neck, and head. Pay attention to how different you feel in your body and how your breathing changes after you do this. Then, return to your reading and notice whether there is also a change in your reading rate, reading comprehension, and/or your thought processes in general.

Because it may be hard to be completely objective in determining your own posture, it might help to keep a mirror handy while reading, or ask a friend to photograph or videotape you during a study session both before and after making changes. Then examine the results to discover whether there are further improvements you wish to make.

◆ RACING THOUGHTS ─────────────

Physical movement also seems be an important factor in enhancing thinking processes. Several creative thinkers have reported that walking or running served as a boost to their cognitive abilities. Inventor Edwin Land was out for a stroll when he hit upon the idea that eventually led to his discovery of the Polaroid camera. Tchaikovsky regularly carried a pencil and composition paper with him during the daily walks that he said provided the inspiration for many of his musical compositions. Thomas Mann wrote: "Much of my composition ... has been conceived on walks. . . . I also regard movement in the open air as the best means of reviving my energy for work."

These anecdotal reports support a growing body of literature over the past decade that points to the role that jogging, walking, dancing, and other forms of regular physical movement have in promoting a wide range of mental functions. Scientists at the Veterans Administration Medical Center in Salt Lake City reported that elderly individuals who took one-hour walks three times a week over a four-month period improved their reaction times, visual organization, and memory over those who remained sedentary or did nonaerobic exercises. In another study of two hundred runners conducted at the Oregon Health Sciences Center, nearly 60 percent claimed that jogging helped them generate unique and spontaneous ideas with very little effort. Many of them actually kept a pencil and paper in their lockers so that they could write down their thoughts as soon as they completed a workout. The following exercise will help you tap your own best ideas "on the run."

WALKING WISDOM

Bring a hand-held tape recorder with you on a walk or jog. (If you are over fifty-five and/or have a medical condition, be sure to exercise under the supervision of a physician.) As you move, simply let your mind wander freely and enjoy the sensory delights of the outdoors. When ideas come to you, speak them into the tape recorder (you shouldn't be running so fast that you're too out of breath to speak clearly). After your exercise session listen to the tape and write down (or sketch) any ideas that you'd particularly like to remember and continue to develop.

Be careful not to overuse the above exercise. Regular jogging or walking should provide an opportunity for you to get away from your daily tasks and problems. Your tape recorder may inadvertently cause you to focus too much attention on personal or professional responsibilities during your workout. You may want to limit the use of this exercise to once a week or have the tape recorder or a notepad available for use *after* your regular exercise session.

Consider using other forms of physical movement to "jog" your mind as well. The other day I happened to be stuck in trying to remember the name of a colleague. As I reached for a book that I knew contained his photo, the name suddenly came to me. It seemed as if the actual process of moving to the bookshelf and handling the book served to jar my memory into action. At other times I've found that if I'm experiencing writer's block or struggling with a problem, some kind of physical movement—rocking in an armchair, putting on music and dancing, practicing yoga—can help get the creative juices flowing again. The next time you have a mental block, try moving through it with a little physical activity and see if the results don't justify the effort.

◆ MENTAL MUSCLES

During the first two years of life, according to Swiss child researcher Jean Piaget, virtually *all* thinking takes place through the body. Piaget referred to this time as the *senso-*

ry-motor stage of cognitive development. The infant grasps, squeezes, crawls, shakes, bounces, turns, twists, and tastes, her way through life, gradually constructing an image of the world. As the youngster grows and gains more control over her body while increasing her contact with the environment, physical actions become internalized. An older youngster can *imagine* tasting a cookie, petting a dog, or building a sand castle, without actually having to *perform* these activities. Physical action goes underground, where it continues to thrive as a vital component of our mind even at the highest levels of abstraction.

A look at some of the world's most brilliant thinkers illustrates how kinesthetic imagery functioned as an important part of their creative process. Albert Einstein, asked to comment on his own problem-solving methods, reported: "The words or the language, as they are written or spoken, do not seem to play any role in my mechanism of thought. The psychical entities which seem to serve as elements in thought are certain signs and more or less clear images. . . . The above-mentioned elements are, in my case, of visual and some of *muscular* type." An example of this kind of kinesthetic thinking is the fantasy Einstein had as an adolescent in which he conceived of himself riding on the end of a beam of light. This high-speed mental thrill ride allowed Einstein to experience at a visceral level the conditions under which time and space exposed their relativity.

Other famous thinkers of our time have drawn upon kinesthetic imagery in working through important professional challenges. Henri Poincaré wrote about his struggle to solve a particularly difficult mathematical problem:

> . . . *every day I seated myself at my work table, stayed an hour or two, tried a great number of combinations, and reached no results. One eve-*

ning, contrary to my custom, I drank black coffee and could not sleep. Ideas rose in crowds; I felt them collide until pairs interlocked, so to speak, making a stable combination. By the next morning I had established the existence of a class of Fuchsian functions, those which come from the hyper geometric series; I had only to write out the results, which took but a few hours.

Similarly, Igor Stravinsky reported that the idea for his masterwork *Le Sacre du Printemps* came to him in a dream of a ritual during which "a chosen sacrificial virgin danced herself to death." Imagery appeared to each of these thinkers in a kinetic form with lots of action, drama, and movement.

Imagery can also be "hands-on." William James wrote about using "mental fingers" to touch the edges of the letters of the alphabet. Such an experience suggests the presence of a kind of invisible "kinesthetic body" that interpenetrates the actual physical body. This "body" consists of proprioceptive images or shadows of internal sensations in skin, muscles, tendons, and other areas of the anatomy. Among those who have lost a limb, for example, there are frequent reports of sensations in the missing appendage. These amputees apparently experience their kinesthetic arms or legs in the absence of these body parts. The following exercise will help you become aware of your own kinesthetic body for use in creative problem solving:

PHANTOM BODYBUILDING

Lie on the floor in a comfortable position. Breathe deeply for a few moments and then begin to focus your awareness on your body, starting with your face and head and working your way down to your legs and feet. After you've spent some time focusing on your *physical* body, become aware of different parts of your *kinesthetic* body. Keep your *physical* arms on the floor and raise your *kinesthetic* or "phantom" arms until they are perpendicular to your body. Feel the muscular sensations in your *kinesthetic* arms as you do this. Then lower them to the floor. Now, raise your *kinesthetic* legs a few inches above the floor, keeping your *physical* legs on the ground. Feel the sensations in your *kinesthetic* legs as you do this. Then lower them to the floor. Now, lying flat on the floor in your *physical* body, get up off the floor in your *kinesthetic* body and begin to walk around. Start to jump up and down in your *kinesthetic* body. Feel each muscle in your *kinesthetic* body as you do this. Imagine there is a trampoline there and start to bounce up and down on it. Feel the sensations in your *kinesthetic* stomach as you bounce. Now, get off the trampoline and imagine someone has placed different textures for you to feel on an imaginary table: sandpaper, sticky flypaper, smooth silk, and some messy fingerprints. Take time to "sit" in your *kinesthetic* body and "feel" the textures of these materials with your *kinesthetic* fingers. Then when you feel ready, return your *kinesthetic* body to the floor, so that it merges with your *physical* body. Lie still for a few moments, feeling the contact your *physical* body makes with the floor, before getting up.

This experience should begin to connect you to subtle kinesthetic sensations in your own imagery processes that you can employ in practical ways. Athletes use this kind of mental rehearsal in learning to master specific physical skills. Jack Nicklaus once knocked ten points off his golf score by using a swing he first learned in a dream (the "dream body" for many people is the same thing as the "kinesthetic body"). Artists employ haptic imagery in formulating creative products. Henry Moore, reflecting on the sculptor's craft, commented: "[The sculptor] gets the solid shape, as it were, inside his head—he thinks of it, whatever its size, as if he were holding it completely in the hollow of his hand." You can use kinesthetic mental rehearsal essentially to "walk" your way through a day, feeling in your bones and muscles the grace, confidence, balance, and poise that you need in any demanding social or personal situation. The next exercise will help you do this.

KINESTHETIC PRACTICE SESSION

Choose a physical skill you currently engage in that you'd like to perform better than you do now. Your goal might be to improve your tennis or golf swing, show particular grace at a business or social event, craft a more handsome piece of furniture, run faster, or excel at any of a number of other activities. Imagine yourself performing the skill flawlessly. Focus particularly on the kinesthetic sensations associated with success in this area. Feel the inner poise in your muscles. Sense the coordinated movement of all necessary body parts working together in harmony to accomplish your objective. Experience the gut-level feeling of achieving your aim. Take five to ten minutes for this exercise. Practice it frequently before engaging in the goal-related activity.

This exercise suggests that although there are many ways for you to become a better thinker using your kinesthetic intelligence, the use of the body—in athletics, sculpture, crafts, mechanics, drama, and many other fields—represents intelligent behavior in its own right. The body is not simply intelligent when it's used in the service of another intelligence—to read better, solve math problems, rectify personal dilemmas, and so forth. It's intelligent when it moves swiftly, turns sharply, manipulates deftly, and springs lightly. To put it another way, Wayne Gretsky is the brain surgeon of the hockey rink and Auguste Rodin is the Einstein of stone. By cultivating your kinesthetic intelligence—for whatever purpose—you can begin to unleash your own inner Gretsky or Rodin to help the mind and body work together as a seamless whole.

25 THINGS YOU CAN DO TO DEVELOP YOUR BODILY-KINESTHETIC INTELLIGENCE

- ◆ Join a work-related or community sports team (softball, basketball, soccer, or other group sport).
- ◆ Take lessons in a solo sport such as swimming, skiing, golf, tennis, or gymnastics.
- ◆ Learn a martial art like aikido, judo, or karate.
- ◆ Exercise regularly and keep track of the ideas that occur to you during exercise sessions.
- ◆ Learn a craft such as woodworking, weaving, carving, or crocheting.
- ◆ Take a class at a community center in working with clay or stone.
- ◆ Learn Yoga or another system of physical relaxation and awareness.
- ◆ Play video games that require the use of quick reflexes.
- ◆ Take formal lessons in dance (modern, ballroom, ballet, or other dance forms) or spend time engaged in free-form creative movement on your own.
- ◆ Take up a "hands-on" hobby around the home like gardening, cooking, or model building

◆ Learn sign language or braille.

◆ Put on a blindfold and have a friend lead you around to explore the environment with your hands.

◆ Assemble a collection of objects having different textures (silk, smooth stones, sandpaper, etc.).

◆ Walk the curbs of sidewalks or balance beams to improve your sense of balance.

◆ Coach a little-league baseball team or some other group or individual sport.

◆ Set up a weight-training and/or aerobics program for yourself under the supervision of a doctor or health club.

◆ Play charades with friends or family.

◆ Engage in sensory-awareness activities that put you in touch with physical sensations and perceptions.

◆ Work with a therapist in a psychophysical discipline such as Rolfing, Alexander technique, bioenergetics, or Feldenkrais work.

◆ Learn how to give a massage to another person and/or how to massage yourself using acupressure, *do-in,* or another massage system.

◆ Develop your eye-hand coordination by bowling, throwing horseshoes, tossing basketballs, or taking up juggling.

◆ Learn a skill that requires a good sense of touch and manual dexterity, such as typing or the playing of a musical instrument.

◆ Keep track of kinesthetic images that occur during your dreams and daytime reveries.

◆ Take a class in acting or pantomime or join a local repertory company.

◆ Learn a practical routine requiring physical grace such as the Japanese tea ceremony.

LOGIC SMART: CALCULATING YOUR MATHEMATICAL AND SCIENTIFIC ABILITIES

Toward the end of the novel *Don Quixote* by Miguel Cervantes, Quixote's ingenuous sidekick, Sancho Panza, is made the governor of a remote island nation and takes an oath to uphold all of its laws. Island customs dictate that every new arrival be questioned by a guard as to the purpose of his visit. If the foreigner speaks the truth, he is allowed free passage onto the island, but if he tells a lie, he is to be hanged. This tourist-control system seems to work for a while. One day, however, a visitor comes to the island who answers the guard's question with a puzzling reply: "I came here to be hanged!" This presents the islanders with a dilemma. If they allow the man free passage onto the island, then he will be guilty of a lie and should have been hanged. Yet if they hang the visitor, he will have told the truth and therefore should have been allowed to live.

This passage provides a doorway into logical-mathematical thinking. For although we can use the four intelligences already covered in this book to enhance the vividness of this scene (visualizing the characters, "hearing" dialogue and background sounds, and experiencing physical sensations), there is still an element that doesn't belong to spatial, linguistic, musical, or kinesthetic intelligences. The juxtaposition of the story's two seemingly incompatible logical relationships stretches our intelligence beyond the confines of the senses into the realms of purely conceptual thought.

◆ THE MATHEMATICAL MIND ——— ——————

This form of imageless thinking, characteristic of scientists and higher mathematicians, is hard to describe since there is little that gives it shape or form. In one survey of the thought processes of theoretical physicists, psychologist Ann Roe commented: "Over half of the total group use[d] imageless thinking, and I suspect that this is an underestimate." Individual scientists described experiencing a "feeling of relationships" or of "just knowing" something. In recounting a conversation with mathematician John von Newmann, philosopher Jacob Bronowski related von Neumann's frustration with him when discussing a specific mathematical concept: "Oh no [said von Neumann], you are not seeing it. Your kind of visualizing mind is not right for seeing this. Think of it abstractly . . ." Similarly, physicist W. I. Beveridge emphasized the necessity of thinking without images in exploring the outer limits of his field: "Physics has reached a stage where it is no longer possible to visualize mechanical analogies representing certain phenomena that can only be expressed in mathematical terms."

We've seen in previous chapters, of course, that mathematical and scientific thinking *do* involve spatial, kinesthetic, linguistic, and musical elements. However, there are core components unique to logical-mathematical thinking. Howard Gardner defines these as "sensitivity to and capacity to discern logical or numerical patterns and the ability to handle long chains of reasoning." The following exercise will help you identify some of these components in your own mind.

BRAIN BUSTERS

Solve the following logical-mathematical puzzles. While you are working on them, pay attention to what's going on inside your mind. In particular, notice thinking processes that seem to have no image content.

- ◆ Insert the missing number: 11 12 14 —— 26 42.
- ◆ A number is multiplied by 3 and divided by 4, and the result is 3/10. What is the number?
- ◆ Pam's brother Ed has two more brothers than he has sisters. How many more brothers than sisters does Pam have?

What's important in the preceding exercise is becoming aware of the process you used in trying to solve the problems and not necessarily getting the right answers. For those who want them, however, the answers are on page 108.

◆ PEAK REASONING ———————————

The abstract thinking you did (or attempted to do!) in the above exercise had its origins in the exploratory play you engaged in during the first years of life. Logical thought initially develops in early childhood through direct sensory contact with concrete objects. The child builds with blocks, manipulates toys, counts squares on the sidewalk, and in many other ways learns about cause and effect, numbers, and other logical-mathematical principles. Yet somewhere around adolescence our logical mind leaves the concrete world behind and soars off into what Jean Piaget called *formal operations* or *hypothetico-deductive thinking*. This form of thought is fundamental to the scientific method whereby one establishes a hypothesis, tests it, and then modifies it in light of the results. Here's an exercise that will illustrate how this type of thinking works.

MIND SWING

Obtain three different lengths of string (one foot, one and a half feet, and two feet) and three objects of varying weight, such as a paper clip, a pen, and a pair of pliers. Attach one of the weights onto the end of a piece of string to make a swinging pendulum. To solve the problem you need to determine which one or combination of four factors will determine how fast the pendulum swings: the heaviness of the weight, the length of the string, the force of the push you give it, or the height of the initial push. Use the materials you've gathered to determine the answer.

What was your method for solving this problem? Did you search back into your memories of high school physics class for clues as to the appropriate law of motion? If so, you were using linguistic intelligence to look for "facts" to help you. If you attempted to visualize the problem (or sense how your body would feel if it were the weight at the end of the pendulum), then you were calling upon spatial or kinesthetic thought. Did you use a trial-and-error process? This indicates a form of logical-mathematical thinking characteristic of children under the age of thirteen.

According to Piaget the formal operational thinker would solve this problem by constructing an overall strategy that varied only one factor at a time while holding the other variables constant. So, for example, you might have experimented with different weights while using the same length of string, force of push, and height of push. If no differences were discovered, you might have varied each of the other factors in turn until determining the variable that affected the pendulum's rate of swing, which in this case turns out to be the length of the string. Formal operational thinking, then, involves the capacity to systematically manipulate several different factors in a consistent way. This process of experimentation, in turn, often results in observations that lead to further logical deductions: for example, the longer the string, the slower the pendulum's rate of swing.

Recent studies indicate that only 30 to 40 percent of the adolescent and adult population in our culture use formal operational thinking. And it's often not consistently used even by those who have the capacity to think in this way. Research does show, however, that the ability to reason systematically *can* be taught. In fact, one of the major applications of cognitive psychology involves teaching students from preschool to postgraduate levels to use logical-mathematical thinking strategies to solve new problems.

One area of study that concentrates on this broad task is the field of *heuristics,* which consists of a loose collection of strategies, rules of thumb, guidelines, and suggestions for problem solving. A major contributor to the field is mathematician George Polya, who, in his book *How to Solve It* describes several heuristic principles that can be used at different stages of solving a problem. If you're having trouble generating a solution to a problem, for instance, you can:

- find analogies;
- separate the various parts of the problem;
- propose a possible solution and then work backward;
- describe the characteristics that a solution should have;
- find a problem related to yours and solve it;
- assume the opposite of what you're trying to prove;
- generalize (proceed from a given set of conditions to a larger set that contains the given one); or
- specialize (move from a given set of conditions to a smaller set).

As an example of how heuristics works, look at the following problem taken from Polya's *How to Solve It:* "To number the pages of a bulky volume, the printer used 2,989 digits. How many pages has the volume?" To assist in your problem solving, use the heuristic guideline *find a related problem to yours and solve it.* If the book has exactly 9 numbered pages, how many digits does the printer use? (Answer: 9) If the book has exactly 99 numbered pages, how many digits are used? How about 999 pages? Use this general approach to guide yourself to a solution. You can also apply other elements of heuristics in solving the problem, including *propose a possible solution and then work backward.* The answer to the problem is on page 108.

◆ THINKING BY THE NUMBERS ──────────

You might have found, in working on the above problem, that you had the right approach but ended up with the wrong answer because of a simple arithmetical error. Thus far in the chapter we've been concerned with reasoning and logic rather than computation. However, the capacity to be *numerate*—or literate with numbers—represents another dimension to logical-mathematical intelligence that deserves some attention.

At its most elementary level, numeracy consists of the ability to calculate accurately and quickly. There was a time, before the advent of computers and calculators, when the capacity to do mental math was highly prized. Even today we marvel at the talents of an individual like Shakutala Devi of India, who was documented by the *Guinness Book of World Records* to have multiplied in her head two thirteen-digit numbers in twenty-eight seconds! There are also people who can extract square roots, derive logarithms, figure compound interest, interpret perpetual calendars and railroad schedules, and factor large sums in short periods of time purely through mental calculation. To a certain extent these accomplishments depend on a highly developed *linguistic* intelligence, where schemas governing number facts, algorithms, and formulas are simply committed to memory, with no understanding of the logic behind them.

In a broader sense, however, numeracy represents the capacity to use numbers to enhance the quality of life. John Allan Paulos, professor of mathematics at Temple University, suggests that large segments of our population may in fact be mathematically illiterate when it comes to having a working knowledge of numbers. He comments: "Many educated people have little grasp for ... numbers and are even unaware that a million is 1,000,000, a billion is 1,000,000,000 and a trillion is 1,000,000,000,000." To help establish a connection with these quantities, Paulos suggests that people link large numbers up to facets of everyday life. For example, a million seconds is roughly equal to 11½ days, a billion seconds takes us back 32 years, and a trillion seconds ago the last remaining Neanderthals walked the earth.

Part of the reason for innumeracy resides in the failure of school math programs to focus attention on topics such as problem solving, probability, and statistics. Too much time has been spent, according to Paulos, on rote computation and paper-and-pencil drills. "Estimation is generally not taught either," says Paulos, "aside from a few lessons on rounding off numbers. The connection is rarely made that rounding off and making reasonable estimates have something to do with real life."

In other cultures estimation is a widely practiced art. Studies show, for example, that Kpelle adults in Liberia succeed much better than American adults at estimating the number of stones in piles ranging from ten to one hundred. In real life, accuracy is not always important—but being in the ballpark is. "If you're ordering wallpaper for your kitchen," says Marilyn Burns, author of *The I Hate Mathematics! Book,* "you'd better overestimate." John Allan Paulos recommends that people hone their estimation skills by playing around with whimsical questions such as those in the following exercise.

GUESSTIMATION

Give your best guess for the following:
- the number of nickels it would take to reach the top of the Empire State Building
- the number of hairs you have on your head
- the number of words you have spoken in your life
- the number of toothpicks it would take to reach from your doorstep to the center of your favorite vacation spot
- the number of grains of salt in the shaker sitting on your dinner table

- ◆ the number of cans of soda (liquid only) it would take to fill up your bathtub to the brim
- ◆ the number of pictures in a year's worth of your daily newspaper
- ◆ the number of windows in your home town
- ◆ the number of people who ate caviar today all over the world
- ◆ the time it would take for you to copy this book down in printed form with your opposite (nondominant) hand

While there are no right answers for the above problems, you can use basic knowledge of certain facts (e.g., the volume of liquid in a can of soda compared to the capacity of your bathtub) to arrive at reasonable solutions.

◆ THE PERILS OF INNUMERACY ————————————

Innumeracy leads to a wide range of individual and cultural ills, according to Paulos and other authorities. Studies show that one's income during the first decade of employment is positively correlated to the number of math courses one took in school. Without "number sense" people are more likely to be taken in by phony advertising schemes, have unrealistic expectations for winning a lottery, and make other poor financial decisions. They're also apt to fail at a wide range of tasks requiring practical math around the home, such as modifying a standard cooking recipe or determining the amount of lumber needed for a remodeling job.

On a collective level, without a sense of what numbers mean, the public cannot adequately grasp important economic, political, and social issues such as the federal budget, the extent of the world's nuclear arsenal, and the risks associated with AIDS. Clearly, then, numerical intelligence should be an important part of one's daily life. The following exercise can provide you with a sense of your own practicable math skills and help you decide whether this area needs some attention. (Answers are on page 108.)

MATH QUIZ

The following questions are designed to sample a wide range of practical number-related skills in everyday life. Use a calculator or pencil and scratch paper if you like, but avoid looking up solutions in a reference book except to check your answers.

◆ What is the population of the United States?
◆ What is the approximate distance from the East Coast of the United States to the West Coast?
◆ If you're at a restaurant and the bill comes to $23.46 before sales tax, how much of a tip would you leave (assuming a standard 15 percent tip)?
◆ You are at a store and want to purchase a sale item originally costing $45 that has been discounted at 50 percent off. You take it to the register only to learn that an additional 25 percent can be taken off the sale price. How much do you pay the clerk?
◆ You want to cover your 275-square-foot family room with carpeting that costs $24.50 a square yard. You have budgeted $600 for the project. Can you afford it?
◆ You're baking a loaf of bread that calls for 2¾ cups of flour. You want to cut the recipe by one-third. How many cups of flour should you use?
◆ The business section of the newspaper says that inflation is going up at the rate of 5 percent per year. If you make $35,000 a year, how much do you need

to make next year to keep up with the pace of inflation?

These questions may have seemed rather easy to you, or they may have triggered memories of embarrassment, frustration, or avoidance in situations in your life where practical math skills were required. Sheila Tobias, author of *Overcoming Math Anxiety,* writes about mathophobes: "These are the people who typically get clammy fingers when it comes time to figure out the tip at the restaurant, who turn down promotions rather than deal with quantitative information, who change college majors to avoid a math requirement." Math-phobic individuals may need to focus more upon process than upon getting "the right answer," allow themselves plenty of time for their calculations, avail themselves of calculators, and link up with others to work cooperatively on difficult problems.

◆ SCIENCE SENSE

Why is the sky blue? What makes a motor work? Answering such questions generally requires a grasp, not of abstract logic or number sense, but of scientific principles. Yet all too often the average person has little awareness of the most basic ideas in science. According to a survey conducted at Northern Illinois University, 93 to 95 percent of adults questioned lacked a fundamental knowledge of scientific vocabulary and methodology and demonstrated a poor understanding of the impact of science on the world. Fifty-nine percent of respondents didn't know that electrons are smaller than the atoms of which they form a part. Sixty-four percent didn't know how lasers worked. Sixty-three percent said that antibiotics kill viruses (they don't—they're used to kill bacteria). This latter finding represents a potentially dangerous assumption, since individuals who believe this might use antibiotics in a futile attempt to fight a viral cold and thereby weaken their immune systems in handling future bacterial infections.

Scientific illiteracy is common even among the so-called highly educated. One informal survey of Harvard graduates indicated that only two out of twenty-three students could correctly explain why it is hotter in summer than in winter. More surprisingly, scientists working outside of their own fields of expertise also seem to have difficulty with basic science concepts. Robert M. Hazen and James Trefil, authors of *Science Matters: Achieving Scientific Literacy,* asked twenty-four physicists and geologists to explain the difference between RNA and DNA. Only three could do so satisfactorily.

Like innumeracy, scientific illiteracy represents a threat to an educated citizenry when it affects their ability to make intelligent decisions about important civic issues. It's difficult to form opinions about issues like gene splicing, the greenhouse effect, and the cost of the space program without an understanding of the scientific principles that form the basis of these questions.

At the same time, an understanding of science brings with it a certain aesthetic satisfaction that one scientist described as the "Lookadat!" effect. Young children seem to have this scientific attitude in their questioning about the most basic natural phenomena. Unfortunately, we seem to lose this attitude of wonder when science "facts" (does anybody remember the formula for Boyle's Law?) crowd out science ideas and the scientific method. The following exercise will help you evaluate your own level of science literacy and provide a number of questions for you to wonder about and investigate.

SCIENCE QUESTIONS

Write down your best responses to the following questions:
- Why is it hotter in summer than in winter?
- How does an atom differ from a molecule?
- What is a superconductor?
- Why is the sky blue?
- What is a black hole?
- What causes acid rain and why is it such a problem to the ecosystem?
- What is DNA?
- What is a laser?
- How does an electric motor work?
- How does a microwave oven cook your food?

To check your answers, refer to a good encyclopedia, a friend knowledgeable in science, or one of several books on science literacy listed in the "Resources" section at the back of this book.

Just as mathematics is not simply rote arithmetic, science is not simply a collection of boring facts—it's a set of patterns in nature and basic laws that run through many disciplines. According to James Trefil and Robert Hazen, "science is organized around certain central concepts, certain pillars that support the entire structure. There are a limited number of such concepts ... but they account for everything we see in the world around us." While these laws are usually understood by using a combination of the intelligences discussed in this book, it's particularly through the regularity-seeking, hypothesis-testing methodology of logical-mathematical intelligence that such laws are discovered and articulated. As such, the impact of scientific thinking on our lives is far-reaching indeed.

25 WAYS TO DEVELOP YOUR LOGICAL-MATHEMATICAL INTELLIGENCE

- Play logical-mathematical games (Go, Clue, dominoes) with friends or family.
- Learn to use an abacus.
- Work on logic puzzles/brain teasers.
- Keep a calculator handy for figuring out math problems you confront in the course of daily life.
- Learn a computer language such as LOGO, BASIC, or PASCAL.
- Buy a chemistry set or other science kit and carry out some of the experiments described in it.
- Have family discussions about math or science concepts in the news.
- Take a course in basic science or math at a local college or community center or buy a self-study guide and work on your own.
- Practice calculating simple math problems in your head.
- Read the business section of your daily newspaper and look up unfamiliar economic or financial concepts.
- Read about famous math and/or science discoveries.
- Visit a science museum, planetarium, aquarium, or other science center.
- Learn to use heuristics in solving problems.
- Form a discussion group or study circle to discuss recent scientific discoveries and their implications in everyday life.
- Watch television documentaries that chronicle important science concepts.
- Circle unfamiliar science concepts or mathematical

expressions in your reading and find explanations in books or from knowledgeable people.

◆ Tape-record yourself talking out loud about how to solve a difficult math problem.

◆ Identify scientific principles operating around your home and neighborhood.

◆ Subscribe to a science news publication such as *Science, Omni,* or *Scientific American.*

◆ Confront, rather than avoid, mathematical problems you encounter in everyday life (figuring tips, balancing your checkbook, determining loan rates, etc.).

◆ Purchase a telescope, microscope, or other magnifying tool and use it to investigate your surroundings.

◆ Teach math or science concepts to someone less knowledgeable.

◆ Visit a science laboratory or other setting where math and/or science concepts are being used.

◆ Use blocks, beans, or other concrete materials in learning new math concepts.

◆ Form a "mathophobe" support group for individuals who feel anxious when forced to deal with numbers.

ANSWER KEY

Page 96: 1. 18; 2. 2/5; 3. 4
Page 99. 1,024 pages
Page 103. 1. 1990 Census estimate, nearly 250,000,000; 2. About 3,000 miles; 3. About $3.50; 4. Around $17.00; 5. No, it will cost about $750; 6. Just under 2 cups; 7. $36,750

7

PEOPLE SMART:
CONNECTING WITH
YOUR SOCIAL SENSE

William Shakespeare, Jane Addams, and Lyndon Johnson.
An unlikely trio to be sure. Yet a common theme runs
through the lives of these three individuals that underscores their greatest achievements. Each had an uncanny
ability to understand other people. Shakespeare was a social chameleon. According to literary critic William Hazlitt,
Shakespeare was "nothing in himself; but he was all that
others were, or that they could become. He not only had
in himself the germs of every faculty and feeling, but he
could follow them by anticipation, intuitively, into all their
conceivable ramifications, through every change of fortune, or conflict of passion, or turn of thought." For Shakespeare this social insight was inner-directed and channeled
into his magnificent plays.

Jane Addams was sympathetic in a more immediate
way, through her active involvement with suffering and
oppressed people. As a young woman she noticed that

she became exhausted after attending lectures and visiting museums but was energized when engaged in charity work. While visiting Europe in her late twenties, she was appalled at the atrocious living conditions of factory workers and vowed to establish a settlement house in the United States where the needs of the poor could be met. In 1889 she founded Hull House, which became a training ground for the first social workers in this country. Through Hull House and other projects, Addams fought for better housing conditions for the poor, improvements in public welfare, stricter child-labor laws, protection of working women, minority rights, community education, and world peace. In conferring the Nobel Peace Prize to her in 1931, the Nobel committee said: "Miss Addams does not speak much, but her quiet, kind-hearted personality creates an atmosphere of goodwill which instinctively calls forth the best in us."

Finally, Lyndon Johnson demonstrated his own highly developed social sense in a far more manipulative way. Recent biographies of Johnson depict him clawing his way up the American political ladder, schmoozing and charming as he went along. One commentator on the Washington scene observed: "Lots of guys can be smiling and deferential. He had something else. No matter what someone thought, Lyndon would agree with him—would be there ahead of him, in fact. He could follow someone's mind around—and figure out where it was going and beat it there."

Each of these powerful individuals possessed a high level of interpersonal intelligence. The core capacity of this intelligence is the ability to make fine distinctions in the intentions, motivations, moods, feelings, and thoughts of other people. According to Howard Gardner, "social primates are required to be calculating beings, to take into account the consequences of their own behavior, to

calculate the likely behavior of others, to calculate benefits
and losses—all in a context where the relevant evidence
is ... likely to change.... Only an organism with highly
developed cognitive skills can make do in such a context."
This chapter will examine the thinking processes that form
the basis for interpersonal intelligence. It will also look at
the ways in which social cognition is translated into action
in the lives of individuals such as business executives and
diplomats who use this intelligence extensively in their
work. Finally, it will provide concrete suggestions for ways
in which you can develop your own social thinking skills,
so that your life might be less of an island and more of
an archipelago, defined by the richness of your contacts
with other people.

◆ SOCIAL THOUGHTS

Over the past twenty years social psychologists have
worked out in sophisticated detail the inner mechanisms
through which individuals think about other people. Research suggests that we build up complex mental frame-
works and that these social schemata guide our attitudes,
beliefs, and responses to the people we meet every day.
These cognitive maps consist of a loose collection of social
stereotypes (for example, the belief that the elderly like
to stay at home and putter around in the garden), personal
traits (for instance, the notion of what it means to be a
"jock"), and typical behaviors in social situations (for example, the expectation that people will generally remain
seated and talk quietly in a fine restaurant). We're constantly using these social maps to record our initial impressions of others, to explain people's actions, and to predict
their future behavior. We're likely to be shocked, consequently, to see an elderly individual in a baseball uniform

dancing wildly on the tables of an exclusive restaurant, because these behaviors contrast so strongly with our pre-existing schemes for social conduct.

Often, however, it seems as if we're fooled into making way-off-the-mark judgments about people because of these same cognitive maps. Not too long ago I was in a post office standing in line behind someone I assumed was a homeless person or psychiatric patient. The evidence was clear-cut—or at least I thought so. Her shirt was half-tucked in, her shoe laces untied, her hair a mess, and she was carrying a load of miscellaneous odds and ends. After a time, however, I got a closer look at one of the papers she was carrying and discovered it was a manuscript she was mailing to a publisher. On the return-address label I caught a glimpse of the name of one of the nation's most popular fantasy/science fiction writers. The following exercise will give you a chance to practice the fine art of thinking about people and show you how active these social guides and prejudices can be in our lives.

SOCIAL MAPS

Go to a busy public area (park, train station, downtown street corner, etc.) and find a comfortable place to stand or sit. Bring a notepad with you. Begin to observe the people around you. Select an individual at random to observe. Write down all the impressions you have of this person based on your quick observations (e.g., "parent," "yuppie," "obsessive exerciser"). After you're done, put a star next to each item listed for which you believe there exists substantial evidence to back up the assertion, and a circle next to each item based on little or no evidence. Then repeat the entire process for at least three more people.

As you observe people in the above exercise, you'll notice far more than isolated individuals going about their day-to-day business. In addition you'll probably observe the complex web of social interactions that make up the human drama—most of it happening without words. Psychologists estimate that nonverbal communication accounts for 60 to 90 percent of all the information transmitted between people. This communication consists of a wide range of behaviors, including facial expressions, distances between people, patterns of touching, posture, gestures, and eye contact. One communications expert, Mario Pei, estimated that humans can perform up to 700,000 different physical signs. Kinesics (body motion) researcher Ray Birdwhistell suggests that the face alone can produce as many as 250,000 expressions, while another researcher, M. H. Krout, has identified 5,000 distinct hand gestures, and kinesics researcher G. W. Hewes cataloged 1,000 different postures.

◆ BREAKING THE CODE

Some of these signals are universal—for example, the facial expressions that go with the emotions of happiness, sadness, anger, and disgust. Most interpersonal cues, however, vary from culture to culture. I remember getting in trouble with a Paris truck driver twenty years ago when he cut me off in traffic and I pointed my finger to my head to indicate he was crazy. In France this gesture has a much stronger connotation than it does in the United States. Another gesture, the thumbs-up signal, seems friendly to an American, but in Nigeria it's the equivalent of giving a person "the finger." Similarly, you may be roughed up in Greece if you hold out your hand to hail a cab. In ancient times Greeks used to parade criminals in the street and smear manure in their face. The remnant of this gesture—a thrusting outstretched hand, palm outward—has been passed down through their culture as an obscenity.

The world's complex grammar of social signals can be used to convey a wide range of feelings, intentions, and thoughts from one person to another. The broadest messages deal with signals of acceptance and rejection or patterns of intimacy and estrangement. According to Albert Scheflen, director of the Albert Einstein College of Medicine Project on Human Communication, cues that suggest affiliation involve side-by-side orientations he calls "withs." An example of a "with" is two people walking in synchrony, assuming similar postures, and using congruent gestures. Scheflen also refers to "frames"—when pairs or small groups of people sit leaning toward each other in such a way as to form a social unit, turning their sides or backs to those they wish to exclude. If you've ever had the experience of walking up to two or three people engaged in conversation and suddenly feeling awkward, you may have just entered "the frame zone."

Other important components of social communication include information about who touches whom (the dominant person in the group often has more permission to touch others), who controls the flow of conversation (dominant individuals generally set the standard for how long or short each person's utterances will be), and patterns of eye contact (the longer people look each other in the eye, the more they tend to be strongly attracted— or repelled—by each other). It's important to remember, however, that there are no fixed meanings for *any* social cue since these can vary from culture to culture and are easily manipulated by those who want to send a different message than the one that's actually there. For example, lovers in a group may consciously avoid staring at each other so that colleagues won't suspect their secret alliance. The following exercise will give you practice in detecting a few of the many crisscrossing connections and covert communications going on in the midst of a typical social gathering:

PEOPLE READING

Attend an informal social gathering where you can remain relatively anonymous (an art gallery opening, a party where you know relatively few people, a public dance, or any other similar setting). Find a place in a corner of the room where you won't be too obvious and set up a comfortable perch. Then, see if you can detect specific alliances in the party by looking at how pairs or groups of people behave together. As people walk into the room, notice examples of "withs" (pairs or trios walking congruently). Look for instances of "frames" (people sitting together as a closed unit). Notice who are the dominant people at the gathering (bosses, hosts, VIPs, etc.) by examining patterns of eye contact, posturing, touching, and gestures. Search for occurrences of "leakage"—people exposing inner feelings to the outer world through specific nonverbal cues. As the party or event begins to come to an end, look for signs of "terminal markers"—behaviors people may engage in to indicate that it's time to go. Find an "insider" (someone who knows many or most of the people there), if appropriate, to check out some of your guesses about alliances, animosities, and pecking orders observed during the event. Afterwards, you may want to take notes of your observations.

◆ THE GREAT COMMUNICATORS ─────────────

It's one thing to understand interpersonal processes and another to be able to use this information in one's life to relate effectively to other people. As noted above, Shakespeare was brilliant in understanding the inner workings of other people, and yet in his own life, he was constantly wrangling with his peers over the production of his plays. More recently the founder of the interpersonal theory of psychiatry, Harry Stack Sullivan, was reputed to have had a terrible time getting along with other people. Individuals who are most effective in relating to others *do* have the kinds of social perception and thinking skills described above. However, they also have the ability to use these insights to negotiate with others, persuade others to follow a specific path of action, resolve conflict among individuals, obtain important information from colleagues, and influence co-workers, peers, and colleagues in many other ways.

"Your intelligence can be in other people," notes Howard Gardner, "if you know how to get them to help you. In life, that's the best strategy: mobilize other people." One place where this ability can best be observed is in the field of business. According to one study, managers spend anywhere from 50 to 90 percent of their time engaged in interpersonal communication with bosses, subordinates, and people outside the organization. Research suggests that the best managers are those who possess the requisite "people skills" to mobilize others toward the company's basic goals. David A. Nadler, a management consultant, and Michael L. Tushman, professor at Columbia University's Graduate School of Business Administration, observe: "A senior manager, usually the CEO, generates a sense of urgency; he acts as the organizational catalyst and establishes a compelling strategic agenda; he builds a bond with large numbers of people in the organization, getting them to 'sign up' for meaningful change.... Such a leader can mobilize individuals, groups, and the entire organization to work enthusiastically toward new goals."

One important quality of interpersonally effective individuals is their capacity to discover the key individuals within a group who can help them meet their goals. Lyle Spencer, a psychologist at McBer and Company, a business consulting firm in Boston, reported in a study of state department officials on one outstanding foreign service officer who "had been able to go to a new assignment in a foreign capital, and very quickly figure out that it was the Prime Minister's mistress's nephew who really called the shots on oil policy—and how to get to this nephew."

Another skill seen by the McBer group as important in managing others is "an objectivity that allows you to see clearly the other person's feelings without your own getting in the way." McBer and Company have devised ways of assessing this capacity by having individuals watch a videotape of people arguing during a business meeting and then asking the participants what the different people in the meeting were feeling and what would have to be done or said to get the people to make specific business decisions. "To do this well," says Spencer, "you have to be able to pick up people's covert agendas. The best executives, we found, do this automatically."

◆ LEARNING HOW TO BE A SOCIAL ANIMAL ———

While it may seem as if the kind of interpersonal abilities related above represent a special mixture of magic, charisma, and good social genes, there is a strong component to social intelligence that is learnable and teachable. Robert Bolton, author of the book *People Skills,* teaches interpersonal communication in four basic areas: listening skills, assertion skills, conflict-resolution skills, and collaborative problem-solving skills. Among the suggestions that Bolton gives for enhancing one's capacity for active listening are:

◆ facing the other person squarely;
◆ maintaining an open position;
◆ avoiding distracting motions and gestures;
◆ making good eye contact;
◆ using appropriate "openers" to communication (e.g., "Care to talk about it?");
◆ providing simple cues during communication to encourage a person to tell his story (e.g., "Tell me more");
◆ maintaining attentive silence while the other is speaking;
◆ paraphrasing the essence of the other's content;
◆ reflecting feelings back to the other person (e.g., "That must be discouraging for you"); and
◆ briefly summarizing the conversation.

Bolton suggests using these skills to start out with in relatively "safe" situations: finding someone you trust to practice with and being willing to make mistakes as you develop your abilities in this area.

Active listening represents only a small part of the total spectrum of interpersonal competencies. A description of all the skills necessary to be an effective communicator would fill many volumes. However, there are some broad strategies known for decades to be crucial in establishing good relations with others. Perhaps the most renowned figure in the field of social-skill development is Dale Carnegie, whose books and courses have made him a legend in the field of personal growth. In his classic text *How to Win Friends and Influence People,* Carnegie lists several points that can lead individuals to greater interpersonal effectiveness, including the following:

- ◆ Don't criticize, condemn, or complain.
- ◆ Give honest and sincere appreciation.
- ◆ Become genuinely interested in other people.
- ◆ Smile.
- ◆ Make the other person feel important.
- ◆ Ask questions instead of giving direct orders.

This kind of social savvy is not typically a part of most intelligence tests, yet it may be among the most important intelligences for survival. According to Robert Bolton, 80 percent of the people who fail at work do so because they don't relate well to other people. In a study conducted by behavioral scientists Morgan McCall and Michael Lombardo with several Fortune 500 corporations, the most important factor in determining an executive's success or failure in being promoted turned out to be her ability—or inability—to understand other people's perspectives.

Similarly, in one's personal life, difficulty in establishing a supportive web of friendships, family relationships, and acquaintanceships can lead to a multitude of emotional and physical problems. In one California study that examined people's social ties (marriage, contacts with family and friends, church membership, and other group affiliations), those who scored low on the combined "social network index" were twice as likely to die in the following nine years. James S. House, chairman of the sociology department at the University of Michigan, reviewed similar sets of data and concluded that "a lack of social relationships constitutes a major risk for mortality." The following exercise will help you become more aware of your own social support network.

CIRCLES OF SUPPORT

Do this exercise on a large sheet of paper. In the middle of the sheet draw a small circle and put your name in the center. Then draw four concentric circles of increasing size so that the circumference of the last circle fills the page. In the first ring (just beyond your name) list all the people who belong to your circle of "intimates." These include spouse or significant other and those few friends and/or relatives that you would call upon in times of crisis. In the second ring list good friends that you regularly go out with, have over, or are otherwise involved with that aren't part of your inner circle. In the third ring list other important people in your social network, including additional family members that you occasionally see, significant people from work, and so forth. In the final ring list as many casual acquaintances as you can.

You have just created a *sociogram*. Sociograms are visual maps that have been used for decades by sociologists, social psychologists, educators, and psychologists as a means of tracking patterns of connectedness between individuals. They provide an instant printout of your social-support network.

Another way of mapping your support system is simply to write your name in the center of a sheet of paper, circle it, and then list the names of significant people in your life randomly around the page. Then, connect the names of these individuals to the center circle using straight lines (double lines if the bond is particularly strong). Indicate the flow of the relationship (whether one-sided or reciprocal) by placing arrows on one side or both sides of each line. After you have finished, notice whether you're a porcupine (lots of lines emerging from your name toward other people); a target (arrows from other people pointed to your name); a mandala (arrows moving

in both directions); or a golf ball (few or no lines at all).
Doing the above exercise can raise some fundamental
questions about your connection as a single individual to
the broader culture around you: Is your support network
central or peripheral to your daily life? Who can you really
count on for help in difficult times? What do the people
in your life mean to you, really?

◆ "WE" CULTURES ────────────────────────

Researchers have recently begun to look at the notion that
certain cultures—including the majority white culture in
the United States—represent "I" cultures, societies that
prize the individual over the group. Other cultures tend
to be "we" cultures, where connectedness, cooperation,
and collaboration are more the rule. While consulting with
the Bureau of Indian Affairs (BIA) in South Dakota a few
years ago, I learned an interesting lesson about "we" versus "I" cultures. A few years before, a large sum of money
had been invested by the Bureau in a handicrafts business
that was to be taken over, in stages, by the members of
the reservation. When the business failed some observers
chalked it up to "lack of Indian initiative." A talk with an
insider, however, revealed a very different story. It turned
out that the BIA had imposed a business model based on
the values of the white American "I" culture: rewarding
individual performance through incentive programs, encouraging competition between individuals, and engaging
in other "I"-related activities. Sioux society—being a "we"
culture—doesn't think primarily in terms of personal rewards and achievements. The guiding principle is more
often "we all move together, cooperatively, or none of us
move at all." So when the native Americans failed to move

up the corporate ladder as single individuals, their actions were misinterpreted as lack of motivation.

"We" cultures tend to make up the greater part of the world's population, including many African, Middle Eastern, Asian, and Latin American societies. Two researchers studying management systems in Kenya, Africa, noted: "In Kenyan tribes nobody is an isolated individual. Rather, his [or her] uniqueness is a secondary fact. . . . First, and foremost, he [or she] is several people's contemporary. . . . In this system, group activities are dominant, responsibility is shared and accountability is collective." In Arabic cultures individuals are known by their *nisba*—or group identification (e.g., Umar Al-Budhadiwi = Umar of the Buhadu Tribe). Similarly, Japanese workers, like the native Americans described above, are embarrassed to be singled out for praise but strive for excellence within a group context.

Ironically, the United States (being predominantly an "I" culture) is learning from Japan that in order to be more competitive in the world marketplace, we must be more cooperative in our businesses and classrooms. As a result businesses are increasingly instituting "quality circles" and other interpersonal structures in their companies. In quality circles employees have the opportunity to meet regularly as teams and contribute ideas and suggestions for improvement of services and products, as well as to solidify their own sense of group involvement in the vision of the organization. In the same way, a growing number of the nation's schools are using "cooperative learning" in their classrooms, a system whereby students collectively work on homework assignments, class projects, and other academic tasks—and often have grades assigned to the whole group rather than to the single individual.

In the broader culture we're also seeing more examples of collaborative projects undertaken by groups united by a common vision, from Hands Across America, a project that took place several years ago in support of world hunger that attempted to have people literally link hands from one side of the continent to the other, to The Names Project, involving thousands of individuals who have sewn quilts in memory of friends and family who have died of AIDS. In addition there has been a powerful surge in the number of support groups springing up around the country. An estimated 15 million Americans currently meet in more than 500,000 self-help groups dealing with issues such as alcoholism, drug addiction, food disorders, physical illnesses, and child abuse.

◆ LINKING UP WITH LIKE MINDS

The nation's movement toward a "we" orientation has resulted in the coining of a new term to describe the forging of productive affiliations: *networking*. While it may conjure up images of yuppies trading business cards at a cocktail party or whole-earth ecologists swapping health-food recipes on their CB radios, networking actually refers to the process of linking up with like-minded people for any purpose whatsoever. According to psychologist Stanley Milgram, anyone in the United States can reach anyone else by going through a statistical average of no more than 5.5 other people. That means that with a relatively minimal amount of effort, you can determine your needs and then find a person or group in the country that has a resource, a point of view, or a supportive attitude to help you in some way. The following exercise will get you started:

JOURNEY TO THE CENTER OF THE NETWORK

At the top of a sheet of paper write down something that you would like to learn more about. Be as specific as you can (e.g., preserving bird populations in your local estuary, writing effective résumés, painting with oils). Select someone in your existing support system (refer to the sociogram above) who might know where to look. Label this person as Stop 1 on your journey, and connect his name to your topic with a straight line. Ask this individual for referrals to others you could talk to concerning the topic. Write these names down as Stop 2 further down on the sheet. Talk with each of the individuals (or write or phone them if they're out of the area) for more information about where to look. Write the referrals given by these people as Stop 3 on your sheet of paper. Continue this process through as many "stops" as necessary until you reach the best possible contact(s) for your topic.

In some cases this process of networking will uncover one expert in the field who can tell you all you need to know about your topic. More likely, however, you'll find yourself connecting with several individuals, each of whom possesses part of the puzzle that you're attempting to put together. In addition you might find as you acquire contacts that you're actually putting together a kind of mini–support system for yourself around a specific issue or area of concern.

Therapist and career counselor Barbara Sher teaches people how to create their own "Success Teams" in order to meet personal and professional goals. In her book *Teamworks!* (coauthored with Annie Gottlieb), Sher gives some basic guidelines for creating and running support networks, including the following:

- ◆ Tell everyone you know about your particular goal (since you never know who the experts might be).
- ◆ Throw an idea/resource party.
- ◆ Brainstorm about each person's goal at the party (three important questions to address: "What's your dream?" "What are the obstacles?" "What do you need to meet your goals?").

◆ Keep an address book of people who attend, including their special skills, interests and abilities.

◆ Print an informal newsletter for support-group members that includes "success" stories, skills and needs Exchange information, and phone numbers.

According to Sher, "People have better ideas for each other than they have for themselves." She also claims that people have more courage for others than for themselves, which is why Sher encourages individuals to form support groups as a way to help them keep moving toward the realization of a dream, even in the midst of doubts, hardships, and setbacks.

Support groups have been particularly useful to me at transitional times in my life. Once, I was thinking about leaving my job as a public school teacher and gathered together a group of similarly dissatisfied teachers to find out if that's what I really wanted to do (it was). Later on, as I was beginning to formulate an image of myself as a writer, I met with a group of people who were also starting new careers. The structure of both groups was the same and consisted of three parts. At the beginning of each meeting, members would share something "new and exciting" that had happened to them since the previous meeting—a quick sharing of one to two minutes. During the middle portion of the meeting, members requested various amounts of time to get help from group members on their individual needs. One person might need half an hour to brainstorm ideas for a project, while another member might only need five minutes to get feedback on an idea. The third and final part of the meeting was given over to a free exchange of ideas, resources, and general enthusiasm.

You might find that the suggestions given for starting a support group, as well as the many other ideas provided in this chapter, are right up your interpersonal alley. On the other hand, it could be that the process of networking with others, actively listening to a colleague, or attending social gatherings is a painful or difficult process for you. If so, the next chapter may be more your style. In it, you'll have the opportunity to value your own "different drummer" tendencies and discover ways of using retreats and other self-development tools to enhance your life.

---

25 WAYS TO DEVELOP YOUR INTERPERSONAL INTELLIGENCE

- Buy a Rolodex, fill it with names of business contacts, friends, acquaintances, relatives, and others, and stay in touch with them.
- Decide to meet one new person each day (or week).
- Join a volunteer or service-oriented group (Rotary Club, Greenpeace, Red Cross, etc.).
- Spent fifteen minutes each day practicing *active listening* with your spouse or a close friend.
- Throw a party and invite at least three people that you don't know very well.
- Attend group psychotherapy or family therapy sessions on a regular basis.
- Take a leadership role in a group you're currently involved with at work or in your community.
- Start your own support group.
- Enroll in a community college course on interpersonal communication skills.
- Collaborate with one or more persons on a project of mutual interest (quilt, article, garden, etc.).
- Have regular family meetings in your home.
- Communicate with other people on a computer network via an electronic bulletin board.

◆ Organize a group brainstorming session at your workplace.

◆ Go on a couples retreat.

◆ Learn the art of proper social behavior by reading a book on etiquette and discussing the material with an individual you consider socially adept.

◆ Strike up conversations with people in public places (bookstores, supermarkets, airline terminals, etc.).

◆ Start regular correspondences with a network of individuals around the country or world.

◆ Attend family, school, or work-related reunions.

◆ Play noncompetitive/cooperative outdoor games with family and friends.

◆ Get to know members of a "we" culture (native American, Japanese, Hispanic, etc.) and adapt the best features of their interpersonal life-style to your own life.

◆ Join a group whose purpose is to help you meet new people (singles club, hiking organization, study group, etc.).

◆ Offer to teach, tutor, or counsel other people through a volunteer organization or on an informal basis.

◆ Spend fifteen minutes a day for a week or two observing how people interact in a public place (street corner, train station, department store, etc.)

◆ Meditate on your connection to those around you, starting with your immediate family and friends, extending this to your community and country, and eventually encompassing the entire planet.

◆ Study the lives of well-known socially competent individuals (e.g., philanthropists, counselors, politicians, social workers) through biographies, films, and other media, and learn to follow their example.

SELF SMART: DEVELOPING YOUR INTRAPERSONAL INTELLECT

Ramana Maharshi, one of India's greatest contemporary sages, was a lad of only seventeen when he had an experience that changed his life forever. He was sitting alone in his uncle's house in South India when a "sudden violent fear of death" overtook him. He was in good health at the time, but the certainty of the feeling that he was going to die caused him to lie down on the floor in imitation of a corpse and hold his breath while his mind went inwards in exploration of the meaning of this "death." He had a deep intuition at that moment that, although his body might die, his Self, the sense of "I," would live on. "All this was not dull thought," he later wrote. "It flashed through me vividly as living truth which I perceived directly, almost without thought-process. 'I' was something very real, the only real thing about my present state. . . . Absorption in the Self continued unbroken from that time on." He was never the same again. After a few weeks he left home and moved to the holy town of Tiruvannamalai, where he remained for more than fifty years, teaching the path of self-inquiry to thousands of people from all over the world.

Maharshi's encounter with selfhood was extraordinary. Yet his experience, for all of its life-transforming power, represents a process that most people engage in to some degree during their lives: a drive to answer the monumental question "Who am I?" The focus of this investigation has many different levels of interpretation, for the self (or Self, depending on one's perspective) is a protean entity that defies exact description. For some it's a Grand Central Station that coordinates the many complex activities we engage in during our lives—planning, hoping, desiring, willing, acting, and performing countless tasks and responsibilities. For others it's a Dewey Decimal System of the mind that stores all our experiences and recalls them as needed to help us cope with the stresses and strains of being human. For the mystical it's a Golden Jewel of Pure Consciousness that transcends the mundane activities of our ego or lower self. Yet regardless of how it's defined, "self" deserves an important place in the study of human intelligence. In this chapter we'll explore the seventh, and final, intelligence in MI theory: intrapersonal intelligence, or self-understanding.

◆ SELF AS A CONCEPT

Ask a three-year-old child to point to herself, and she'll probably put her finger on her belly button. Ask an older child or an adult the same question, and the hand will more often gesture toward the chest or the head. Over the past twenty-five hundred years ideas about the locus of the self have undergone several radical changes, with some touting the heart or liver as the source of selfhood and others vying for the pineal gland or some other brain-related organ as a central origin of consciousness. Moreover, specifying the extact nature of the self has proved far more difficult than locating it somewhere in a human being.

Perhaps the real problem with arriving at a solid definition of the self lies in the fact that the object of our search is the same entity that is doing the searching. To put it another way: if the self were so simple that we could understand it, we'd be so simple that we couldn't. As far back as 500 B.C. Buddhist thinkers regarded the self as a *concept*. They contended that there was no tangible self existing at the core of consciousness, only thoughts, feelings, sensations, and ideas that adhered to the illusion of selfhood. More recently, cognitive psychologists have taken up the same line of thought in suggesting that the self is nothing more than a very complex mental map or system of schemas that allows us to organize information about the world more efficiently.

Another contemporary psychological perspective suggests that there actually is a *real self* that develops out of interactions with the environment and with significant others. This real self is the ultimate source of one's inner creativity, vitality, spontaneity, and emotional well-being. William James may have summed up this idea of self best when he wrote: "I have often thought that the best way to define a man's character would be to seek out the particular mental or moral attitude in which, when it came upon him, he felt himself most deeply and intensely active and alive. At such moments there is a voice inside which speaks and says: 'This is the real me!'" According to psychiatrist James Masterson, author of *The Search for the Real Self,* the real self has several components, including:

- the capacity to experience a wide range of feelings deeply with vigor, excitement, and spontaneity;
- the capacity for assertion;
- an acknowledgment of self-esteem;
- the ability to soothe painful feelings in oneself;
- the wherewithal to make and stick to commitments in work and relationships;
- the capacity for creativity and intimacy; and
- the ability to be alone.

Masterson points out that this real self persists over time and space. "Whether up or down, in a good mood or a bad one, accepting failure or living with success," says Masterson, "a person with a real self has an inner core that remains the same even as he grows and develops."

Early childhood seems to be the critical time for the development of this self. An infant provided with love, encouragement, strong role models, and appropriate "mirroring" (the sparkle in a mother's eye that says "You're here and you're marvelous!"), develops a positive concept of self and has his real self continuously affirmed. However, a young child who grows up in a home filled with fear, depression, hate, or apathy forges a negative self-image that will follow him into adulthood with distressing results. This can lead to the formation of a "false self": a rigid or perfectionistic mask that a person puts on to buffer himself from the world or to protect himself from feelings of worthlessness and inadequacy. Taken to the extreme, a child who experiences severe physical or emotional abuse can experience a complete fracture in his self-structure, resulting in a profound disintegration of the self such as is found in multiple personality disorder.

Even among normal individuals, though, it's relatively common to develop several "subselves" in early childhood as a way of coping with the inevitable stresses and strains

of growing up. Schools of psychological thought character-
ize these selves in different ways, with Gestalt therapy referring to the "topdog" and "underdog," transactional
analysis identifying the child, parent, and adult roles, and
psychoanalysis touting the id, ego, superego, and ego-ideal
as fundamental components of personality.

In psychosynthesis, a therapeutic system developed by
Italian psychiatrist Roberto Assagioli, clients provide their
own names for a wide range of subpersonalities, such as
"the spoiled child," "Mr. Wizard," "the pervert," "Crazy
Suzie," and "the thought police." These "little selves" co-
exist with our basic sense of self, often remaining at an
unconscious level before springing into action at the
slightest provocation. The next exercise will help you identify these subselves and assist you in defining more clearly
your "core" sense of self, or real self.

SELF COLLAGE

Gather together art materials for creating a collage, including glue, scissors, paint, crayons, pencils, old magazines and
newspapers, and a large sheet of newsprint. Then, draw,
write, and glue pictures onto the paper that correspond to
the different aspects of yourself. (You might also include Xe-
roxed copies of photos of yourself at different ages.) In the
center of the sheet include words and images that correspond to your core or *real self*—the sense of self you feel
when you are most alive and vital inside. Then, identify specific subpersonalities or "little selves" and depict them in
words and images around the images of your real self.

This exercise can help articulate your self-concept and
provide a blueprint for the development of your inner

sense of self. Most self-esteem experts agree that cultivating a positive self-image generally involves a process of freeing ourselves from the limitations of the small selves ("the bad child," "the perfectionist," "the lazy girl," and so forth) and gradually identifying with our central core. Here are some suggestions for moving in the direction of a positive self-image:

- ◆ Avoid putting yourself down with negative self-talk.
- ◆ Do something nurturing for yourself every day.
- ◆ Write down twenty positive statements about yourself and say them to yourself on a regular basis.
- ◆ Form mental images of your real self.
- ◆ Surround yourself with positive role models.
- ◆ Read self-help books that reinforce your emerging positive sense of self.

As Dorothy Corkille Briggs, author of *Celebrate Your Self,* puts it: "Your self-image—who you think you are—is literally a package *you put together* from how others have seen and treated you and from your conclusions as you compared yourself to others." By focusing on the inner core of your personal aliveness, vitality, and creativity, you can escape the prison of a negative self-image and find freedom in a much broader and expansive sense of 'I am.' "

◆ GOING FOR THE GOAL ─────────────

An important key to developing a positive self-image involves cultivating an inner sense of mastery and competence, or what psychologist Robert W. White terms *effectance*—the internalized feeling that we have an *effect* upon the world. I discovered in my work as a special-education teacher that self-esteem exercises such as those given above were often not terribly productive unless they were linked to students' feelings of *accomplishment* after meeting goals they had set for themselves.

The development of a sense of *self-mastery* seems crucial in helping people establish a solid sense of self. Yale intelligence researcher Robert Sternberg refers to this kind of tacit ability as the intelligence of *managing self*. According to Sternberg, this skill involves "knowledge about how to manage oneself on a daily basis so as to maximize one's productivity. Examples . . . include knowledge about the relative importance of the tasks one faces, knowledge about more and less efficient ways of approaching tasks, and knowledge about how to motivate oneself to maximize accomplishment."

Few people appear to have totally developed their self-management abilities. One indication of this can be seen in the relatively small number of New Year's resolutions that are actually kept from year to year. Motivational specialist Dennis Waitly observed: "It is obvious that the majority of people spend more time planning a Christmas party or a vacation than they do planning their lives. By failing to plan, they actually are planning to fail by default."

A look at many of the great achievers of society shows that they possessed this self-directedness and used it to help them reach their life's goals. Benjamin Franklin, for example, was only twenty when he set up a master plan for how he would conduct the rest of his life. It included guidelines for frugality, honesty, industriousness, and moral integrity. In his later life he reflected back on his life plan, noting that it "had been faithfully adhered to thro' old age." A more contemporary cultural icon, former Chrysler chairman Lee Iaccoca, reflected in his autobiography on the importance of setting short-term goals and organizing time efficiently. "Ever since college I've always worked hard during the week while trying to keep my weekends free for family and recreation," wrote Iaccoca. "Every Sunday night I get the adrenaline going again by making an outline of what I want to accomplish during the upcoming week."

Of course, the mere listing of goals does not ensure that they will be reached. Several other factors need to be included in the goal-setting process. First, an individual must choose goals that are *achievable*. Someone who selects "win the Nobel Peace Prize" as a major life goal is almost certain to be disappointed. Knowing your own strengths and limitations constitutes an important component of self-intelligence (a faculty, you are developing as you read and work through the exercises in this book). By choosing goals that are at a level of "just manageable difficulty," you can ensure that they will be challenging and attainable.

This brings up the second important criteria of goal setting: that your goals be *desirable*. Charles Garfield, author of *Peak Performers*, notes that "one can outline ninety-nine . . . goals but it is the excitement of knowing that these goals matter deeply to you that cuts through the old 'why bother?' attitude." Make sure that your goals emerge from the promptings of your real self and that they're not simply part of somebody else's agenda (more on this in chapter 9).

Finally, the goal should be *measurable,* so that you know when you've reached it. Use specific, concrete language to describe what it is you intend to do and when you intend to accomplish it (not: "I will make a lot of money" but "I will make $75,000 a year as an interior decorator by 1998"). The following exercise should help you begin the process of goal setting and assist you in honing your self-management capabilities.

GOAL TENDING

On a blank sheet of paper, list ten significant goals that you'd like to achieve in your personal and/or professional life. Be specific as you write them down and make sure they represent goals that matter to you and that are attainable. Then, order the goals, with the most important one at the top and the least important at the bottom. Take a second sheet of paper and put the most important goal from your list on the top of this new page (include next to it the date you intend to reach the goal). Write down all the things you need to do in order to accomplish this goal (brainstorm with a friend if necessary). On a third sheet of paper, list the activities for that goal in the order required for you to complete the goal (what you need to do first, what you need to do second, and so on). Then, begin doing the activity at the top of the list. After you've accomplished it, check it off and go on to the next one. Continue this process until you've reached your goal. To assist you in your process, write on a card the following epigram from Goethe: "Whatever you can do or dream you can, begin it. Boldness has genius, power, and magic in it. Begin it now!" Keep that card on your desk or find another passage that inspires you to reach your goal.

◆ HOW TO KNOW THYSELF ─────────────

Some readers may be hesitant to try the goal-setting exercise above because they aren't sure what they really want to do with their lives. These individuals may need to focus on another important component of self-understanding: awareness of one's inner life. Howard Gardner characterizes this capacity as the core component of intrapersonal intelligence. According to Gardner a person with strong intrapersonal intelligence can discriminate among a wide range of internal emotions and eventually label them, symbolize them, and "draw upon them as a means of understanding and guiding one's behavior." Such people include therapists, the wise elders of society, and writers.

Marcel Proust, for example, spent much of his adult life lying in bed thinking back over his life in amazing detail. The result of his introspection was one of the great literary works of Western civilization, the multivolume novel *Remembrance of Things Past*. The novel begins with more than fifty pages about the protagonist's feelings as a child waiting for his mother to come up to his room to kiss him goodnight. Each subtle emotion and thought is explored in intricate detail.

The founder of psychoanalysis, Sigmund Freud, on the other hand, engaged in a very different kind of introspection. Starting at the age of thirty-nine, he devoted the last half-hour of every workday to self-analysis. Using the same psychological tools that he employed with his patients, including free association, dream work, and (like Proust) recollection of childhood memories, Freud carried on this adventure of the psyche for more than forty years—a process that contributed significantly to the development of psychoanalytic theory.

Yet another model of introspection comes from Southeast Asia, where Theravadan Buddhist monks typically spend several hours a day engaged in intensive meditation designed to focus their attention on the phenomenology of the mind. Buddhist Abhidharma psychology has worked out an intricate psychological system of the mind that classifies mental processes based on the inner experiences of these masters of consciousness. It has identified, for example, eleven positive mental events, twenty sources of mental instability, nine phases of mental control, and numerous other categories of mental functioning.

You don't have to be a writer, psychiatrist, or monk, however, to engage in deep introspective work. Let's look at a few simple tools you can use to help focus your attention in an inward direction:

Keeping a journal. Modern-day explorers of the inner self often find journal keeping to be invaluable in helping them probe the depths of their souls. Although journals are a linguistic medium used by intrapersonally intelligent individuals, they tend to be more a tool for self-exploration than a means of literary expression. Thomas Mallon, author of *A Book of One's Own: People and Their Diaries,* characterizes these self-wise journalists as "generally very serious people, more in the way of pilgrims ..." Examples of the writings of these individuals include the philosophical broodings of Thoreau, the intense personal disclosures of Anaïs Nin, and the spiritual yearnings of Thomas Merton. Techniques used by journal keepers to reach self-understanding vary widely. Author Joanna Field recorded the happiest moment of each day as a starting point for her diary entries. Psychiatrist Carl Jung drew images of dreams and waking fantasies in his black leather–bound journals. Former United Nations Secretary General Dag Hammarskjöld assembled a patchwork of poems, quotations, questions, and other assorted bits of wisdom over a period of thirty years.

New York psychologist Ira Progoff has combined many of the best features of journal keeping in an approach that anyone can learn and use as a means of self-understanding. The journal, kept in a three-ring binder, is divided into several sections which represent different aspects of one's inner experience. These include:

◆ dreams;
◆ twilight imagery (daydreams);
◆ life-history material;
◆ inner dialogues with significant others;
◆ inner dialogues with oneself and one's work; and
◆ a daily log.

Typically, an individual might begin by recording an entry in one section of the journal but then move to other sections as associations are triggered. An entry in the daily log, for example, might trigger a dream memory that would be recorded in the dream log, which in turn might lead to an early-childhood memory that could be recorded in the life-history section. Progoff feels that this dynamic approach to journal keeping overcomes the limitations of the typical diary format, which is too static and doesn't allow people to "loosen the soil" of their inner life.

Meditation. For those who don't want to be tethered to the printed word, meditation offers perhaps the best and most time-honored tool for self-knowledge. Whether it involves focusing attention on a candle flame, reciting a mantra, or simply observing the thoughts that rise and fall in one's mind, meditation provides a means of consciously looking at inner experiences that are typically glossed over in the course of one's busy daily existence. As psychiatrist Lawrence LeShan, author of *How to Meditate,* points out: "We meditate to find, to recover, to come back to something of ourselves we once dimly and unknowingly had and have lost without knowing what it was or where or when we lost it." The following exercise will give you an opportunity to practice one very simple form of meditation adapted from Vipassana or Buddhist "insight" meditation.

EXPLORING THE INNER MINDSCAPE

Sit in a comfortable chair in a quiet room. Close your eyes, and begin to focus attention on your breathing. Breathe normally and notice the sensation of air passing through your nostrils with each inhalation and exhalation. If your concentration begins to wander, simply return your attention back to your breathing. You might find that your attention keeps wandering off to a certain thought, feeling, sensation, or perception. If this happens, simply notice the experience ("oh yes, that's anger . . ." or "itching . . . itching . . ." or "I'm remembering yesterday's party . . ."). After identifying the experience, return to your breathing. Keep your attention focused on your breath. If your mind wanders again, repeat this process of identifying the experience and returning to your breath. Continue meditating like this for 20 minutes.

Dream work. Sigmund Freud called dreams "the royal road to the unconscious." Remembering and learning to understand your dreams can be a powerful method of exploring the inner self. Historically, dreams were used as sources of prophecy, divination, and inspiration. More recently, figures such as Gandhi, Henry James, and Beethoven used dreams as triggers for their creative work. Dreams can unlock repressed emotions, dislodge forgotten memories, activate creative ideas, and give birth to new perspectives on life and self. "Dreams are dynamic mosaics that express the movements, conflicts, interactions, and developments of the great energy systems within the unconscious," says Robert Johnson, Jungian analyst and author of *Inner Work*. To remember your dreams, keep a tape recorder or journal at your bedside and record them immediately upon waking during the night or in the morning. Johnson suggests a four-step plan for interpreting a dream:

◆ *Making associations:* Take each image from the dream and write down all the connections you can make to it. Example: The image of a vacant lot might be associated with emptiness, potential, natural growth, a lot you played on as a child, or lack of use.
◆ *Connecting dream images to inner dynamics:* Relate the dream images to what's going on in your own life.

Example: "I feel like I'm moving through a vacant lot in my own creative life."

◆ *Interpreting:* Put together your associations and personal connections from the first two steps and view the dream's meaning as a whole. Example: This dream is telling me that there's a part of me that's lying unused—a potential that I need to explore."

◆ *Performing Rituals:* Do something concrete to bring the dream from the world of the imagination into the real world. Example: Go to a nearby vacant lot and walk around it thinking about what it is in you that may need to be developed.

Johnson emphasizes the importance of "going where the energy is" in working with dreams. You'll know that you're getting close to the central meaning of the dream when you get a sudden surge of interest, vitality, or an emotional charge from the images.

◆ THE UNDISCOVERED SELF

Self-discovery tools such as meditation, journal keeping, and dream work can open us up to unexpected experiences that challenge our conceptions of who we are. As Carl Jung pointed out, "most people confuse 'self-knowledge' with knowledge of their conscious ego personalities." Jung's own conception of selfhood was much broader, encompassing what he called the *collective unconscious,* a storehouse of archetypal symbols and images shared by humanity. William James, the founder of modern psychology, reflected on this wider conception of self when he wrote: "Our normal waking consciousness . . . is but one special type of consciousness, whilst all about it, parted from it by the flimsiest of screens, there lie potential forms of consciousness entirely different."

For thousands of years world cultures have articulated · highly detailed systems of selfhood that incorporate these "potential forms of consciousness." The Vedanta (Hindu) religion of India speaks of different *sheaths* of the self that include physical, emotional, mental, intuitional, and spiritual domains. Tibetan Buddhist philosophy, though denying the presence of a "self," nevertheless posits the existence of thousands of peaceful and wrathful entities (bodhisattvas, dakinis, yoginis, herukas, and other beings) within an individual's consciousness. Sufi psychology, the mystical branch of Islam, has an elaborate system that speaks in poetic language about the various stages of development in the growth of the self toward truth. The mythologies, cosmologies, and folklore of many other cultures weave intricate symbols together in patterning complex portraits of the self.

Typically, individuals who are in touch with this level of intrapersonal intelligence have served as mediators or guides for other members of the culture to the farthest shores of the human psyche. These include the priests, prophets, shamans, sorcerers, mystics, gurus, tzaddiks, and visionaries of a culture. Such figures stand outside the society and often experience harrowing rites of initiation involving encounters with both dark and light dimensions of the inner self. They often undergo what mythologist Joseph Campbell called the *hero journey*. This journey consists of three basic stages: separation, initiation, and return. Campbell writes: "A hero ventures forth from the world of common day into a region of supernatural wonder; fabulous forces are there encountered and a decisive victory is won; the hero comes back from this mysterious adventure with the power to bestow boons on his fellow men."

One important component of this journey is solitude. Individuals in quest of a deeper conception of selfhood must often separate themselves from their everyday existence and find a place outside of the culture, often in nature, where they can open themselves up to the miraculous or mysterious. The greatest of all intrapersonal explorers in the history of civilization—the founders of the world's great religions—each had important periods of isolation in the course of their mission: Buddha sitting under the bo tree, Jesus resisting temptation in the desert, Mohammad seeking refuge in the Cave of Hera during the month of Ramadan. In shamanic cultures individuals often isolate themselves for days at a time, sometimes in the company of animals, where they can receive their personal vision.

In our own culture intrapersonally intelligent individuals typically seek out periods of isolation for self-renewal. Admiral Byrd, for example, volunteered to operate an advanced weather base by himself in the Antarctic in the winter of 1934 because of a desire to find some inner solitude. Although he nearly died during that winter, Byrd later wrote in his autobiography *Alone,* "I did take away something that I had not fully possessed before: appreciation of the sheer beauty and miracle of being alive, and a humble set of values. . . . I live more simply now, and with more peace." Writer May Sarton, author of *Journal of a Solitude,* similarly noted that her own existence truly began only when she was apart from others.

The desire to be alone can run counter to societal pressures that often demand that a person "relate" to others in order to be considered emotionally healthy. Psychiatrist Anthony Storr, author of *Solitude: A Return to the Self,* observes: "In a culture in which interpersonal relationships are generally considered to provide the answer to every form of distress, it is sometimes difficult to persuade well-meaning helpers that solitude can be as therapeutic as emotional support." Our culture does provide for structured periods of solitude, often in the form of retreats, sabbaticals, or leaves of absence. However, you don't have to wait for such a time to come around in your life in order to benefit from solitude. Anyone can use a free weekend or holiday to create her own period of self-renewal in isolation from others. The following is an exercise designed to help you do just that.

DO-IT-YOURSELF RETREAT

Consult your yearly calendar and block off one or more days as a retreat time for yourself. Arrange in advance to stay at a location apart from your own home (a hotel, a formal retreat center, a monastery, a friend's house). Make sure that you have a room of your own and that you have no obligations during your stay. Also, see that regular meals are provided for you (or can be obtained at a local restaurant) so that you don't have to think about eating arrangements. Spend all of your time alone or as much of it as possible.

Use your retreat in any way that you'd like. However, make sure to build into it three basic components:

◆ *Taking-in time:* to assimilate experiences from the outside world. Examples: reading a book, walking in nature, or looking at beautiful art

◆ *Do-nothing time:* to incubate the experiences you've taken in. Examples: meditation, sleeping/dreaming, daydreaming, or simply thinking things over

◆ *Expression time:* to externalize your inner experiences. Examples: writing in a journal, drawing or painting, dancing, and/or other creative expressions

Pay attention to new insights, intutitions, images, or conceptions of self that emerge from your retreat. After you've come back to the world, make sure to refer back to your experience periodically by reading your journal, putting an important image on your wall, or engaging in activities that call up the retreat for you. In this way, you can integrate what you've learned into your daily life.

Some people may find that they already engage in "mini-retreats" while involved in their favorite solo hobbies such as fishing, gardening, handicrafts, and hiking. These kinds of experiences help the solitary self find strength and meaning in the midst of a busy and frequently off-center world. In a society where images of who we're *supposed* to be pounce on us from all sides, it's especially important to be true to our own deepest selves. Theologian Martin Buber tells a story about a man who died and went to heaven expecting Saint Peter to ask him "Why weren't you more like Moses during your life?" Instead, he was surprised, and mortified, when the question was "Why weren't you more like *yourself?*" By striving to become truly ourselves, whatever that may mean, we can ensure our salvation in this life, if not the next.

---

25 WAYS TO DEVELOP YOUR INTRAPERSONAL INTELLIGENCE

- Do individual counseling or psychotherapy work as a client.
- Study "maps of the self" in Western psychology and/or Eastern philosophies.
- Learn to meditate.
- Listen to motivational audio- and videocassettes.
- Write your autobiography.
- Create your own personal ritual or rite of passage.
- Record and work with your dreams on a regular basis.
- Read self-help books.
- Establish a quiet place in your home for introspection.
- Teach yourself something new such as a skill, a

language, or a body of knowledge in an area of interest to you.

- ◆ Start your own business.
- ◆ Develop an interest or hobby that sets you apart from the crowd.
- ◆ Enroll in a class on assertiveness training or developing self-confidence.
- ◆ Take a battery of tests designed to assess your special strengths and weaknesses in a broad range of areas.
- ◆ Set short- and long-term goals for yourself and then follow through on them.
- ◆ Attend a seminar designed to teach you about yourself or your "selves" (e.g., psychosynthesis, transitional analysis, psychodrama, gestalt work, or another psychological school of thought).
- ◆ Keep a daily journal or diary for recording your thoughts, feelings, goals, and memories.
- ◆ Study the biographies and autographies of great individuals with powerful personalities.
- ◆ Engage in daily self-esteem–enhancing behaviors (e.g., using positive self-talk, affirming your successes).
- ◆ Attend the house of worship of your choice regularly.
- ◆ Do something pleasurable for yourself at least once a day.
- ◆ Find out what your personal "myth" is and live it in the world.
- ◆ Keep a mirror handy to look into when you are in different moods or states of mind.
- ◆ Take ten minutes every evening to mentally review the various thoughts and feelings you had during the day.
- ◆ Spend time with people who have a strong and healthy sense of self.

9

AWAKENING
YOUR LATE-BLOOMING
INTELLIGENCES

If Conrad Ferdinand Meyer had died at the age of forty, he would hardly have been missed. As a child and student he had been restless, distractible, and morose. As an adult he wandered from job to job without focus or direction. At the age of twenty-seven he entered a mental institution where he suffered from hypochondria and the delusion that "all people found him disgusting." He came close to putting an end to his own life.

Then at forty, everything changed. As Ernst Kretschmer, author of *The Psychology of Men of Genius,* wrote: "Until his fortieth year he appeared stunted and lean as a skeleton, and only at this age did his beard begin to grow and his figure to take on the later fullness and stateliness. And at this age for the first time appeared a collection of poems." He continued to write for the next twenty-seven years and became one of Switzerland's most beloved poets.

Meyer's poetic genius is remarkable for its sudden appearance. But in a larger sense his story shows us how an ability can remain hidden for years like an underground stream and burst forth unexpectedly as a fountain of vitality. We all have potential like Meyer's, waiting for the opportunity to express itself. Each of us possesses hidden intelligences that lie dormant like seeds in winter, waiting for the spring to blossom. This chapter will help you identify your own late-blooming intelligences and will suggest ways in which you can nurture them and bring them to fruition in your own life.

◆ THE ORIGINS OF INTELLIGENCES IN CHILDHOOD

Childhood is probably the best place to begin searching for late-blooming intelligence. As Carl Jung pointed out, "The child is potential future . . . the [inner] 'child' paves the way for a future change in personality." For Jung this turned out to be especially true. In his late thirties he experienced a depression, due in part to his estrangement from his teacher and mentor, Sigmund Freud. It was a childhood memory, he wrote later, that helped him move through this crisis. He remembered being a child of ten or eleven building cities and castles out of stones and mud. This memory brought with it a strong emotional charge. " 'Aha' I said to myself," Jung wrote, "there is still life in these things. The small boy is still around, and possesses a creative life which I lack."

So, at the age of thirty-eight, Jung began playing once again like a child during lunchtime breaks from his psychiatric practice. He made little civilizations in mud and stone near his lakeside home. This daily practice, he later said, unleashed a stream of fantasies and visions that provided the basis for most of his future life's work. Interestingly, it seems to have been the spatial and bodily-kinesthetic intelligences that Jung called up from childhood that helped him balance a strongly linguistic adult self. "At any time in my later life," he wrote, "when I came up against a blank wall, I painted a picture or hewed stone. Each such experience proved to be a *rite d'entree* for the ideas and works that followed hard upon it."

Childhood is the original spawning ground of all seven intelligences. Children's early language is quite musical in character. Their first spatial representations often have a kinesthetic quality about them. For example, a two-year-old child may draw a picture of a rabbit by actually skipping the pencil along the paper in short hopping motions. In the area of logical-mathematical thinking, Jean Piaget pointed out that the infant appears to reason entirely on a physical or *sensory-motor* level. Young children also seem to have frequent experiences of *synesthesia*. That is, they can often hear colors, see sounds, and mix the senses (and intelligences) together in unique and interesting ways. One classic image of a child is of someone moving along the road dancing, singing, counting, talking, relating, daydreaming, all at the same time.

Out of this multimodal mix of behaviors and experiences a certain pattern of strengths begins to emerge. One youngster will show greater musical and interpersonal gifts. Another will evidence kinesthetic and spatial abilities. Gardner calls these early signs of intellectual strength *proclivities,* and suggests that they are to some extent hardwired into us through genetics and other biological factors, but that culture plays a huge role in forming and shaping them. Using the checklist below, I'd like you to take a look back at your own childhood and think about which intelligences you were most "at promise" to express. To help jog your memory you might consider getting background information from some of the following sources before completing the checklist:

- ◆ *Interviews.* Talk with parents and other relatives about their remembrances of your special strengths as a child, such as early walking, talking, and reading.
- ◆ *Documents.* Visit childhood haunts, look at childhood photos, and retrieve childhood memorabilia. A toy drum, a catcher's mitt, or a 4-H ribbon tucked away in an attic or basement may remind you of talents you'd forgotten about.
- ◆ *Dreams.* Record and think about your dreams. Look for images that point back to childhood. These may bring up lost memories that point the way to a neglected ability.
- ◆ *Play.* Observe children at play and be playful yourself. These experiences may remind you that you were once a skillful runner or drew really well, or had a great sense of rhythm.

CHECKLIST: INTELLIGENCES IN CHILDHOOD

LINGUISTIC:

_____ I often had an easy time memorizing stories, poems, history facts, or other tidbits of information in school.

_____ I was an early reader.

_____ I liked to write poems, notes, or stories, even as a very young child.

_____ I was very talkative when I was young.

_____ I loved to look things up in the encyclopedia or dictionary as a kid.

_____ I had many favorite books as a child.

_____ I was an early talker.

Other linguistic memories:

LOGICAL-MATHEMATICAL:

_____ I enjoyed playing around with a chemistry set or other science materials as a child.

_____ I had an easy time understanding new math concepts in school.

_____ I enjoyed counting things as a child.

_____ I frequently asked parents and teachers questions about how things worked or why things in nature happened the way they did.

_____ As a youngster I liked watching such television shows as "Mr. Wizard" and "The Wild Kingdom," which dealt with science or nature themes, or the parts of "Mr. Roger's Neighborhood," "Sesame Strect," or "Captain Kangaroo" that involved numbers and science experiments.

_____ As a child I liked to experiment with cause-and-effect while playing with blocks or other toys.

_____ I tended to look for patterns and regularities in the world when I was small (e.g., noticing every third step on the stairs had a notch on it etc.).

Other logical-mathematical memories:

SPATIAL:

_____ I enjoyed scribbling, drawing, and painting as a very young child.

_____ I was especially delighted by certain colors when I was young.

_____ I enjoyed figuring out how to take apart and put back together toys, simple machines, and/or puzzles.

_____ I liked building card castles or sand castles, or playing around with Erector Sets, Tinker Toys, Lincoln Logs, Legos, or other construction materials.

_____ I had vivid and colorful visual dreams as a child.

_____ I used to be able to close my eyes and visualize things in my head that were almost as real as objects in real life.

_____ I had an instinctive ability to find my way around my neighborhood as a kid.

Other spatial memories:

BODILY-KINESTHETIC:

_____ I was an early crawler and/or walker.

_____ I enjoyed messy hands-on activities like finger painting, clay, and papier-mâché.

_____ I was a physically active youngster.

_____ I liked to "ham it up" as a child in little skits, puppet shows, plays, or other performances.

_____ I showed special ability in one or more sports from an early age.

_____ I was attracted to dance, ballet, gymnastics, creative movement, or other kinds of physical motion as a child.

_____ I loved being outdoors.

Other kinesthetic memories:

MUSICAL:

_____ People tell me that I had an especially musical quality to my babbling as an infant.

_____ I liked to bang on toys, furniture, kitchen utensils, or other objects in a rhythmic way as a very young child.

_____ I loved listening to favorite records or tapes.

_____ I liked to make up my own special songs.

_____ I enjoyed playing a musical instrument as a child.

_____ I would really perk up whenever music was played in my home (e.g., on the radio, record player, or in a live performance).

_____ I seemed to have a good ear for different kinds of nonverbal sounds (dogs barking, ice cream vendor, wind blowing, etc.).

Other musical memories:

INTERPERSONAL:

_____ I seemed to warm up naturally to strangers as a young child.

_____ I had an easy time making friends in school.

_____ I was often called upon by my peers to help solve disputes in the neighborhood or schoolyard.

_____ I was a leader in clubs or other groups when I was a child.

_____ I usually knew what was going on socially with kids in the neighborhood (feuds, romances, and other gossip).

_____ I could often tell what a friend or relative was feeling as soon as the person walked into the room.

_____ I often felt compassion or caring for an individual or group of people as a child and wanted to take some kind of specific action.

Other interpersonal memories:

INTRAPERSONAL:

_____ I was a particularly self-reliant and independent youngster.

_____ I had lots of hobbies or other activities that I preferred to do on my own.

_____ I had a special secret place that I went to in order to get away from everybody and everything.

_____ I frequently thought about what I wanted to be when I grew up.

_____ I spent a lot of time by myself feeling and thinking about things that were happening to me in my life.

_____ I had unusual experiences of a religious, psychic, or aesthetic nature as a child that I couldn't really talk to anyone about.

_____ I was aware of having a separate identity fairly early in my childhood.

Other intrapersonal memories:

◆ INTELLIGENCE SHUTDOWN ────────────

If, after completing the above checklist, you discovered the same strengths in childhood that you now have as an adult, then you're probably on the right track in making the most out of your potential. Keep in mind, however, that there still may be gifts that you've hidden so deeply inside that you're unable to recognize them in any of the items in the checklist. If you suspect this might be the case, keep on digging into your memories and dreams. You're likely to hit gold eventually.

On the other hand, if you identified abilities and strengths in childhood that are no longer part of your adult life, you should ask yourself what happened to them. They were so important then. Why aren't they an important part of your life now?

An intelligence can shut down for many reasons. One of the most common reasons is not having the time to develop it. You grow up, marry, have kids, and get a mort-

gage, and there's simply no space in your life left for painting that picture, acting in a play, inventing, cartooning, or
doing the other things that may have brought you such
enjoyment as a child or adolescent. Sometimes when these
family and financial pressures are released, neglected intelligences have a chance to develop.

As a child, novelist Jean Auel read voraciously, loved
listening to the Saturday morning radio show "Let's Pretend," and created her own imaginative playmates. As an
adult, however, Auel engaged in far more practical pursuits. She raised a family, worked as a credit manager in
an electronics firm, and obtained an M.B.A. degree. But at
the age of forty, she found herself wondering what she
wanted to do with the rest of her life. "I had been spending practically every minute of my life raising my family,
working, and going to school, and now suddenly I had my
degree," she said.

One day an idea came to her for a short story set in
prehistoric times about an orphaned girl who finds herself
among people of another, more primitive race. She became
obsessed with the idea, began going to the library to research it, and over the next two years wrote the best-selling
novel *Clan of the Cave Bear*. She now has four novels in
print with sales of more than 20 million copies. Auel apparently needed to fulfill personal and professional responsibilities before she could turn to her more creative side.

Sometimes, however, intelligences remain hidden for
more psychological reasons. A parent may shame a child for
being musical, artistic, or proficient in some other area that
is threatening to the adult, and the child will respond by
turning that ability off. In the classic children's tale *The Little
Prince,* Antoine de Saint-Exupéry describes being a child of
six trying to show adults his spatial conception of a boa
constrictor swallowing an elephant. "The grown-ups' response ... was to advise me to lay aside my drawings of boa

constrictors, whether from the inside or the outside, and devote myself instead to geography, history, arithmetic, and grammar. That is why, at the age of six, I gave up what might have been a magnificent career as a painter."

One also thinks of late-bloomers such as Vincent van Gogh, who didn't begin to paint until he was twenty-seven, and Pulitzer prize–winning author Anne Sexton, who began writing poetry at the suggestion of her psychiatrist at the age of twenty-eight. Both of these highly creative individuals came from dysfunctional families where a toxic emotional atmosphere may have stunted their abilities until later in adulthood. Sadly, in both cases, emotional illness led to their creative impulse being cut short through suicide.

Ironically, parents or teachers can subvert a hidden potential by encouraging it for the wrong reasons. In *Pictures of Childhood* Alice Miller writes about her rediscovery of a long-lost interest in painting at the age of forty-five:

> *If my mother had displayed pictures of mine to her friends—the way she did my school note-books—as evidence of her pedagogic talents, I might later have gone on to art school and gotten a diploma there. But no doubt I would have lost all desire to paint spontaneously as a means of expression ... once my mother took possession of what I created. She didn't have the chance to do so, because my need to paint disappeared deep within me in time to protect me from her pedagogical intervention and abuse. There it survived, and when I discovered it again after forty-five years and gave it free rein, I was amazed at the childlike curiosity and the intense delight in looking at things that came to light, still intact.*

How many other potentials lie lost within us because of

our fear of what adults either did or might have done had we fully expressed ourselves?

Finally, in a broader sense, culture itself works to shut down certain intelligences even as it seeks to cultivate others. As mentioned throughout this book, we live in a strongly linguistic and logical-mathematical society. Consequently, children who are "at promise" in these areas will get lots of positive reinforcement from the adults around them. But children with talent in musical, spatial, bodily-kinesthetic, or personal intelligences will often have these potentials actively discouraged, or more often they will simply be neglected by parents and teachers who believe that these intelligences do not contribute enough of substance to the culture at large. Multigifted children soon learn to lie down in what psychoanalyst Ernest Schactel refers to as the "Procrustean bed of the culturally prevalent experience schemata which allow for certain experiences, forbid others, and omit a great many for which the culture has either no frame of reference or only an unsuitable one."

Ultimately, an intelligence will flourish or languish in an individual's life as the result of a dynamic interaction between his or her biology (good or bad genes), psychology (good or bad family environment), and cultural context (favorable or unfavorable historical epoch). To illustrate, let's consider what might have happened to Wolfgang Amadeus Mozart if, instead of being born in eighteenth-century Austria—a musical mecca—and having a composer for a father, he was instead born into a family of tone-deaf individuals in Puritan England, where music was considered Satanic. Do you think it likely that he would have fully expressed his musical intelligence in such a setting? Probably not. On the other hand, the great mathematician Srinivasa Ramanujan might have soared to even greater heights if he had been born a century earlier or had grown up in England instead of India. Because he lived in an area cut off from the mainstream of mathematical thought, he spent his creative life intuitively re-creating much of what had already been written about in Western mathematical circles.

Timing and circumstances, then, have a great deal to do with what happens to our innate talents and abilities. Scientists have studied in detail what happens to animals when they're deprived of or exposed to certain experiences at "critical periods" in their development. Monkeys with one eye sutured shut during a critical period in their visual development will develop *amblyopia*, or dimness of vision in that eye. Ducks will follow around as "'mother" any moving object that happens to be around them fifteen hours after they hatch. The important moments for humans, postnatally, tend to be somewhat looser and are termed "sensitive periods" by developmental psychologists. The period of six to twelve months, when an individual creates an emotional bond to a primary caretaker, may be particularly important for the development of interpersonal intelligence. Other sensitive periods exist for linguistic development, logical-mathematical intelligence, and also, probably, for each of the other intelligences.

The existence of sensitive periods in early childhood, however, doesn't prevent the possibility of substantial development later in life. Recent research indicates that we continue to develop, even neurologically, into old age. University of California brain researcher Marian Diamond, in her book *Enriching Heredity,* writes: "We have learned that every part of the nerve cell from soma to synapse alters its dimensions in response to the environment . . . the experiential environment is a major factor in maintaining the healthy old brain." She also notes: "Several of our measurements have indicated that even the deprived brain can adapt by changing in structure as a result of enriched living conditions."

These findings should offer hope for adults who feel that they're past their prime or might have "blown it" in the early years by not receiving the right kind of help to develop in a desired direction. Certainly there are biological limitations to what each of us can become. A sixty-year-old just taking up long-distance running will not be able to win the marathon event in the Olympics no matter how hard he tries. But he may be able to win the Boston marathon in his age group. A fifty-year-old beginning to study calculus will probably never make a major contribution to mathematics. She could, however, develop into an excellent math teacher. On the other hand, an eighty-year-old just starting to paint might well become another Grandma Moses (who started when she was seventy-eight years old)! The real message here is that it's never too late to develop your late-blooming intelligences.

◆ DEVELOPING YOUR NEGLECTED INTELLIGENCES

Happily, there exist some relatively straightforward guidelines for cultivating a neglected intelligence. Harvard philosopher Israel Scheffler, in his book *Of Human Potential,* suggests a threefold approach for actualizing one's untapped abilities. First, you have to eliminate those factors that block the realization of a potential. If you have a broken foot, you can't continue to develop your potential to run until the bone heals and you resume practice (unless, of course, you practice "running" in your kinesthetic mind!) Second, you have to be exposed to experiences that promote the potential. If you have a gift for math, you won't go very far with it unless you're introduced to teachers, courses, and books or tools related to the subject at your level of understanding. Finally, you have to make a personal commitment to develop the potential. You may have a great talent for painting, but if you refuse to paint you will almost certainly not develop in that area.

The process of removing obstacles to growth can be as simple as forgoing certain daily habits. Researchers estimate, for example, that roughly half of an American adult's leisure time is spent in front of a television set. Over a period of forty years, that represents tens of thousands of hours that could more profitably be spent learning a foreign language, practicing a musical instrument, developing a new business idea, building a crafts project, or engaging in hundreds of other activities spanning all seven intelligences. Similarly, other common leisure-time activities, such as reading magazines and newspapers, talking with others, or "spacing out," do virtually nothing to move you into exploring new intellectual terrain. By simply choosing to stop engaging in these activities, or cutting them back, you can open up windows of time to pursue the development of your hidden potentials.

Sometimes the obstacles to realizing one's potential are more pernicious. Drugs, alcohol, and other addictions are particularly toxic to the awakening of talents and abilities. In such cases it may be imperative that a person get out of an unhealthy environment before she can find the space in which to grow. Motivational speaker Og Mandino tells the story of how he had reached the end of his rope at the age of thirty-five. A failure in his work life, divorced, and alcoholic, he spent much of his time in bars. One rainy night he contemplated buying a gun and ending it all but instead sought refuge in a local public library. The quiet in the library provided him with the opportunity to think clearly for the first time in years. It also exposed him to books, especially books on philosophy and self-esteem, which he began to devour over the next few months. This led to the discovery of his real talents as a salesman and motivational expert. His book *The Greatest Salesman in the World* has sold several million copies, and his speaking talents are sought after throughout the world. For other people, recovery groups, psychotherapy, or other forms of renewal may be instrumental in getting them out of negative patterns of feeling, thinking, and behaving that stand in the way of their becoming who they really are.

◆ PASSION FOR LEARNING

Removing obstacles is not enough, however, to activate hidden intelligences. There must be a spark in the early stages of intellectual growth to get the fires burning. This spark may be a book (as it was with Mandino), or it could be an experience, a person, or some other event that creates a passion for learning. David Henry Feldman, professor of psychology at Tufts University, calls these potent motivators *crystallizing experiences* and suggests that they're instrumental in propelling creative individuals toward the realization of their greatest achievements in life.

Howard Gardner and Thomas Hatch interviewed several master teachers about their own crystallizing experiences. One photographer remembered being in the navy and going to the Museum of Modern Art while stationed in New York. That experience awakened him to the value of the visual arts. "I remember that day like yesterday— the weather, the people on the street," he recalled. "I guess you could say it was an 'epiphany.'" Similarly, a topologist identified some mathematical "tricks" taught him by his father as being an especially important influence in directing his work. Earlier in this book we looked at several other examples of crystallizing experiences: Carl Jung's childhood memory, Martin Luther's reading of the Bible, and Ramana Maharshi's death experience. In each case there was a distinct turning-point, a moment that set the person on the road to the fulfillment of a particular destiny.

Once the passion to explore a certain intelligence has been awakened, it needs to be nurtured into mature development. Philosopher Alfred North Whitehead wrote of a "rhythm of education" that consists of three primary stages in learning something new: a period of *romance,* where one celebrates the vitality and passion that accompanies a crystallizing experience; a period of *precision,* where one must commit sometimes substantial energy toward acquiring specific skills on the way to mastery of a subject; and a period of *generalization,* where the competency can then be directly applied to practical life situations. Often an individual will experience a real delight in exploring a new intelligence but then find a year has passed and nothing has been done to take that experience to the next level. I remember getting very excited after reading Betty Edwards's book *Drawing on the Right Side of the Brain,* doing some of the exercises in her book, and realizing "I can draw!" That was twelve years ago, and I've done little in the meantime to continue to develop my drawing ability.

That's why it's important, after you've been "awakened," to seek out ongoing sources of support, such as a study circle, extension program, correspondence course, or apprenticeship that can take you step by step along the pathway toward growing proficiency.

An estimated 40 million American adults participate every year in educational activities through these and other learning channels. Through adult education programs a person can engage in a wide range of learning activities across the spectrum of intelligences, from quilt design, journal writing, and tai chi, to mastering personal finances, playing the tuba, and helping the homeless. There are even educational brokering services that can assist you in identifying your needs, setting goals, and linking up with educational resources in your area. (For a partial listing, see Ronald Gross's book *The Lifelong Learner*.)

Many individuals choose to develop their intelligences through personal study and individualized learning projects. Patrick Penland, a University of Pittsburgh adult education researcher, reported that three out of every four adults plan one or more informal learning projects on their own each year. These projects include activities like putting in a garden, repairing a car engine, or making a dress, and average 156 hours for completion. Think about what kind of project or ongoing educational program you'd like to develop. Take some time to look over the "25 Ways to Enhance Your Intelligence" lists in chapters 2 through 8. Then do the following exercise. It will help you become more aware of a late-blooming intelligence and enable you to develop a plan for realizing it.

AUTOBIOGRAPHY OF A LATE-BLOOMER

Choose one of the seven intelligences to focus on for this exercise. You might choose an intelligence that appears to be strong based on your childhood-memory questionnaire. Or you might choose instead to focus on an intelligence connected to a specific project or dream that fills your mind during odd hours of the day. You might even decide to choose an intelligence based on the criterion "If I died tomorrow, which intelligence would I regret not having developed in my life?"

Write the name of the intelligence at the top of a piece of paper. Then, write the story of your life in terms of that intelligence. You might start by writing about the earliest memories you have of displaying some aspect of that intelligence. Include examples of crystallizing experiences, if any, in childhood. Also, talk about negative incidents that may

have caused you to shut that intelligence down—experiences
of shame, humiliation, trauma, or neglect. Include people
who were significant to you in either encouraging or discouraging the intelligence. Continue by writing about how the
intelligence may have emerged at different stages of your
life (later childhood, adolescence, early adulthood) as you
attempted to develop it in some way. Finally, write about
how you are currently dealing with this intelligence (is it active, dormant, or being expressed in small ways?).

Below your autobiography write down in specific terms
five things you plan to do in the coming months and years to
further the development of that intelligence. That plan might
include some of the following elements:

- ◆ courses of study
- ◆ people who can help you
- ◆ books you can read for direction
- ◆ organizations you can join
- ◆ software you can use
- ◆ learning tools you can acquire

The "Resources" section at the back of this book includes books, software, organizations, and other materials
that promote the development of each of the seven
intelligences.

Spatial learners may prefer to do this exercise as a time
line, a photo essay, or a series of drawings. Interpersonal
learners, on the other hand, may simply want to tell their
story to a trusted friend.

The above exercise should help you become aware
that your so-called hidden intelligence has a unique history of its own. Use the autobiography as a map to help
create a plan for developing this intelligence. You may

want to apply this exercise as well to the other six intelligences so that you can compare each of their histories.

Once you've created a specific plan for actualizing an intelligence, make sure to affirm it in some tangible way. Using the multiple intelligences approach, there are at least seven different ways for you to do this:

- ◆ Linguistic: Put the words *Just Do It!* on a poster as a constant reminder.
- ◆ Spatial: Visualize yourself doing something concrete related to the intelligence.
- ◆ Musical: Play a motivating song such as "You Gotta Have Heart," or "Get on Your Feet" by the Miami Sound Machine
- ◆ Bodily-Kinesthetic: Use a thumbs-up sign to signal your determination whenever you begin to feel doubts about your plan.
- ◆ Logical-Mathematical: Create a poster on which is written the number of days it will take before you meet your goal.
- ◆ Interpersonal: Tell another person exactly what you plan to do and when you plan to do it.
- ◆ Intrapersonal: Experience deep inside yourself the feeling of determination that you *will* reach your goals.

It's this latter quality of determination that is particularly important in helping an individual move through hardships and difficulties on the way to greater accomplishment. Israel Scheffler writes:

> As the studies required for the [learner's chosen goal] progress, the sense of its content and significance alters, the demands enlarge and become more specific, the costs in effort become

plain. To bear these costs means that the object of desire is capable of overriding them even with an enlarged perception of what is involved. Desire here blossoms into commitment, perseverance, loyalty—a kind of love of the project embarked on, with which one identifies oneself and which helps shape one's self-respect.

This commitment, blended with the other ingredients described in this chapter, can work miracles. In his book *See You at the Top,* Zig Ziglar writes about cosmetics mogul Mary Kay Ash, who got off to a miserable start in her career selling home products and had to scrimp as a single parent even to come up with enough money to attend her sponsor's national convention. During the crowning of the Queen of Sales at that event, she made a decision that started her on the road to success. Getting in the reception line to meet the queen, she stopped and told the organization's executives that during the next year *she* would be the queen. Her determination led her to succeed in that goal and in many others on her way to forming her own multimillion-dollar cosmetics business.

Not every person can do what Mary Kay Ash did. But every person *can* formulate his *own* goals for success and realize them. The Hopis have a belief that every person is born with a gift and that the purpose of life is to realize that gift in some tangible way. In like manner, all people need to "follow their bliss" as Joseph Campbell has said, and hold fast to their deepest dreams. For as another late-bloomer, novelist Tom Clancy (who started his first book at age thirty-five), put it: "Nothing is as real as a dream. The world can change around you, but your dream will not. Responsibilities need not erase it. Duties need not obscure it. Because the dream is within you, no one can take it away."

STRENGTHENING YOUR WEAKEST LINK: MULTIPLE INTELLIGENCES AND LEARNING DIFFICULTIES

His writing was atrocious. As one observer noted: "The words are severed and broken ... the spelling is that of a servant ... or recruit." He wrote backward much of the time. He made simple mistakes in arithmetic calculations. He had trouble reading some of the basic texts of his time. On his deathbed he expressed regrets that he had not lived up to his potential. Yet he was by many accounts the most gifted person who ever lived: Leonardo da Vinci, painter, sculptor, musician, poet, architect, engineer, geologist, anatomist, botanist, physiologist, astronomer, and philosopher.

It's hard to imagine da Vinci as someone who had to struggle with basic academic skills and who might even have ended up in a class for the learning disabled in today's society. But his situation was no different in some ways from that of many people. We've all known someone a little like Leonardo: a person with excellent spatial and logical-mathematical abilities who struggles with reading,

writing, or speaking. Most of us know individuals of superior linguistic ability who can't add or subtract to save their
lives, or who have the drawing abilities of a five-year-old.
Canvas a crowd of people and you'll find individuals with
specific problems in all seven intelligences: people who
can't act, sing, dance, relate, dream, express feelings, reason clearly, or do many other things that *we* might take
for granted. Yet we too have our learning weaknesses,
often safely hidden from all but our most trusted compan-
ions. This chapter will guide you into exploring your own
weak links in the seven-intelligences chain and help you
devise sound strategies for strengthening them or at the
very least learning to live with them in a new way.

◆ THE SELECTIVELY IMPAIRED MIND ────────────

Learning problems show up most clearly in the lives of
people who have suffered brain damage due to illness or
accident. As far back as the mid-nineteenth century, French
surgeon and anthropologist Pierre-Paul Broca demonstrated a clear connection between brain injury and specific cognitive impairments. Working with soldiers and
others who had received head wounds, Broca noticed that
lesions in a specific region of the left hemisphere of the
brain seemed to impair a patient's ability to express himself verbally. Further research during the late 1800s revealed lesions in other areas of the brain that could
selectively interfere with reading ability, mathematical calculation, and a number of other competencies.

What was remarkable about these findings was the ten-
dency of a brain lesion, when restricted to a specific area of
the brain, to wipe out one type of cognitive function while
leaving intact abilities associated with other areas of the
brain. A classic example of this is the French composer Mau-

rice Ravel, who suffered a stroke in his later years that left him virtually unable to speak or write. Because the damage was limited to the linguistic functions of the left hemisphere, however, the musical regions of his right hemisphere were generally healthy. As a result he still had a keen sense of pitch and could recognize melodies, point out the slightest errors in a musical performance, and exercise excellent taste and judgment in evaluating a style of music.

Another well-known case is that of Phineas Gage, a Vermont construction foreman who experienced a freak accident that caused a three-foot rod to pass through his skull. He miraculously survived the incident and could generally function normally, but he changed from being a soft-spoken and reliable worker into an obnoxious and foulmouthed rake who wandered from job to job until his death. Apparently the accident had damaged that portion of his brain related to his personal intelligences while leaving intact most of his other abilities.

In his book *The Shattered Mind,* Howard Gardner provides several additional illustrations of this kind of selective damage: artists who, after a stroke, can't speak but can draw with finesse; writers who can't write but can sing; telegraph operators who can recognize Morse code as flashing lights but not as hand signals; and many other examples. As you'll recall from Chapter 1, it was partly through his studies of brain damage that Gardner came to understand the existence of separate intelligences and the fact that one intelligence might be harmed while others are spared.

◆ LEARNING DISABILITIES: HIDDEN POTENTIALS? —

Specific brain injury accounts for learning problems among only a few individuals in the general population. A somewhat wider circle of troubled learners includes the so-called learning disabled. This group comprises people who don't have identifiable brain lesions yet experience considerable learning difficulty in one or more academic areas. The term was first developed during the early 1960s to describe a group of children who couldn't read, write, do math, or perform other academic functions yet appeared to be of average or above-average intelligence. Since that time more than 2 million American children have been identified by schools as learning disabled, and attention is increasingly being focused on the estimated 5 to 10 million American adults who are apparently similarly afflicted.

Symptoms of "LD" include everything from difficulty in reading and writing, to disorganization, awkwardness, poor sociability, and even depression. Theories about what causes learning disabilities vary widely and include hereditary factors, traumas before or during birth, and developmental difficulties during early childhood. The term itself continues to be quite controversial, and little consensus exists about who qualifies for the label.

The real problem in defining learning disabilities is that there isn't any *one* set of symptoms that characterizes a person as learning disabled. It's more accurate to think of *specific learning disabilities.* Just as individuals with brain damage perform well in certain areas and not in others, so too a person with specific learning disabilities often has her learning problems restricted to only a few specific skills or tasks. One person can read but can't write. Another can write well but has difficulty doing arithmetic. Still another may be proficient in most school subjects but have trouble recognizing the face of an acquaintance (*prosopagnosia*) or learning a new step on the dance floor (*dyspraxia*).

The theory of multiple intelligences provides a model for making sense out of all the different learning disabilities that people experience. It suggests that there are specific learning disabilities in each of the seven intelligences. Since our culture is heavily oriented toward linguistic and logical-mathematical intelligences, most of the learning disabilities focused on by the media tend to cluster around logical and verbal skills: *dyslexia* (trouble reading), *dysgraphia* (trouble writing), *dyscalculia* (trouble with arithmetic calculation), and other academic problems. But there are learning disabilities for musical intelligence, bodily-kinesthetic intelligence, and spatial intelligence, and even disabilities in the personal intelligences.

Harvard neurologist Norman Geschwind once said: "... practically all of us have a significant number of special learning disabilities." They may not be in school-related areas and thus may have evaded detection for years. Geschwind himself was grossly unmusical and couldn't carry a tune. Yet the chances are great there are tests available—out of the literally thousands that have been developed over the past fifty years—that can detect something wrong with the way just about anybody in our society learns.

Pragmatically speaking, whether or not you're actually *identified* as learning disabled may have more to do with how many specific learning disabilities you have and their relative level of severity as measured by a learning specialist or psychologist. I prefer not to use the label *learning disabilities* because people tend to identify too strongly with the term. There's a certain quality of fatalism that accompanies the label—the idea that it's somehow an indelible part of one's learning life rather than something that can be transformed. Instead, I'd like to think of these weak links as learning *difficulties* or even learning *opportunities* because they can challenge one to new heights. The following checklist will help you zero in on those areas that have been problematic for you in the past.

There's room at the end of each section to write in additional difficulties that you've noticed.

LEARNING DIFFICULTIES CHECKLIST

LOGICAL-MATHEMATICAL:

_____ I have difficulty keeping my checkbook balanced.

_____ I get easily confused when someone is explaining a scientific concept to me.

_____ I frequently make errors when computing simple arithmetic.

_____ I had difficulty in school mastering postarithmetic subjects like algebra or trigonometry.

_____ I avoid the business page of a newspaper because economic or financial news confuses me.

_____ I still count on my fingers or use some other concrete method when calculating numbers.

_____ I usually get stumped when working on a brainteaser requiring logical thinking in a puzzle book.

Other Logical-Mathematical Difficulties:

SPATIAL:

_____ I find it hard to see clear images in my mind's eye.

_____ I sometimes don't recognize the faces of people who should be familiar to me.

_____ I have difficulty finding my way around an unfamiliar town or building.

_____ I sometimes have problems telling right from left.

_____ My drawings of people are still at the stick-figure level.

_____ I had a hard time in geometry class as a high school student.

_____ I'm color-blind or have other difficulties distinguishing shades of color.

_____ I have difficulty copying simple shapes and designs on a sheet of paper.

Other Spatial Difficulties:

LINGUISTIC:

_____ I frequently experience problems understanding what I read.

_____ I have difficulty translating my thoughts into written words.

_____ I often don't pronounce new words the way they should be pronounced.

_____ I often have a hard time coming up with the right word to describe an object, situation, or concept.

_____ I'm still reading at an elementary school level because of my difficulty in decoding the printed word.

_____ I have problems telling the difference between subtle sounds in the language ("b" and "p," "th" and "sh," etc.).

_____ I am frequently corrected by others (or am afraid of being corrected) for ungrammatical phrases in my speaking or writing.

Other Linguistic Difficulties:

MUSICAL:

_____ I have a hard time carrying a tune.

_____ I have difficulty keeping time to a rhythmic piece of recorded music.

_____ I have problems recognizing musical passages that seem to be familiar to my family and friends.

_____ I find it difficult to enjoy listening to music.

_____ There are only a very few songs (or no songs) that I can actually remember.

_____ I would have a hard time naming the musical instrument a piece of music was being played on (e.g., cello versus violin).

_____ I would have a difficult time matching my voice with a note on a piano.

Other Musical Difficulties:

BODILY-KINESTHETIC:

_____ I'm "all thumbs" when it comes to doing something that requires delicate fine-motor coordination (sewing, crafts, etc.)

_____ I'm uncoordinated on the athletic field.

_____ I have a hard time learning new dance steps.

_____ I'm resistant to touching things in my surroundings.

_____ I have a hard time expressing concepts through my body (in charades, acting, mime, etc.).

_____ I'm relatively unaware of my body most of the time.

_____ I'm clumsy when engaged in simple physical actions like walking, making the bed, or setting the table.

Other Bodily-Kinesthetic Difficulties:

INTERPERSONAL:

_____ I'm painfully shy when meeting new people.

_____ I get into frequent misunderstandings or disputes with others.

_____ I often feel hostile or defensive toward others.

_____ I frequently have a hard time feeling empathy for other people.

_____ In a time of crisis I would be virtually without any social support.

_____ I go through life generally unaware of the interpersonal interactions going on around me.

_____ I have a problem "reading" other people's moods, intentions, motivations, and temperaments.

Other Interpersonal Difficulties:

INTRAPERSONAL:

_____ I frequently feel a sense of low self-worth.

_____ I have little sense of where I'm going in my life.

_____ I'm generally unaware of how I'm feeling from moment to moment.

_____ I'm often afraid of being abandoned or engulfed by people whom I'm intimate with.

_____ I dislike spending time alone.

_____ I sometimes have feelings of unreality—as if I didn't really completely exist.

_____ I get easily disturbed by simple events in my life.

Other Intrapersonal Difficulties:

◆ COGNITIVE BYPASSING ——————————

The single most important guideline to keep in mind when tackling learning problems is this: *don't let your learning difficulties get in the way of being a successful human being*. I've already pointed out that I don't like the term *learning disabled* because there's a danger that a person might overidentify with it and begin to see herself as a handicapped individual. Psychologists tell us that a negative "self-fulfilling prophecy" can have a devastating effect upon one's sense of self-worth. See yourself as an intact and whole human being before anything else. Then regard your learning difficulties simply as something that makes you an even richer and more unique human being. Above all, don't let these problems keep you from living your life.

Many successful individuals with learning problems have discovered that they can *bypass* their difficulties and find alternative ways of getting the job done. The famed inventor and industrialist Henry Ford had difficulty reading and remembering basic facts. He once sued a newspaper for libel because they called him an *ignorant pacifist*. During the trial the paper's lawyers put Ford on the witness stand and asked many factual questions about history and current events in order to discredit him. Unfortunately, Ford did rather poorly on these questions. At one point he gave the date of the Revolutionary War as 1812. Finally growing exasperated, Ford responded to the lawyers,

> *If I should really want to answer the foolish question you have just asked, or any of the other questions you have been asking me, let me remind you that I have a row of electric push-buttons on my desk, and by pushing the right button, I can summon to my aid men who can answer any question I desire to ask concerning the business to which I am devoting most of my efforts. Now, will you kindly tell me why I should clutter up my mind with general knowledge, for the purpose of being able to answer questions, when I have men around me who can supply any knowledge I require?*

There are probably hundreds, if not thousands, of businesspeople in the country like Ford, or like John Corcoran, a real-estate developer who couldn't read yet built a multimillion-dollar enterprise by surrounding himself with lawyers, secretaries, and other specialists who could do all his written work. And there are probably many professional people who can't do math, like architect Hugh Newell Jacobsen, who has won ninety different awards for design yet says, "I was terrible at math. I failed math time and time again. I never did pass algebra or geometry. I still can't. As an architect I hire engineers; someone else has done that for me for years."

In bypassing their so-called handicaps, successful individuals often develop creative ways of doing things that make them even more effective in their fields. Hans Christian Andersen cultivated his marvelous storytelling ability in part because he couldn't read or write. Nelson Rockefeller became an accomplished extemporaneous speaker because of his difficulties in reading a printed text of his speeches. In each case a minus was turned into a plus when the person, instead of wallowing in his weakness, focused his energies upon what he *could* do.

◆ ENABLING TECHNOLOGIES

"My motto is find out what you cannot do and discard it. Find another way," says Dr. Florence Haseltine, director of the Center for Population Research of the National Institute of Child Health and Human Development. Dr. Haseltine has difficulty with writing tasks and frequently uses the telephone instead of writing notes to communicate with others on the job.

Modern technology has now rendered many learning disabilities virtually obsolete by providing learners with access to alternative ways of getting information and expressing themselves. Poor spellers have access to spell checkers. Individuals with illegible handwriting can use a word processor to produce a neat typescript. People with dyscalculia (difficulty with math calculations) benefit from having a pocket calculator handy when a math problem comes up. Similarly, learners with poor memories can tape lectures, discussions, and other verbal exchanges. Individuals with faulty visualization skills can use computer-aided design (CAD) software programs that allow them to manipulate three-dimensional objects on screen. Book-shy people now have audiotapes, videotapes, and a range of computer programs available for getting information on a wide variety of topics. There is even a machine—the Xerox/Kurzweil Personal Reader—that can translate printed information into the spoken word. Soon portable versions will be widely available that can actually read printed books off the shelf for those who have difficulty with reading.

Another way learning-challenged individuals can gain access to skills and information is by using alternative symbol systems that match their strongest intelligences. A person who has problems reading the English language as a set of linguistic symbols, for example, can often be more successful when a spatial symbol system is used. Educators in Philadelphia had an easier time teaching a group of so-called learning-disabled children to read Chinese characters than to read letters of the English alphabet. That's because Chinese characters are based on a spatial symbol system and thus are more closely matched to the children's strong spatial intelligence.

Similarly, in work with brain-damaged individuals, setting a string of words to a melody appears to be an effective way of helping patients relearn a body of facts wiped out by a stroke. Braille and sign language have also been effective bodily-kinesthetic methods of teaching reading to severely reading-impaired individuals with normal hearing and sight. Finally, students with problems in math often find Chisanbop (a method of calculating rapidly with the fingers) to be an effective bodily-kinesthetic route to logi-cal-mathematical competence.

SEVEN WAYS TO LEARN ANYTHING

If you're having difficulty learning a new concept, skill, or task, try linking what you're learning to as many different intelligences as possible. As a general rule of thumb, take the information to be learned and:

- talk, read, or write about it (linguistic approach);
- draw, sketch, or visualize it (spatial approach);
- dance it, build a model of it, or find some other hands-on activity related to it (bodily-kinesthetic approach);
- sing it, chant it, find music that illustrates it, or put on background music while learning it (musical approach);
- relate it to a personal feeling or inner experience (in-trapersonal approach);
- conceptualize it, quantify it, or think critically about it (logical-mathematical approach); or
- work on it with another person or group of people (interpersonal approach).

To illustrate, if you're consistently misspelling a specific word, try one or more of the following techniques: spell the word out loud; visualize the word in your mind's eye; make the letters of the word out of clay; sing the letters of the word in rhythm to a piece of music; spell the word with feeling; think about the spelling rules the word might follow; and have a friend test you in spelling the word. You may not always be able to find seven different ways to learn some-thing new, but the more intelligences you activate, the more bridges you will build cognitively and neurologically from the weak sectors of your brain to the strong areas.

I often hear people talk about an individual "compensating" for her disability when she uses one of the above learning methods or approaches. I think this word is unfair because it sends a subtle message that "if you were healthy, you'd do it the normal way." This *is* the normal way for that person. In fact, it often takes a great deal of craft and cunning to develop ways of getting around a learning problem. It also takes a person who has the inner confidence and self-knowledge of her own strengths and limitations to develop such a plan in the first place. I would much rather think about an individual "tailoring an activity to her own unique learning style" than "compensating for her problem."

Of course this doesn't mean that a person should seek to sugarcoat his problem in nice phrases or avoid dealing head-on with a learning difficulty. Often the best approach is to admit that you have a problem and tackle it directly. The Greek orator Demosthenes had a severe speech impediment and was also extremely shy. His father died and left an estate that would have made Demosthenes extremely wealthy. In order to claim the estate, however, he needed to establish his right to ownership in a public debate. He couldn't do this because of his poor linguistic and interpersonal abilities. He decided to work intensively on his problem, using, among other things, his famed technique of speaking to the sea with stones in his mouth. The rest, as they say, is history.

◆ THE MASKS OF LEARNING DIFFICULTY ─────

If a learning difficulty has caused you humiliation, shame, defeat, or anxiety, as it often does while we are growing up, then it's likely that you sealed it away in some private compartment of your life and developed defensive strategies for dealing with it. Sally Smith, author of *Succeeding Against the Odds: Strategies and Insights from the Learning Disabled,* and director of the Lab School in Washington, D.C., says that there are many different "masks" that people with learning problems wear to protect their self-esteem. There's the mask of the "clown," which uses humor as a way of deflecting attention away from a learning problem, the mask of the "victim," which refuses to take responsibility for difficulties, the mask of "invisibility," which causes an individual to blend into the woodwork so as not to be seen and helped, and many other masks that protect and defend against the painful feelings connected with not feeling "okay" as a learner.

Sometimes these masks actually are helpful in furthering a person's work life or relationships. Smith points to learning-disabled celebrities like Henry Winkler and Cher, who began their careers by acting out the part of the "class clown" or the outrageous noncomformist as a way of coping with their difficulties. But at other times these masks get in the way of growth and need to be discarded. Many individuals with learning problems talk about the relief they felt once they began to speak openly about their difficulties. A student at Sally Smith's night school for learning-disabled adults said, "I feel like a leaden weight has been lifted off my shoulders by not having to pretend to be having a riotous time and not having to think up all those quips. I have energy now for my studies."

Self-revelation allows an individual to get the help he needs so that he can focus intensively on his learning difficulties. After financial setbacks forced John Corcoran to lay off the people who had helped him bypass his academic troubles, he was forced to confront his reading problem. This led to his enrolling in an adult literacy program in southern California, where he spent forty to fifty hours a week for almost two years learning how to sound out words. Organizations such as the Learning Disabilities Association of America (4156 Library Rd., Pittsburgh, PA 15234; 412–341–1515) and the National Network of Learning Disabled Adults (808 North 82nd St., Suite F2, Scottsdale, AZ 85257) can link people up with resources in their area for getting help with specific learning difficulties, particularly in the linguistic and logical-mathematical areas.

For individuals facing difficulties in other intelligences, long-term strategies may involve physical therapy or rehabilitation programs (bodily-kinesthetic), support groups and psychotherapy (personal intelligences), intensive music or art instruction, or one's own patient process of self-care and personal development (see books, software, organizations, and games listed in the "Resources" section for help in developing each intelligence). The next exercise will get you started in developing a concrete plan for dealing with your learning problems.

GAME PLAN FOR WORKING WITH YOUR WEAKEST LINK

At the top of a sheet of paper, write down an area of learning difficulty that troubles you and that you'd like to come to grips with in some tangible way (use the checklist at the beginning of this chapter to help you focus on an area). Be specific. For example: "difficulty reading," "problems drawing pictures," "inability to get along with colleagues at work," "tone deaf," "math phobia," "clumsy when playing sports," and so forth.

Write a brief history of the problem: how it shows up in your everyday life, how you may have developed a mask to hide it from others, and how it gets in the way of your living your life. Then brainstorm ways of dealing with this problem by listing as many different strategies as you can on a separate sheet.

Consider the following questions in developing your strategies:

- How can I bypass the problem using a technological aid?
- How can I bypass the problem using an alternative symbol system?
- What sort of specialist could help me deal with this problem?
- What specific books, software programs, games, or other learning tools can I borrow, rent, or buy to help me deal with this issue?
- What personal qualities (such as courage, determination, persistence) do I need to develop to help me with this situation?
- What special courses, apprenticeships, support groups, or other formal or informal educational programs or organizations are available to help me?
- What activities can I do to link areas of weakness with my strongest intelligences?
- How can I get people around me to accommodate my learning needs so that this is no longer as much of a problem?
- What other things can I do to help cope with this difficulty?

From the many ideas that emerge, choose five suggestions that seem to be most helpful, and begin taking steps to implement them.

If your problem happens to be in the writing area, then consider doing this exercise in another way: using a tape recorder, making diagrams in a sketchbook, talking with another person, or through one or more of the other intelligences.

While you're engaged in the process of looking at your learning difficulties, it's vital that you focus on what's *right* with the way you learn. An individual's positive traits often make his learning problems endurable and solvable. Olympic champion Bruce Jenner, who was honored with an "Outstanding Learning Disabled Achievers Award," told Sally Smith's Lab School students, "I found sports, and I could hold my head up with all my friends, and feel good about' myself. And that gave me confidence that I could lick the reading problem or at least cope with it." Another award winner, singer-actress Cher, commented, "You have to find the place that you can shine if you don't fit in with what everybody else is doing."

It sounds paradoxical, but it may also be true that our greatest strengths can actually be found *within* the very difficulties that we're struggling to overcome. I'm reminded of the Disney movie *Dumbo,* in which a baby elephant learns that his greatest handicap, his big ears, are in fact his greatest asset when they allow him to fly. The renowned psychoanalyst Alfred Adler pointed out years ago that there is a deep impulse within the human psyche to surmount limitations. He said that we're ultimately driven toward our greatest accomplishments in life as a direct result of the obstacles that are placed in front of us. Television executive Fred Friendly seemed to affirm this belief when he said, "If I could make a Faustian deal today, at age seventy-four, if I could make a deal that I didn't have to be dyslexic and have my whole life to live again, I would take dyslexia. Because it gave me, when I was fourteen years old, forty years old, sixty years old—all my life—the drive and motivation that made me somebody to whom someone would say many years later: if you can make it, anybody can make it."

WORKING SMARTER: MATCHING INTELLIGENCES TO CAREER GOALS

Not long ago I was in a large discount toy store purchasing some items for my wife, who is a child psychotherapist. The clerk rang up my order, and as I began writing out a personal check for the toys, he started to describe the way the store handled personal checks in its accounting system. He went on explaining in intricate detail what all the different numbers on my check represented, and how they were cross-referenced by different components of the system, and he provided numerous other details that were unimportant to me since logical-mathematical intelligence is down toward the bottom of my multiple-intelligence totem pole. In the meantime a line of customers began to form, but the clerk seemed entirely oblivious of the presence, let alone the impatience, of the other customers.

It occurred to me that this individual was the right person in the wrong job. In the company's accounting department, or in a high school math classroom, he could have been a star. But in that clerk's position, where customer service and quick and friendly interpersonal relations were so important, I could imagine it would only be a matter of time before he was fired.

This story underscores the importance of making sure that our work lives match our personal gifts and interests. MI theory tells us that we each have multiple talents. The task is to find work for ourselves that pays us to do what we'd want to be doing anyway with our natural gifts. This chapter will help you determine whether or not you're in a career that makes the most of your potentials, and if it doesn't, will show you ways of changing your current job situation to maximize what it is that you do best in life.

◆ WORK: PRISON OR PARADISE?

Work ought to be one of our greatest satisfactions. Yet everywhere we look the opposite seems to be true. So many people appear to be engaged in what Studs Terkel calls "a Monday through Friday sort of dying." Stress complaints on the job now account for 10 percent of all occupational disease claims, up from virtually zero ten years ago. The business consulting firm Robert Half International reports that the average office worker "steals" four and a half hours a week from company time by arriving late, leaving early, feigning illness, and engaging in other non-work-related activities. The most recent Gallup poll results show job-satisfaction indicators falling 3 to 8 percentage points from the previous year.

Do our work lives have to be so irksome? A look at our cultural roots offers conflicting views. The Greek word for work (*ponos*) actually means "pain," and the Bible describes work as a punishment God delivered upon Adam and Eve for disobeying Him. Moreover, history is filled with images of sixteen-hour-a-day sweatshops, Protestants working to save their souls, and more recently, Willy Lomans toiling in obscurity for few, if any, tangible rewards. As Studs Terkel puts it: "There are, of course, the happy few who find a savor in their daily job ... [but] for the many, there is a hardly concealed discontent.... 'I'm a machine,' says the spot-welder. 'I'm caged,' says the bank teller, and echoes the hotel clerk. 'I'm a mule,' says the steelworker.... Blue collar and white call upon the identical phrase, 'I'm a robot.' "

On the other hand, the idea of career or "vocation" has an almost mystical significance attached to it: the word *vocation* derives from the Latin, *vocare* meaning "to call." A person works, in this context, because of a summons or call from above that inspires and gives meaning to even the dreariest of tasks. One thinks of the story of the three masons working side by side who were asked to describe what they did for a living. The first mumbled, "I lay bricks." The second replied, "I put up walls." The third exclaimed, "I build cathedrals!" It's this sacralization of work that led Thomas Carlyle to say, "Blessed is he who has found his work; let him ask no other blessedness." Even a nonbeliever like Jean-Paul Sartre made it clear that work represents "the significance of an individual." According to trend watcher Daniel Yankelovich, there has been a recent change among the country's younger workers from a work-for-money ethic to one that emphasizes meaning and personal satisfaction. "Younger and better-educated jobholders," says Yankelovich, "have made the momentous discovery that work, rather than leisure, can give them what they are looking for—an outlet for self-expression as well as material rewards."

◆ FLOWING TOWARD JOB SATISFACTION ————

This search for deeper job satisfaction has recently been the subject of intensive research by University of Chicago psychology professor Mihaly Csikszentmihalyi (pronounced "chick-sent-mĭ-hī-yee"). The professor coined the term *flow* to describe what happens when a person is totally and rapturously absorbed in an activity. According to Csikszentmihalyi, the author of *Flow: The Psychology of Optimal Experience,* during an experience of flow an individual experiences a heightened sense of vitality, alertness, strength, control, satisfaction, and even transcendence. Interestingly, he points out that while people report their motivation on the job is low, they actually have *more* flow experiences while working than they do during their off-hours. He writes: ". . . people do not heed the evidence of their senses. They disregard the quality of immediate experience and base their motivation instead on the strongly rooted cultural stereotype of what work is *supposed* to be like. They think of it as an imposition, a constraint, an infringement of their freedom, and therefore something to be avoided as much as possible."

Csikszentmihalyi says that flow experiences tend to occur most often in jobs where there is an optimal level of engagement with work tasks. People in jobs that don't challenge them usually become bored with their work. On the other hand, individuals in jobs with too many demands experience anxiety or other symptoms of burnout. The flow experience occurs when work tasks involve challenges that are themselves deeply interesting and when the worker feels a sense of meaning and empowerment in what he does. "The more a job inherently resembles a game," says Csikszentmihalyi, "with variety, appropriate and flexible challenges, clear goals, and immediate feedback—the more enjoyable it will be regardless of the worker's level of development."

That means that people can experience flow whether they're CEOs of large corporations or factory workers. One of the early studies of flow examined Joe Kramer, a Chicago welder who refused several promotions to administrative posts and stayed in the same welding job for thirty years. His co-workers considered him to be the most important person in the plant, since he could fix each of the factory's complex machines and take anyone's place if they were absent from work. During one interview Kramer said he'd been fascinated with machines since childhood, especially when they weren't working properly, "like when my mother's toaster went on the fritz. I asked myself: If I were that toaster and I didn't work, what would be wrong with me?" Ever since then, he's been using this problem-solving method to fix machines, both at home and at work.

Similarly, a piano tuner named Eugene Russell interviewed by Studs Terkel appeared to have frequent experiences of flow in his work (one of the few in Terkel's study to do so consistently). Russell commented: "I was tuning a piano for a trombone player who once played for Jan Savitt. As I was tuning, I played around with Savitt's theme song, 'Out of Space.' I got those big augmented eleventh chords progressing down in ninths. It's a beautiful thing." Russell regards his craft as more than the technical process of matching the tone of a piano string to the sound of a tuning fork. For him, it's a creative expression of his own love of music. "There seems something mystic about music, about piano tuning," says Russell.

◆ SEVEN KINDS OF WORK SMART ————————————

The cases of Joe Kramer and Eugene Russell illustrate what can happen when an individual's strongest intelligences match the requirements of his job. Kramer's strong spatial/bodily-kinesthetic intelligences matches beautifully the tasks involved in working with heavy machinery. If he'd been promoted to an administrative post he would likely have become a victim of the Peter Principle, whereby "each person rises to his own level of incompetence." In a managerial position requiring high levels of interpersonal, linguistic, and perhaps logical-mathematical intelligence, his own strongest intelligences would have had little opportunity to be expressed.

In a similar way Eugene Russell epitomizes the highly musically intelligent individual working in a job that maximizes his acute sense of pitch, rare sensitivity to tone and timbre, and a deep appreciation of different musical styles. If he were to end up working as a piano salesman instead of a piano tuner, and had much less time available for hands-on work with the sounds of a piano, it's likely that he would grow bored or stressed-out.

Few things are sadder than seeing a person with great potential waste away in a position that makes little use of his natural gifts and abilities. We've all known examples like the clerk described in the beginning of the chapter. MDs with poor "people skills" working as family physicians when they should be in a research laboratory. Artistic individuals with horrible spelling skills working as secretaries instead of graphic artists. Incompetent plumbers who consistently botch the job when they could be using their superior social skills to run an after-school recreational program.

I was flying to the East Coast a couple of years ago and heard the pilot come on the intercom with his usual postflight debriefing: "The weather in Pittsburgh is sunny and seventy-six degrees ... [silence] ... correct that, I mean sixty-seven degrees." At first thought, my heart jumped and I thought, "Is this guy dyslexic?" The idea of having a person in charge of my life misreading instrument panels didn't sit well with me. But then I remembered from my work as a learning-disabilities specialist that dyslexic individuals often have superior visual-spatial skills. Spatial intelligence is *exactly* what I want a pilot to have while navigating the three-dimensional skies. This reassured me a little, but as a rule of thumb I think it's a good idea for any cockpit to include one person with strong spatial skills, someone with strong logical-mathematical abilities (to handle computer data), and an individual with good interpersonal/linguistic capabilities (to communicate effectively with air-traffic control). Naturally, having two or three individuals strong in all of these areas is even better.

The following chart shows how different careers match up with the seven intelligences. While I've listed sample professions according to the primary intelligence used, it's important to keep in mind that no job uses only one intelligence. Lawyers, for example, are listed under the linguistic category. That's because lawyers have to read, understand, and memorize law cases, argue and write persuasively, and work with words in many other ways. At the same time, a trial lawyer must have strong interpersonal skills, a tax attorney should have excellent logical-mathematical abilities, and an entertainment or sports lawyer needs to have some appreciation for musical or bodily-kinesthetic intelligences. Likewise, each of the other vocations is similarly complex in its unique blend of intelligences. However, this list should give you some sense of which skills and jobs match up with each of the seven intelligences.

◆ LINGUISTIC INTELLIGENCE ————————————————

Job Skills: talking, telling, informing, giving instructions, writing, verbalizing, speaking a foreign language, interpreting, translating, teaching, lecturing, discussing, debating, researching, listening (to words), copying, proofreading, editing, word processing, filing, reporting
Sample Professions: librarian, archivist, curator, editor, translator, speech pathologist, writer, radio/TV announcer, journalist, legal assistant, lawyer, secretary, typist, proofreader, English teacher

◆ LOGICAL-MATHEMATICAL INTELLIGENCE ———————

Job Skills: financing, budgeting, doing economic research, hypothesizing, estimating, accounting, counting, calculating, using statistics, auditing, reasoning, analyzing, systematizing, classifying, sequencing
Sample Professions: auditor, accountant, purchasing agent, underwriter, mathematician, scientist, statistician, actuary, computer analyst, economist, technician, bookkeeper, science teacher

◆ SPATIAL INTELLIGENCE ———————————————————

Job Skills: drawing, painting, visualizing, creating visual presentations, designing, imagining, inventing, illustrating, coloring, drafting, graphing, mapping, photographing, decorating, filming
Sample Professions: engineer, surveyor, architect, urban planner, graphic artist, interior decorator, photographer, art teacher, inventor, cartographer, pilot, fine artist, sculptor

◆ MUSICAL INTELLIGENCE ———————————————

Job Skills: singing, playing an instrument, recording, conducting, improvising, composing, transcribing, arranging, listening, distinguishing (tones), tuning, orchestrating, analyzing, and criticizing (musical styles)
Sample Professions: disc jockey, musician, instrument maker, piano tuner, music therapist, instrument salesperson, songwriter, studio engineer, choral director, conductor, singer, music teacher, musical copyist

◆ BODILY-KINESTHETIC INTELLIGENCE ———————

Job Skills: sorting, balancing, lifting, carrying, walking, running, crafting, restoring, cleaning, shipping, delivering, manufacturing, repairing, assembling, installing, operating, adjusting, salvaging, performing, signing, miming, dramatizing, modeling (clothes), dancing, playing sports, organizing outdoor activities, traveling.
Sample Professions: physical therapist, recreational worker, dancer, actor, model, farmer, mechanic, carpenter, craftsperson, physical education teacher, factory worker, choreographer, professional athlete, forest ranger, jeweler

◆ INTERPERSONAL INTELLIGENCE ———————————

Job Skills: serving, hosting, communicating, empathizing, trading, tutoring, coaching, counseling, mentoring, assessing others, persuading, motivating, selling, recruiting, inspiring, publicizing, encouraging, supervising, coordinating, delegating, negotiating, mediating, collaborating, confronting, interviewing
Sample Professions: administrator, manager, school

principal, personnel worker, arbitrator, sociologist, anthropologist, counselor, psychologist, nurse, public relations person, salesperson, travel agent, social director

◆ INTRAPERSONAL INTELLIGENCE ─────────────────

Job Skills: carrying out decisions, working alone, self-promotion, setting goals, attaining objectives, initiating, evaluating, appraising, planning, organizing, discerning opportunities, looking inward, understanding self
Sample Professions: psychologist, clergyperson, psychology teacher, therapist, counselor, theologian, program planner, entrepreneur

If your job, or another profession you have in mind, isn't listed above, use the general principles discussed in this book to determine the primary intelligence required. Keep in mind the principal tasks of the job, and ask yourself whether those tasks involve:

◆ words (linguistic);
◆ images or pictures (spatial);
◆ physical activity (bodily-kinesthetic);
◆ music or rhythm (musical);
◆ logic or numbers (logical-mathematical);
◆ interaction with other people (interpersonal); and/or
◆ involvement with one's inner life (intrapersonal).

The next exercise will help you decide whether or not your current job matches your strongest intelligences.

MATCHING STRENGTHS TO CAREER

At the top of a sheet of paper, describe your job as briefly and succinctly as possible (for example, "language arts teacher for multiply-handicapped elementary school children" or "freelance writer of pamphlets on automotive repair"). Number and list all the different tasks you do as a part of your job description, *in order of importance* (for example, "teach children specific language skills," "develop curricula," "write educational objectives," "meet with parents and administrators"). For each task decide on the primary intelligence required and write this information after it in parentheses (for example, "meet with parents and administrators" [interpersonal]." Look over the top five tasks involved in your job and decide whether the accompanying intelligences are among your three strongest intelligences, as indicated in the checklist you filled out in chapter 1. If at least three tasks make use of your strongest intelligences, then write *match* at the bottom of the page. If not, then write *mismatch*. Finally, write two or three sentences about your response to this exercise and whether it helps explain your current level of job satisfaction or dissatisfaction.

Remember that it's possible to have a "mismatch" and still enjoy your work. Csikszentmihalyi's model of optimal experience suggests that one can experience "flow" on the job if there is just the right degree of challenge. A strongly linguistic person who wants to stretch her mind may find it invigorating to take on a role in a weaker area—such as graphic arts—as long as she perceives the tasks as being within her abilities.

In the same way it's not at all unusual for an individual to register a "match" and still feel unhappy at work. Participants in my multiple-intelligences workshops frequently report feeling "bored" by things that they're very good at doing. Examples include a burned-out bookkeeper with logical-mathematical strengths, a frustrated editor who is strongly linguistic, a talented carpenter who would rather be doing other things with his time, and many other dissatisfied workers. There are several reasons why a person can be dissatisfied with work that they're highly qualified to do: trouble with superiors, bad working conditions, or low wages, to name only a few. But from the multiple-intelligences perspective, it's also possible that they've simply become so familiar with what they do that the thrill is gone.

Generally speaking, though, if you find that you greatly enjoy your work and registered a "match" on the above exercise, there's at least one important reason why you like what you do: it makes use of your most powerful intelligences. Organizational consultant Sherrie Connelly lists seven signs of what she calls "work spirit"—indicators of exceptional job satisfaction:

- ◆ a sense of enormous energy
- ◆ a positive, open state of mind
- ◆ a sense of purpose and vision
- ◆ a full sense of self
- ◆ awareness of oneself as a creator and nurturer
- ◆ a sense of living in the moment
- ◆ a sense of a higher order and oneness

If you find at least a few of these traits present some of the time during your work life, and you recorded a "match" on the exercise, then you're probably in very good shape careerwise and can go on to the next chapter.

However, if you recorded a "mismatch" on the exercise and find yourself moderately to severely dissatisfied in your current job, then you should read on. It's particularly important that you devote time to the rest of this chapter if you suffer from any of the symptoms of job stress listed below:

- feelings of helplessness
- chronic fatigue
- resistance to going to work
- clock watching
- workaholism
- sadness/depression
- irritability
- drug or alcohol abuse
- accident-proneness
- crying
- cynicism
- inflexibility
- physical complaints
- forgetfulness
- asocial behavior
- lack of pleasure in life

These factors may serve either as warning signs or as full-blown indicators that you've burned out on the job. If they're accompanied by a "mismatch" on the above exercise (fewer than three of the top five job tasks tied into strong intelligences), then you may be in need of a career switch—to a position that makes better use of your talents and abilities. That's what the final section of this chapter will help you accomplish.

◆ INTELLIGENT CAREER COUNSELING ─────

People end up in frustrating jobs for many reasons, including family pressures, financial responsibilities, and just plain ignorance. It's reassuring to know, however, that even for the most hopelessly entrapped, there's light at the end of the tunnel. Psychologists Ayala Pines and Elliot Aronson point out that in order for people to burn out, they need to have been on fire at some time in the past. Hence, a first step in getting on the right career track involves discovering what ignites you with passion, vocationally speaking. Go back to the checklists and exercises in chapters 1 and 9 and explore your natural gifts once again. Focus on your top two or three intelligences and decide how they can best be expressed in the workplace. There are two major choices open to you in matching your intelligences with your work life: you can modify your existing job in some way to take account of your strengths and abilities; or you can seek new employment.

◆ MAKING CHANGES IN YOUR PRESENT JOB ───

The easiest option, and the one that's available to the largest segment of the work force, is to modify one or more aspects of your current job so that it better reflects what it is that you do best. You can accomplish this by negotiating formally or informally with your employer for a change in your work responsibilities, either through adding tasks associated with your highly developed intelligences or by subtracting tasks related to your weaker ones. In her book *Succeeding Against the Odds,* Sally Smith writes about a woman named Doreen who worked as an assistant in a school library. Doreen was weak in the linguistic and logical-mathematical areas, and as a result she consistently reversed numbers and had difficulties replacing books on the appropriate shelves. She talked about her difficulties with the library committee and shared with them her perception of her strong interpersonal intelligence. As a result they put her in a job that involved more interaction with people and she developed a successful after-school storytelling program.

You might find you need to shift into working more with others, or less with others; more with numbers and words, or less with numbers and words; more with pictures and graphics, or less. Depending on the flexibility of your work environment, you may be able to keep your current job title, salary, and benefits, and simply shift the emphasis in what you do.

For those who have jobs or employers that lack this kind of give and take, however, there is still a great deal you can do to bring your strongest intelligences into the workplace:

Find ways of indirectly expressing your strongest intelligences. Sometimes you can carry out your job responsibilities in a slightly modified way, one that puts the accent on the positive. Organizational consultant Marsha Sinetar writes about a client with strong bodily-kinesthetic skills who expressed his need for physical movement in an office position by wandering through the halls. "By nature restless, he thinks best when strolling around," writes Sinetar. "Because he has come to accept this about himself, others have too. After many years of working with him, colleagues now expect him to walk the halls. Of course, his superior thinking has made millions of dollars for his company, and he has earned the 'right' to stroll as much as he wishes." Musical individuals might find that rhythmic foot or finger tapping helps them focus better on their work or think more productively. Spatial learners could keep a scratch pad nearby as a creative outlet for their visual intelligence.

Change your physical surroundings to reflect your strengths and interests. If you're a strongly intrapersonal individual working in the midst of lots of people, you might consider moving your work location to a quieter area of the office or putting up wall dividers to ensure greater privacy. If you're a spatial individual, think about decorating your office area with visual images such as cartoons, artwork, or sculpture. Musical people might try to convince management to install a background music system in the workplace or seek permission to work with a portable cassette player and headphones.

Use work breaks to express your strongest intelligences. These empty spaces during the day can be seen as little pockets of opportunity for developing or exercising one's intelligences. Author Cornelius Herschberg used his lunch hour and subway ride to and from work each day to read great literature. "I have read on subways, trains, and buses for forty years," says Herschberg, "and on these conveyances, and during my lunchtime, I've done approximately ten hours of reading a week for about two thousand weeks. . . . Those 20,000 hours add up to at least five college degrees."

It's even possible for individuals in highly routine jobs to find time during the workday itself to focus on their natural gifts and talents. American author Nathaniel Hawthorne wrote four novels, including *The Scarlet Letter,* while working at the Customs House in Salem, Massachusetts. Longshoreman-philosopher Eric Hoffer spent countless hours working out ideas for his books while laboring in California railroad yards. And peak-performance psychologist Charles Garfield writes about a man he met working in a tollbooth next to the San Francisco-Bay Bridge who engaged in creative movement while he worked. "I'm going to be a dancer someday," said the man. "My bosses are in there [pointing to the administration building] and they're paying for my training."

The most important thing to remember in revitalizing your career is to keep your strongest intelligences alive at all costs. Ayala Pines and Elliot Aronson point out that people who perform boring activities are most at risk for experiencing burnout, while those who engage in activities that allow them to use much of their mind rarely experience it. Nobel prize–winning geneticist Barbara McClintock used to imagine actually being the corn that she studied. Zen master Dogen wrote in *Instructions to the Zen Cook:* "See the pot as your own head; see the water as your lifeblood." The most boring job can become exciting when engaged in with this kind of spirit.

◆ LOOKING FOR A NEW JOB ─────────────

If you find that the above suggestions don't pull you out of your job blues, then it might be time to make the switch to a totally new career. Most people would agree that when Vincent van Gogh left his job as a minister to become a painter, when John Steinbeck abandoned marine biology for a writing career, and when Pyotr Ilich Tchaikovsky quit working as a law clerk to become a musician, each made the right career move. In our own lives, however, striking off in a new direction can be a daunting prospect. That's why it's probably a good idea to think about making changes that do less—at least initially—to disturb the status quo. This is especially important if you have a family to feed, bills to pay, and other obligations that require continuity in your life. Here are some ways to get your feet wet in another career without risking your standing in your current job:

Volunteer. Volunteer work provides the opportunity for you to acquire valuable on-the-job experience that can pave the way to a paid position in a career that maximizes your gifts. Corporate guru Peter Drucker calls volunteerism "the third sector" of the nation's economy—an estimated 90 million people in this country work as volunteers, either part-time or full-time. Examples of volunteer positions that take advantage of the seven intelligences include:

- docent in an art museum (spatial);
- folk singer in a hospital (musical);
- library assistant (linguistic);
- counselor for the homeless (interpersonal);
- meditation teacher in a nursing home (intrapersonal);
- tour guide at a park (bodily-kinesthetic); and
- math tutor in an elementary school (logical-mathematical).

Most large communities have volunteer centers that will match an individual's interests and abilities to a specific job.

Start your own business. Turn activities that you already enjoy doing for free into money-making enterprises. Connecticut housewife Linda Bronstein had been designing Victorian-style notecards and sending them to friends as a hobby. Then she took a seminar entitled "How to Earn a Living Without a Job" and transformed her artistic talent into a primary means of livelihood. According to recent statistics, at least 16 million Americans work out of their homes in activities ranging from accounting to zither making. Paul and Sarah Edwards's book *Working from Home* provides specific guidelines for getting started.

Moonlight. According to recent surveys, some 6 million workers in this country now hold two or more jobs. By taking on a part-time job in an area of interest, you can experience a different work milieu and find out whether it allows you to express more of your musical, or spatial, or kinesthetic mind. A frustrated bookkeeper who spends two hours each evening working in an architect's office has the opportunity to discover whether this new environment provides an outlet for his long-stifled spatial skills. Make sure that the additional job you decide to take on provides at least minimal opportunities for exposure to a new intelligence.

Combine Careers. Often you can take job skills you've acquired over the years in a field that doesn't make use of your potential and put them to use in a job that does. Steve Crowley was an accountant who dreamed of someday going into broadcasting. He found a way to incorporate his logical-mathematical expertise into a new career by becoming a producer and host of a television program on personal finances. Similarly, a bodily-kinesthetic person who has invested several years in becoming certified as a high school English teacher can make the switch to a more appropriate position as a physical education instructor or sports coach with relatively little additional training.

If you do decide to make a clean break with the past and seek out a radically different career, make sure it's in an area that consumes you passionately. It sometimes takes years of intense focus in an area of deep interest before you reap financial benefits. Remember, though, that it's the activity itself and not the money that will bring the richest rewards. As psychotherapist Viktor Frankl advises: "Don't aim for success—the more you aim at it and make it a target, the more you are going to miss it. For success, like happiness, cannot be pursued; it must ensue ... as the unintended side-effect of one's personal dedication to a course greater than oneself."

WHEN INTELLIGENCES COLLIDE: HARMONIZING THINKING STYLES IN RELATIONSHIPS

One of the questions I'm asked most frequently in multiple intelligences workshops is how sex differences fit into the seven kinds of smart. I used to be hesitant about answering this sort of question, feeling like I was about to walk into a hornet's nest of controversy. Now, however, I feel more comfortable about sharing what the research suggests are some of the basic cognitive differences between males and females, realizing that the differences aren't carved in stone and can change as culture evolves.

More important, though, I've become interested in how multiple intelligences can shed some light on, and even raise an olive branch in, the war between the sexes. I've noticed that certain things in my own marital relationship become easier to explain (and therefore easier to take) when looked at from the perspective of the seven intelligences. For example, the inevitable collisions that take place after dinner when it comes time to put the dishes in the dishwasher now seem a bit clearer to me. I load the dishes by "feel" (kinesthetically). In other words, if I can jam it in, I've accomplished my goal. I'm also usually so wrapped up in internal linguistic mind chatter that I don't pay much attention to what I'm doing. My wife, on the other hand, is spatial and logical in her approach. She can't understand why I'm unable to appreciate the need for order. ("If you put a dish there," she'll say, "it'll block the nozzle that sprays the dishes with water.") I nod to her that I understand, but I don't really. Not, at least, until I realize that it's our mind styles that are clashing and not our personalities or egos. I hope this chapter will help couples find some peace in their relationships by seeing that certain areas of conflict are resolvable once you begin to realize how your communication patterns, your selection of leisure-time activities, and even your household habits are influenced by the way you think.

◆ VIVA LA COGNITIVE DIFFERENCE ─────────

Over the past twenty-five years a growing body of scientific evidence has accumulated suggesting that there are basic differences in the way that men and women think. Although the jury is still out on whether these differences are biological, cultural, or some combination of the two, the facts are plain: there *are* differences and they show up in a number of ways across the seven intelligences.

Regarding spatial intelligence, for example, it appears that from adolescence on there is a relatively clear and consistent advantage among males in visual-spatial skills such as those involved in mental rotations of objects and right-left directionality. According to Jo Durden-Smith and Diane Desimone, authors of *Sex and the Brain,* "Males are better at maps, mazes and math; at rotating objects in their minds and locating three-dimensional objects in two-dimensional representations. They're better at perceiving and manipulating objects in space. And they're better at orienting themselves in space. They have a good sense of direction." This latter observation, however, should be tempered by recent studies suggesting that men and women have different *styles* for finding their way around unfamiliar territory. Males tend to use mental vectors and coordinates in orienting themselves, while females tend to rely on landmarks. It has been suggested that using landmarks is actually a superior method of negotiating one's way around.

On average males appear to have an advantage in logical-mathematical intelligence—at least with respect to higher mathematics. Johns Hopkins University researchers Camilla Benbow and Julian Stanley studied the performance of thousands of gifted high school students on the math section of the Scholastic Aptitude Test and discovered that the higher the score, the more likely it was that the test taker was a male. Interestingly, follow-up studies suggested that among this same group of adolescents, the girls were more likely to receive higher math grades and pursue a math major in college. Although some observers point to this as an indication that males have a natural flair for math while women must work hard to achieve the same results, more recent studies show that women in fact *are* catching up and narrowing the gap in logical-mathematical areas.

For linguistic intelligence the situation appears reversed. Anthropologist Margaret Mead asserted that in every society she studied, women surpassed men in linguistic behavior. In psychological studies infant females tend to "vocalize" their excitement more consistently than males. However, Stanford researcher Eleanor Maccoby suggests that females don't show superior performance on

verbal skills until around age eleven. In one study of
eighth graders, girls relied more on their verbal ability to
deal with numbers and shapes as well as words, while
boys tended to rely on math and spatial abilities even to
tackle linguistic subjects. Furthermore, there's clear evidence that males are far more likely to experience specific
linguistic difficulties such as stuttering, and reading and
writing disabilities.

The situation may not be as simple, however, as saying that women are good at linguistic skills while men are
not. In one study researchers tape recorded conversations
at several university faculty meetings and discovered that,
with one exception, men spoke more often and for longer
periods of time than women. Georgetown University psy-
cholinguist Deborah Tannen suggests in her book *You Just
Don't Understand!* that men engage in *report-talk* while
women prefer to communicate via *rapport-talk*. Men talk
to preserve their sense of independence and report their
knowledge to others in a public setting. Women, on the
other hand, discourse as a means of establishing connections and negotiating relationships, and they prefer to do
this in private surroundings.

These observations may also be important in looking
at how the sexes differ with respect to the personal intelligences. There's evidence to suggest that in men, the personal intelligences are skewed toward seeking personal
identity and self-definition (more intrapersonal concerns),
while women tend to seek a web of connectedness or a
sense of relatedness that is more interpersonally focused.
Feminist psychologist Nancy Chodorow writes that "girls
emerge from [the first three years of life] with a basis for
'empathy' built into their primary definition of self in a
way that boys do not." Studies in social psychology generally show females outperforming men in several different
components of social intelligence, including sensitivity to

nonverbal emotional cues and judging intention, and in their ability to negotiate conflict. Harvard psychologist Carol Gilligan suggests that these fundamental interpersonal attributes of women have typically been neglected by developmental researchers: "The discovery now being celebrated by men in mid-life of the importance of intimacy, relationships, and care is something that women have known from the beginning."

Again, though, it's not as simple as saying that men are intrapersonal and women are interpersonal. Howard Gardner defines a core component of intrapersonal intelligence as the ability to make fine distinctions in one's inner emotional life. Psychotherapist Lillian Rubin, in her book *Intimate Strangers,* suggests that it is these very intrapersonal characteristics that men have so much difficulty with when going through therapy: "Repeatedly, when therapy begins, I find myself having to teach a man how to monitor his internal states—how to attend to his thoughts and feelings, how to bring them into consciousness." It may be, then, that a certain combination of the personal intelligences—those characterized, perhaps, by the ambitious CEO who networks (interpersonal) and promotes himself (intrapersonal) to the top of the corporate career ladder— are more typically male. And still other aspects of the personal intelligences—for example, those of the marriage and family counselor who shows deep levels of sensitivity to internal emotional states (intrapersonal) and demonstrates the ability to relate to others on the basis of those emotions (interpersonal)—are more typically female.

When we look at musical intelligence, the evidence is similarly mixed. University of South Florida psychologist Diane McGuinness points to research suggesting that women can sing in tune six times more often than men. Studies done in English music colleges likewise show a distinct advantage among women when it comes to displaying sensitivity to musical dynamics, or the ability to distinguish changes in loudness in a musical passage. On the other hand, a study of preschool children done by Carol Knox and Doreen Kimura indicated that boys are more attentive to environmental sounds and animal noises —stimuli that certainly have a musical character— while girls are more attentive to verbal sounds (again, attesting to their linguistic strength). On tests of pitch and rhythm, no significant sex differences have been found by researchers.

Finally, in the area of bodily-kinesthetic intelligence, no clear advantage for males or females is apparent. However, there are some suggestions that women may have an advantage in fine-motor skills while men excel with respect to gross-motor skills. Studies done with boys and girls aged two to eighteen years at the Youth Sports Institute at Michigan State University indicate that boys outperform girls in tests of strength, speed, and agility, while females showed superiority in the area of muscle flexibility.

On the other hand, a British research project conducted with three- to fifteen-year-olds involving moving pegs rapidly along holes in a board showed a female advantage. This female superiority in small-motor tasks also seems to hold true with respect to executing more complex sequences of physical activity. Students of McGuinness observed men and women learning a new dance step. All the women learned the sequence quickly, but many of the men had great difficulty with the movements.

The results reported above should be interpreted with caution. There is still considerable controversy over whether many of these sex differences are the result of biological factors or are due to cultural conditioning. The fact that we're seeing a narrowing of the gap between males and females in logical-mathematical intelligence suggests that socialization is indeed a significant factor in the differing ways that males and females think. The old stereotype that "girls aren't good in math" seems to be disappearing, and this may be creating more opportunities for females to show their true abilities. On the other hand, it seems plausible that there *are* certain factors "hard-wired" into the genes of men and women that create differences not just in the procreative functions but also in the cognitive ones. It's likely that "nature" interacts with "nurture" in complex ways to create the kinds of differences observed in the research studies summarized above.

Keep in mind that these sex differences are *group* differences and don't apply in individual cases. As you'll recall from the beginning of the chapter, I am strongly linguistic, while my wife tends to be more spatially and logically oriented. These differences are in marked contrast to the studies given above. You too may find that the differences between you and your significant other don't fit with the research results. As Purdue University social psychologist Alice Eagly observes: "The public needs to be warned that knowing a person's sex doesn't allow you to predict much of anything about him or her." The important point isn't necessarily what males and females can and cannot do differently from one another but rather how your particular profile of intelligences differs from your partner's mind-style—regardless of how you both may relate to the norm. The following exercise will enable you to look at this aspect of your relationship.

DETERMINING YOUR PARTNER'S MULTIPLE INTELLIGENCES

Go back over the checklist you filled out in chapter 1 and rank your intelligences from strongest to weakest. Then, have your significant other fill out the same checklist, ranking his own intelligences. (It's best if you duplicate the checklist first so that your partner isn't influenced by your results.) After you've both finished, take one hour to discuss the results with each other. Spend twenty minutes sharing your own profile, twenty minutes listening to your partner share his profile, and twenty minutes discussing how your differences and similarities in multiple intelligences affect your relationship. You might also want to do this with the other two checklists in the book related to childhood intelligences and learning difficulties (chapters 9 and 10).

◆ SPEAKING THE SAME MIND LANGUAGE ────

Effective communication between partners is probably the single most important dimension of any relationship. In one recent survey of failed marriages, 70 percent of women and 59 percent of men cited poor communication as a major cause of their divorce. Although each partner in a successful relationship needs to have enough interpersonal intelligence to be able and willing to attend to the needs of the other, and sufficient linguistic intelligence to talk things out effectively, all seven of the intelligences come into play when couples communicate.

Tracy Cabot, author of *How to Keep a Man in Love with You Forever,* suggests there are certain cognitive strategies a woman (or man) needs to know about in order to communicate effectively with his or her mate. In her model there are three cognitive channels: auditory, visual, and kinesthetic. This model can easily be expanded, however, to comprise the seven intelligences of this book. Cabot explains that conflicts in a relationship often arise when one partner fails to "speak the love language" of the other. To establish harmony, according to Cabot, a person needs to use words that resonate with his or her mate's strongest learning style. Here are some examples, translated into the terminology of each intelligence, of how you might explain to your partner that you're understanding him or her:

Musical:	"I'm *in tune* with what you're saying."
Spatial:	"I *see your point.*"
Linguistic:	"Your *words speak* loud and clear."
Bodily-kinesthetic:	"I'm *in touch* with where you're *coming from.*"
Logical-mathematical:	"Everything you say just *adds up.*"
Interpersonal:	"I can *relate* to that."
Intrapersonal:	"I have a *good feeling inside* about what you just said."

In learning to speak your partner's "MI (multiple intelligence) language," keep in mind the following points. Musical language emphasizes melodic terms and metaphors but also includes sensory data like environmental noises and animal sounds. Spatial language is highly visual, with lots of color and detailed imagery. Bodily-kinesthetic language includes words that have texture ("Let's *smooth* things out") as well as words suggesting movement and action. Logical-mathematical language makes frequent reference to numbers and quantities as well as reason and logic. Intrapersonal language is highly feeling-oriented ("That's a *sad* argument"), while interpersonal language tends to be more interactive and includes frequent references to other people. The next exercise will give you an opportunity to practice speaking a couple of these "MI languages" with your partner.

SPEAKING YOUR PARTNER'S MI LANGUAGE

Set aside twenty minutes for this exercise. Before beginning decide on your strongest or preferred intelligence, as well as your weakest or least preferred intelligence, and ask your partner to do the same. Then spend three minutes talking to your partner using words and phrases based on her *least* preferred intelligence. Afterward, have her describe her experience of listening to you talk (whether she felt pushed away, attracted, or neutral). Then take three more minutes to talk to her using words directly related to her chosen intelligence. Again, have her share her response. Then switch sides and repeat the exercise.

Through the above exercise we've infused the other six intelligences into what is essentially a linguistically based medium of expression. There are many other ways to communicate, however, that encompass all seven intelligences. In their book *Married Etc.*, family educators Buff Bradley, Murray and Roberta Suid, and Jean Eastman, write: "Partners communicate with each other in a nearly infinite variety of ways. They talk and they touch and they read each other's books. . . . Some people write notes to each other, some use silences; some tell jokes or whistle or procrastinate or cook a special meal or speak through the children or read aloud a passage from a book that says what they can't . . ."

Several of these alternative methods of communication, especially those that rely on nonverbal intelligences, may be especially helpful in bridging the gap between the silent partner in a relationship and the more verbal one. In *Intimate Strangers* Lillian Rubin recounts the lament of a wife who felt abandoned by her nonverbal spouse: "It's always the same. I'm the one who tries to get things going.

I'm always doing my bla-bla-bla number, you know, keeping things moving and alive around here. But he's the original Mr. Shutmouth most of the time, so I'd just as leave be with a friend and I go call somebody up and talk to her for a while ... then he gets mad at me, or jealous or something, for talking on the telephone."

Rubin suggests that "words ... are not at the center of the definition of intimacy for most men; nonverbal activities will do for them at least as well, often better." In one case a man married for five years said about his wife: "She tells me that every time I whistle she knows something is bothering me. It's the only time I whistle." Another couple communicated by staging improvised puppet shows: "Sometimes the stuffed animal ... becomes a way for one of us to express something to the other in a more indirect, less risky way." Other ways of communicating through the seven intelligences include the following:

Linguistic:	sharing books, writing notes, sending letters
Logical-mathematical:	creating secret codes, establishing logical social cues, setting up communication contracts
Musical:	singing, trading favorite musical selections, playing instruments
Spatial:	drawing pictures, sending cards, using facial expressions
Bodily-Kinesthetic:	touching, gesturing, giving massages
Intrapersonal:	sharing dreams, using "I feel ..." statements, mental telepathy
Interpersonal:	active listening, taking turns, mirroring

◆ NEGOTIATING LEISURE TIME ───────────────

Although today's couples have about one third less leisure time than did couples twenty years ago, hobbies and outside interests are still tremendously important in their lives. Studies show that shared time together, especially activities that involve playfulness and fun, is a major contributor to the success of long-term relationships. However, alliances often go awry when there's a multiple-intelligences clash over leisure-time choices. One couple argues over whether to spend the weekend reading books (her linguistic choice) or hiking in the woods (his bodily-kinesthetic preference). Another couple can't make up their minds about how to spend a free evening. He would like to go to a friend's party (interpersonal) while she would prefer a movie (spatial).

Successful couples find ways of dealing with such differences in personal taste. One approach is to alternate activites from day to day or week to week. In a survey of eighty-seven couples who had been together fifteen years or more, one participant observed: "Tony likes to relax on vacations and I like to be on the run. So one summer we travel a lot, and the next summer we rent a house and look at the view." One of the most famous and enduring celebrity couples, Paul Newman and Joanne Woodward, have differing recreations. He likes to race cars and she likes the ballet. So he'll go to the ballet once in a while, and she goes to the races from time to time.

Another way of choosing pastimes is to search for common ground in an activity so that both of your needs can be met. For example, a strongly bodily-kinesthetic person and a deeply musical individual might seek activities that combine these two intelligences, such as dancing, hiking with Walkmen, doing aerobic exercises to music, or playing musical instruments. Similarly, a linguistic person and his spatial mate might spend leisure time looking at illustrated books, going on a guided tour of an art museum, attending a lecture-slide presentation in an area of mutual interest, or engaging in other activites that combine words and pictures.

If you find that you and your partner have strongly mismatched intelligences, the next exercise can help you develop an appreciation for your partner's preferred ways of expressing her intelligences and lead to more creative ways of spending leisure time together.

APPRENTICE FOR A DAY

Set aside a day, or part of a day, to participate with your partner in leisure-time activities related to her strongest or preferred intelligence. Let her select the activities, materials, settings, and ways of proceeding through the day. If she's highly spatial, that may mean you'll do some painting together, look at pictures or illustrations, go to the movies, share favorite art, and/or take photographs. At the end of the day, talk about your experience together—what you liked, didn't like, and would like to do again. Then, make plans for another day, so that you can switch roles and plan a day for both of you based on *your* strongest or preferred intelligence.

◆ HANDLING HOUSEHOLD HABITS ─────────

After enjoying leisure-time pursuits, a couple still must return home to face daily chores and errands. How they handle these tasks may determine the *real* quality of their relationship. Arlie Hochschild, professor of sociology at the University of California, Berkeley, says that the happiest households are those in which couples *share* housework, while the unhappiest are those in which women bear all or most of the burden for chores. It's important, then, for couples to be able to divide up the tasks in such a way that each individual has the opportunity to make the most of their strongest intelligences. The following chart suggests household chores that correspond to specific intelligences:

Linguistic:	correspondence, phone calls
Logical-Mathematical:	bill paying, tax returns, banking
Bodily-Kinesthetic:	cooking, cleaning, gardening, pet care
Spatial:	machine repair, renovating, decorating
Interpersonal:	shopping, dealing with service people, child care
Intrapersonal:	setting up household goals

In many cases you won't have to argue too much about certain chores because it will become apparent, especially after reading this book, who is most qualified to do a specific task. For example, my wife and I are in the process of decorating and landscaping our house right now. I know my spatial limitations and feel fine about my artistic wife taking major responsibility in this area. Similarly, couples in my workshops often talk about how they had little trouble deciding who would pay the bills in the family—there always seemed to be one partner who was more logical-mathematical than the other. However, when you finally reach items on your list like "clean the toilet" and "take out the garbage," it's likely that there won't be a rush, even among the most bodily-kinesthetic individuals, to take on these responsibilities. These you'll have to divide up as best you can.

Whether you're grappling with communication patterns, leisure preferences, household habits, or any other aspect of a relationship, it's particularly important to have *respect* for your partner's way of doing things. Validating your partner's uniqueness can be an important first step in finding ways of accommodating differences in intelligences around the house. The final exercise in this book will give you some practice in doing this.

MULTIPLE INTELLIGENCES TROUBLESHOOTING

Choose a problem that keeps coming up in your relationship. It can be related to faulty communication, conflicts over household responsibilities, philosophical differences, differing attitudes to work or leisure, problems with friends or relatives, or some other difficulty. Write the problem down on a sheet of paper. Then spend thirty minutes brainstorming ways in which this problem may be related to differences in your multiple intelligences. For example, problems in keeping the house clean may be related to one person being more spatial, where *order* is most important, while the other person is more kinesthetic, where *comfort* is the predominant need. If you determine that a difference in multiple intelligences *does* have an impact on the problem, spend five minutes in silence contemplating the *value* of the other person's strengths in this area. Then, take turns saying something positive about the other's strongest intelligence. Finally, determine whether or not this renewed respect for the other's way of thinking has affected the original problem in any way. If solutions to the problem come to mind, take some time to work them out in writing or discussion.

It has been said that we enter a relationship with another person in order to become more whole. Ironically, it often seems that the very things that bother us the most about our partner are qualities that we have not yet fully realized in ourselves. I remember one highly logical friend who was attracted to a very introspective partner because she had a feeling life he wished he had. But because he had not learned to accept his own inner emotional self, he rejected it in her and the relationship died. Most of you can probably think of similar examples. That's why it's so very important for us to work toward acknowledging and accepting our *own* intelligences—even the weak and hidden ones—so that we can truly accept them in the ones we love.

Once we've made that leap and accepted ourselves and the other, then both our own abilities and our partner's unique talents become a gift to the relationship. We learn to combine our intelligences in ways that are more powerful together than they are apart. Instead of regarding our partner's abilities as alien or threatening, we learn to acknowledge her expertise as a valuable asset we can both draw upon. As one happily married person put it: "You have just so much time, energy, and intellect, and it's good to be able to depend on your spouse to fill in the gaps."

MIND-STYLES
OF THE FUTURE:
INTELLIGENCES OF THE
TWENTY-FIRST CENTURY

"Alpha children wear grey. They work harder than we do, because they're so frightfully clever. I'm really awfully glad I'm a Beta, because I don't work so hard. And then we are much better than the Gammas and Deltas." So reads a passage from Aldous Huxley's *Brave New World,* a novel that foresees a time when people will be separated into different intelligence types while still incubating in test tubes. It's unsettling to think that someday we could unwittingly create our own "brave new world" peopled with "logicals," "spatials," "verbals," and "musicals" by misusing the theory of multiple intelligences.

In such a world parents and teachers would test children at a young age for any sign of artistic ability, logical aptitude, verbal facility, or social grace, and then make concerted efforts through sophisticated educational measures to bring particular forms of intellect into maturity. These kids would then go off to their appointed stations in life—the logical child to an accountant's position, the verbal child to an editor's post, and so on—each person being directed to his assigned place in an educationally sound and neuropsychologically based twenty-first-century caste system. In some parts of the world this sort of hothouse pedagogy is already being employed to develop future gymnasts and musicians. How awful!

If I can leave you with any single message concerning the theory of multiple intelligences, it would be that *each person possesses all seven intelligences and has the ability to develop each one to a reasonable level of proficiency.* There's a real danger in thinking "I'm a kinesthetic person" and then focusing your energies on that one area of your life to the exclusion of the others. I'm reminded of the child prodigy whose parents directed all their resources toward developing his verbal and logical gifts. At the age of forty he was discovered floating facedown in a friend's swimming pool—a suicide victim. He'd become so unbalanced that he couldn't roll with the punches that life inevitably delivers. As an increasingly specialized society, we've lost touch with the kinds of cultural influences that created the Renaissance men, the jack-of-all-trades, and the generalists, synthesists, and liberal artists of the past. The theory of multiple intelligences ought to be a medium for broadening our conceptions of what we may be, not a means of narrowing them down to only "what we're good at" or what we think society will demand of us.

In the final analysis the concept of seven *separate* intelligences is somewhat misleading. Howard Gardner suggests that these seven categories are actually *fictions,* and that in real life they're always linked together in complex ways. Chess players look at the game board with a spatial *and* logical-mathematical mind. Mechanics fix carburetors by drawing on spatial *and* bodily-kinesthetic intelligences. Even something as simple as cooking a meal requires several intelligences: linguistic for reading the cookbook, logical-mathematical for dividing a recipe in half, bodily-kinesthetic for measuring, mixing, and pouring; and the personal intelligences for planning a menu that appeals to different tastes. There's virtually no activity in life that can be undertaken with only one intelligence. That in itself is an argument in favor of staying loose and relatively balanced with respect to all seven.

Moreover, society is changing, and as it continues to change, the primary intelligences required for successful adaptation will likely change as well. I presented a prehistoric scenario at the beginning of this book suggesting how important bodily-kinesthetic intelligence was several thousand years ago. Even one hundred years ago it was the strapping young lad who could milk cows and raise barns who held the day in the average American household, not the spectacle-clad bookworm. Intelligences come and go like fall fashions. Certain kinds of logical-mathematical abilities that were unimportant thirty years ago now receive a great deal of attention because of the fact that computers have come along to make effective use of them. The "nerd" who had no place in the 1950s is now making money creating software programs in Silicon Valley.

The future is likely to bring with it a demand for intelligences that aren't considered so important today. As our country continues to shift from an industrial base to a service-oriented economy, the importance of interpersonal intelligence will grow. Similarly, with information becoming increasingly available through a variety of visual forms—videotape, computer graphics, and the like—the importance of spatial intelligence and the need for expert visual thinkers will become increasingly acute.

The best advice is: don't place your bets on any one intelligence—it may well be "obsolete" by the time you've mastered it. Instead, look to cutting-edge technologies like hypertext and multimedia computer software—which combine intelligences in creative ways—for clues to the importance of cultivating competence in several intelligences at one time.

Ultimately, there may be intelligences on the horizon that we don't even know about. Howard Gardner has certainly left room in his model for that possibility. One candidate that has emerged for consideration is spiritual or moral intelligence. As Harvard psychiatrist and Pulitzer prize–winning author Robert Coles points out, it's quite possible to be highly intelligent and still be wicked. He writes: "We are reminded that in 1933 and 1934, some of the most prominent and distinguished intellectuals in Germany signed up with Hitler. They were doctors, and lawyers, and intellectuals; philosphers, psychoanalysts, psychologists, journalists, authors of books—high-IQ people, even in the seven categories . . . "

It may be important, even essential for the survival of the planet, that we acknowledge and cultivate an intelligence within us that somehow guides the other seven, making sure that their use is directed toward the common good of humankind. That intelligence may be outside of ourselves, as it was conceived of in ancient and medieval times, in a transpersonal, religious, or celestial realm. It may even be located deep within the soul of the earth, as supporters of the Gaia hypothesis have proposed. Or it may be in ourselves—but located in our hearts rather than our minds. However we conceive of it, to cultivate such a supraordinate intelligence may be the single most intelligent thing we will ever do.

14

NEW INTELLIGENCES: THE NATURALIST AND THE EXISTENTIAL

Since the publication of the first edition of *7 Kinds of Smart,* Harvard researcher Dr. Howard Gardner, the originator of the theory of multiple intelligences, has added a new intelligence to his list—the naturalist—and has begun to speak of a possible ninth intelligence—the existential.* In this chapter I describe the two "new" intelligences and give some ideas of how you can assess and develop these intelligences in your own life. Then, in the next chapter, I will discuss how Dr. Gardner came up with these two new intelligences, and examine in detail the different criteria he uses to determine whether or not an intelligence should appear on his list. Finally, I will speculate on the possibilities of other intelligences being added to his list in the future.

*See Howard Gardner, *Intelligence Reframed: Multiple Intelligences in the Twenty-first Century* (New York: Basic Books, 1999).

◆ THE NATURALIST INTELLIGENCE ────────────

According to Howard Gardner, the naturalist is a person who shows "expertise in the recognition and classification of the numerous species—the flora and fauna—of his or her environment." As with each of the first seven intelligences, there are many different ways to express an intelligence in the world. Perhaps most obviously, the naturalist reveals the intelligence of the "green thumb"— that knack that some people have to garden, to nurture household plants, create wonderful landscapes, or in other ways show a natural care for flora. The reverse of this would be the person who lives amidst dying plants. Perhaps there is a "learning disability" for natural things— if so, I believe I have it. My wife has moved all the plants out of my office to give them a fighting chance for survival!

Similarly, one might have an intelligence for animals. It's amazing how many veterinarians, in particular, have a special knack for calming the most skittish of beasts. In Oliver Sacks's book *An Anthropologist on Mars,* he writes about Tempil Grandin, a woman who is labeled as "autistic" (having difficulties with the "personal" intelligences), but who is a genius with animals. She uses her extraordinary understanding of the needs of cattle, for example, to design machinery that helps calm them while they're being led to the slaughterhouse. And for those who fail to see any compassion in that sort of business, there is also the intelligence of the animal-rights activist. I believe that my niece has this particular kind of "animal smart." She has been a vegetarian since she was six. She refuses to wear animal products. Instead of presents for her birthday, she asks that donations be made to an animal-rights organization like Greenpeace or PETA. There are also "earth angels," or natural ecologists who demonstrate this kind of care for ecosystems—helping to save rain forests, coral reefs, or other endangered land.

As is evident from my niece, a person can begin showing certain "proclivities" toward being a naturalist at an early age. Jane Goodall, the chimpanzee expert who has spent so much time observing them and championing their cause around the world, wrote about following a hen into a chicken coop at the age of five. She wanted to find out where the eggs came from, and so she hid in the back of the hen house and waited patiently for over four hours until her family, distressed at not finding her anywhere, called the police. "Then finally," Jane writes, "my mother, calling in the gloaming, saw this excited little girl come running across a field with shining eyes and straw all over her. And instead of scolding me, which would have taken away all the joy, she sat down to hear my story."

This sort of encouragement from relatives or others can certainly contribute to the forming of a naturalist, but it doesn't always work that way. Charles Darwin, perhaps the most famous of all naturalists, was considered a dunce by his family. His father once told him: "You care for nothing but shooting, dogs, and rat-catching. You will be a disgrace to yourself and all your family." Fortunately, his father was wrong, and Charles transferred his "rat-catching" ability to other species as well (sparked by a life-transforming voyage to the Galapagos Islands in his twenties), and thereby changed the way we view the evolution of us all. Sometimes chance intervenes to determine the shape that a naturalist's life will have. E. O. Wilson, twice a Pulitzer Prize winner and author of the autobiography *Naturalist,* writes that his own fascination with the fauna and flora of the world was made very specific for him when he had a childhood accident that damaged his eyes. Not able to see more than a few feet in front of him, he decided to focus on insects as a specialty and became one of the world's leading expert in ants!

Most of us, when we think back to our own childhoods, will recognize the naturalist within us. Perhaps you remember having a speciality of your own when you were growing up: worms, beetles, butterflies, lizards, poppies, daisies, maple trees, or even clouds. Young children are natural-born naturalists. I remember investigating worms, for example, scraping off the dirt and looking at the rings that allowed them mobility, examining the dirt mounds they emerged from, and even biting into them to examine their innards. Here are a few questions to help jog your own memory about your childhood naturalist experiences:

_____ I loved to look at animal tracks and guess what kind of animal made them.

_____ I enjoyed collecting insects in bottles, leaves in scrapbooks, or other kinds of natural collections.

_____ I liked to spend most of my time outdoors when I was young.

_____ I used to dislodge big rocks from the ground to discover all the living things that lay beneath.

_____ In school I enjoyed studying topics about nature.

_____ I used to have an aquarium, terrarium, or ant farm as a hobby.

_____ I loved to watch birds or other animals and to follow their habits (e.g., nesting, feeding) or find out other things about them.

_____ I wanted to be a veterinarian, forest ranger, botanist, or a related profession that involved nature when I was growing up.

_____ I derived a lot of pleasure just from looking at natural phenomena like clouds, trees, mountains, or other formations.

_____ I had pets that I spent a lot of time with.

Interestingly, Dr. Gardner says that if a child grows up in an urban environment, and has no exposure to the natural world of living things, then he or she may transfer the components of the naturalist to objects of the city. For example, instead of being able to differentiate among certain kinds of leaves, or flowers, or birds, the child may use this capacity to discriminate among certain types of CD album covers, sneakers, or automobiles.

As we grow up, many of us may find that the natural world recedes to the background (unless we become veterinarians, forest rangers, or botanists). Relationships, jobs, children, and other social responsibilities come to the fore and require that we develop other intelligences (although having children may call us back to the natural world through their interests). However, most of us have found ways to bring the intelligence of the naturalist into our life in peripheral ways, through hobbies, interests, and avocations. Here is another checklist to help you determine where the naturalist is in your life now as an adult:

_____ I have a garden and love to putter around in it.
_____ I enjoy spending time going backpacking, hiking, or just walking in nature and enjoying its riches.
_____ I am involved in a volunteer ecological organization (e.g., Greenpeace, Sierra Club) to help save nature from further destruction.
_____ I love to have animals around the house (more than just a dog or cat).
_____ I have a hobby that involves nature in some way (e.g., bird watching, butterfly collecting).
_____ I have taken adult education courses relating to nature (e.g., botany, zoology, ecology).

_____ I love to visit zoos, natural history museums, or other places where the natural world is studied.

_____ I enjoy watching nature shows on television (e.g., the Discovery Channel, *National Geographic, Nova*).

_____ For vacations I prefer to go off to a natural location (park, campground, hiking trail) than to a hotel/ resort or city/cultural location.

_____ I'm very good at telling the difference between different kinds of birds, dogs, trees, or other types of fauna or flora.

Perhaps after taking these two surveys you've discovered that you were very much the naturalist in childhood (as many kids are), but have left the world of nature behind as an adult, and that, like the French philosopher Jean-Jacques Rousseau, you'd like to shake off the constraints of social convention and get back to nature! Or possibly instead you've discovered that you really haven't been very much of a nature-boy or -girl, and would like to develop that intelligence in your life. Here are some ideas for putting more "nature-smart" into your world:

◆ Get to know the natural things in your own backyard (insects, birds, plants, etc.).

◆ Ask your children (or neighborhood children) to share what they know about the natural world.

◆ Investigate Internet sites that have to do with nature (use a search engine like Yahoo!, Lycos, or Alta Vista, and select search words such as *ecology, nature, botany, birds,* etc.).

◆ Go through the TV listings for the week and record shows having to do with an aspect of nature that you'd like to learn more about (e.g., volcanoes, chimpanzees, hurricanes).

◆ Get involved in a political or social cause that relates to the preservation of nature (e.g., write your congressperson about saving wetlands in your area, join the Sierra Club, start a petition to save a historic tree in your community that's about to be cut down).

◆ Find a place in your community where the natural world is displayed and studied (e.g., nature museum, zoo, park) and go there regularly to attend lectures and study exhibits.

◆ Choose a specific type of animal or plant (e.g., beetles or lilies) and learn as much as you can about it through books, the Internet, interviews with experts, and direct observation.

◆ Take up gardening or landscaping as a hobby, or if you already garden or landscape, investigate some new aspect of it (e.g., topiary, bonsai).

◆ Volunteer to take a group of kids into the natural world to learn more about some aspect of it (e.g., Scouts, Explorers).

◆ Subscribe to a magazine related to nature (e.g., *National Geographic*) and read it regularly.

◆ Read biographies or autobiographies of famous naturalists (e.g., E. O. Wilson's autobiography, *Naturalist,* Jane Goodall's *My Life with the Chimpanzees,* or Linda McMurray's biography of George Washington Carver).

◆ Go on a camping or backpacking trip and devote some time every day to observing nature.

◆ Make a list of all the animals (including types of birds) that live in your area.

◆ Keep a "naturalist's journal" that includes observations you make, questions you have about how different aspects of nature work, and resources you discover.

◆ Buy a set of binoculars and a magnifying glass, and go out once a week to a "wild" area in your neighborhood (e.g., vacant lot, park) to explore the natural world.

After devoting some time to studying the natural world, you might discover you want to consider a naturalist's career. There are a wide range of vocations that tap the naturalist's intelligence including: farmer, horticulturist, agronomist, botanist, veterinarian, entomologist, zoologist, animal husbandry specialist, forest ranger, viticulturist (wine making), evolutionary biologist, marine biologist, and ornithologist, as well as a wide variety of careers in environmental studies and ecology. It's especially important today, when the natural world is under assault worldwide from many social, cultural, political, and economic forces, to have the benefit of individuals who are "green" in their outlook, who view other species with respect, and who feel a sense of stewardship for planet earth. The addition of the naturalist to the list of multiple intelligences helps underline the importance of such people to contemporary life in the new millennium.

◆ THE EXISTENTIAL INTELLIGENCE ─────────

Howard Gardner has begun to speak of a possible ninth kind of smart: existential intelligence. Although some people may associate this new intelligence with the post–World War II writings of Jean-Paul Sartre and Albert Camus, it really has little to do with any specific philosophical school of thought. Rather, Gardner defines existential intelligence as the intelligence of concern with ultimate life issues. Such questions as "What is life?" "What's it all about?" "Why is there evil?" "Where is hu-

manity heading?" and "Does God exist?" are strong starting points for an exploration into these deeper concepts.
Dr. Gardner defines the core abilities of existential intelligence as twofold:

- ◆ To locate oneself with respect to the furthest
  reaches of the cosmos—the infinite no less than
  the infinitesimal;
- ◆ To locate oneself with respect to the most existential features of the human condition—the significance of life, the meaning of death, the ultimate
  fate of the physical and psychological worlds, such
  profound experiences as love of another human
  being, or total immersion in a work of art.

Gardner makes no assumptions about an ultimate answer
to these questions. In other words, he doesn't think some
people have more existential intelligence because they've
found an "ultimate truth," while others are less existentially intelligent because of their failure to do so. Gathered
among the existentially smart can be found theologians,
pastors, rabbis, shamans, ministers, priests, yogis, lamas,
and imams, each of whom could have a different conception of what the nature of absolute truth might be. But
there also are agnostics, atheists, skeptics, gadflies, here-
tics, and blasphemers who demonstrate high levels of existential intelligence, because they too may be grappling
with the same questions at a similarly intense and sophisticated level. In addition, Dr. Gardner points out that
many artists, scientists, writers, and individuals in careers
spanning the other intelligences are engaged in existential
pursuits. One thinks here of an artist like Vasily Kandinsky, whose book *Concerning the Spiritual in Art* argues
for the necessity of art to explore mystical and cosmic
depths, or of the physicist J. Robert Oppenheimer, who

when he observed the first atomic bomb go off (a bomb he helped to develop) quoted a passage from the ancient Hindu sacred text, the Bhagavad Gita, about cosmic destruction. His existential concerns with the "fallout" from the development of the atomic bomb led to the loss of his security clearance with the United States, and the questioning of his loyalty to the government.

As with the other intelligences, existential intelligence begins to emerge in early childhood. Not yet having the cultural blinders of adulthood, young children are open the mysteries of life, constantly asking big questions that the adults around them may be hard put to answer. In my book *The Radiant Child* I chronicled the many ways in which children show wisdom beyond their years in such matters. I included many accounts of children's nonordinary experiences, including archetypal dreams, peak experiences, psychic perceptions, near-death states, mystical encounters, and existential confrontations. One study I reviewed from Manchester College, Oxford, England, included the memories of an adult recalling an event that occurred to him fifty years before.

> *During the year when I was eight . . . as I stood dressed to go out on one of those interminable and awful walks through the country lanes, I was actually thinking and considering my position, something like this—"Here am I, a little boy of seven; I wonder where I was eight years ago." At that tremendous thought I stood rooted to the carpet (remember I was alone in the room) with a wave of tremendous feeling sweeping over me. I suddenly felt old and aware of being somebody very ancient, weighed by Time, of almost unbeginning individuality. Eight years ago, thought I, why not eighty or eight hundred? I felt ancient*

and old and full of Time. Nowadays, of course,
I cannot find the wording to state clearly what
I mean. I remember it quite exactly, nevertheless.

Most of us remember lying on our backs as children, looking up at the stars and wondering how far the universe extended (I remember having to stop myself from doing this several times when it got too intense to think about). We may have had special experiences in nature that caused us to think more deeply about life and its meaning. Or we may have pestered our parents, teachers, or others with big questions about life, death, and the reason for it all. The following checklist may help you look back to the development of your own existential intelligence in childhood and adolescence:

_____ I used to think a lot about life and death as a child or adolescent.

_____ I got into serious discussions with my parents, religious authorities, or others as a child or adolescent about religious, spiritual, or philosophical issues.

_____ I had special experiences in nature that lifted me out of the everyday concerns of life and into a deeper perspective about the universe.

_____ I used to spend time by myself thinking about the meaning of life, existence, God, death, or other existential themes.

_____ I had dreams as a child that had to do with the nature of existence, the purpose of life, the meaning of our time on this planet, or other similarly cosmic issues.

_____ I had a brush with death as a child or adolescent that caused me to look at life in a totally different way.

_____ I felt different from my peers as a child or adolescent because of my preoccupation with existential questions.

_____ I used to read a lot as an adolescent in philosophy, religion, and/or the cosmic dimensions of science.

_____ I had special psychic, mystical, spiritual, or other nonordinary experiences as a child that I couldn't really explain to anyone around me.

The fact of the matter is, many kids who had existential experiences were not able to share them with the adults around them, adults who were too busy with their mundane lives to be able to care much or truly understand. As a result, many kids simply forgot about these experiences, or repressed them (one psychologist refers to the "repression of the sublime"). On the other hand, you may have found mentors in your growing-up years— sensitive parents, pastors, rabbis, imams, priests, gurus, or nonreligious but highly philosophical or "wise" individuals—who understood what you were going through and provided a context within which you were able to continue to pursue your understanding of these big life questions. Or, perhaps you lost sight of these concerns as you grew up, but came back to them in adulthood as a result of a significant life change (accident, death in the family, job loss), or had children that you wished to guide, or simply opened up in a spontaneous way to deep experiences that brought these existential issues back to center stage in your thoughts. Here are some statements to consider in evaluating the nature of your current awareness with respect to existential themes in your life:

_____ I find meaning in regularly attending some form of worship or study in a church, synagogue, mosque, temple, or other religious or philosophical organization.

_____ I spend time regularly meditating or reflecting upon the questions of life and death.

_____ I read materials (sacred texts, books on spirituality or philosophy) that help me think or reflect about existence in a more profound way.

_____ I enjoy getting into philosophical or religious discussions with people.

_____ I think more about the meaning of life than most of the people around me.

_____ I find myself expressing my feelings and ideas about spiritual, philosophical, or existential themes through writing, artwork, research, service, or some other means of creative work.

_____ I take time out regularly to go to a place of retreat to reflect upon the meaning of life, God, and/or other big life questions.

_____ I have had special spiritual or philosophical experiences as an adult that have caused me to think about life in a deeper way.

_____ I am attracted to movies, plays, or other performances that have spiritual, philosophical, or existential themes.

_____ I am, or have thought about being, involved in a career that allows me to focus on existential issues with other people.

Every society has created formal roles for individuals that help to guide the existential concerns of the entire community. These include the formal or orthodox leaders of religious institutions: ministers, pastors, priests, bishops, imams, rabbis, gurus, and lamas. Within the academic community, existential issues are explored in a more intellectual way through the work of theologians, philosophers, religious studies professors, and the like. There are also roles in some societies that are informally assigned to people who show a particular aptitude for experiencing the deep questions of life, including shamans, yogis,

· sheiks, medicine men, and healers. However, as Dr. Gardner has pointed out, existential intelligence can be brought into many roles in society that seem to be more associated with other intelligences, including writer, artist, and scientist. Perhaps existential intelligence is more integral than other intelligences in its ability to interpenetrate virtually any vocation or aspect of life. Because it's not as easily analyzed into specific "skills" or discrete components as other intelligences, it's also more difficult to enumerate exactly what one must do to develop it. Life often brings unexpected events which serve to stimulate the existential dimensions within us. However, there may be certain things that we can do to help create a context or prepare a favorable environment for existential awareness, so that when life creates challenges for us, we can make the best use of them. Here are a few suggestions:

◆ Engage in some type of prayer, meditation, reflection, self-study, or inward discipline that creates a space within which existential themes can be encountered and explored.

◆ Attend some form of worship, study, group reflection, or community service that takes place within a religious, philosophical, or otherwise existential context.

◆ Read sacred books that evoke existential thoughts, feelings, or moods (e.g., the Hebrew or Christian Bible, Koran, Bhagavad Gita, Dhammapada, Analects of Confucius, Tao Te Ching) or philosophical books that explore the meaning of life (e.g., Viktor Frankl's *Man's Search for Meaning,* Spinoza's *Ethics*).

◆ Watch films that have big life questions as their major themes (e.g., *Resurrection, The Ten Com-*

mandments, Meetings with Remarkable Men, Schindler's List).

◆ Keep a journal that records your thoughts about philosophical, religious, aesthetic, or other existential questions or ideas.

◆ Form a discussion group with others to read, study and/or discuss the big questions of life.

◆ Listen to music that creates a mood for exploring existential themes (e.g., Vaughn Williams' *Fantasia on a Theme by Thomas Tallis,* Bach's *B Minor Mass,* Beethoven's *Ninth Symphony,* chants from any religious tradition, contemporary gospel, New Age music).

◆ Attend lectures, sermons, talks, performances, or other events involving notable individuals who have devoted a significant amount of time to the exploration of existential issues (e.g., Dalai Lama, Billy Graham, Elie Wiesel).

◆ Take courses at a local college or community center in religion and philosophy, or courses in literature, art, history, and other subjects that are taught from a spiritual or philosophical perspective.

◆ Create a space in your home, out in nature, or elsewhere that can serve as a "launch-pad to infinity" to use Ram Dass's phrase, or a centering ground for the development of existential intelligence.

Just as it's hard to specify exactly what to do to develop existential intelligence, it's hard to tell how far you've developed over time. As pointed out above, development of existential intelligence isn't necessarily about moving along some cosmic continuum toward an "absolute truth." Certainly, different spiritual and religious groups and systems have developed their own often highly detailed pathways to enlightenment, grace, paradise, salvation, or truth. However, in the absence of any universally agreed-upon definition of reality, the path of existential intelligence is an uncertain one, and one best navigated by each person in accordance with her own deepest intuitions about the mysteries of life.

WILL THERE BE MORE
INTELLIGENCES?

The addition by Howard Gardner of an eighth and possibly ninth intelligence to the theory of multiple intelligences raises some potentially troubling questions. Here's one from a hypothetical disgruntled critic of the model: "If Dr. Gardner is so smart, how come he can't figure out how many intelligences there are?" To fully answer that query, however, I first need to describe how Gardner came up with the first seven. Only then will it become apparent why he's decided to add to his original list. In his book *Frames of Mind* Dr. Gardner describes a set of eight criteria that he used to come up with his first seven intelligences. At the start he actually considered scores, and perhaps hundreds, of potential candidate intelligences (there are, in fact, theories in psychology that refer to the existence of over a hundred intelligences). But the seven that formed the basis for the original theory of multiple intelligences—linguistic, logical-mathematical, spatial, bodily-kinesthetic, musical, interpersonal, and intrapersonal—were the only candidates that met all eight of his criteria. Since the publication of *Frames of Mind* in 1983, he has concluded that the naturalist, and possibly the existential, also meet the same criteria.

In order to understand why the original seven were selected, why two more were added, and whether there will be additional intelligences in the future, we need to take a detailed look at the eight criteria used to establish the theoretical foundations for the multiple intelligences.

Potential isolation by brain damage. Dr. Gardner has worked as a neuropsychologist at the VA Hospital in Boston for some years, and through his experiences there and as an adjunct research professor of neurology at Boston University School of Medicine he came to understand that brain injuries or illness were oftentimes selective with respect to intelligences. That is, an individual could have a lesion in one area of the brain which might devastate a particular intelligence while leaving other cognitive faculties alone. In his book *The Shattered Mind,* he writes about the French composer Maurice Ravel, who in his seventies had a stroke which affected Broca's area—an area of the frontal lobe in the left hemisphere that is important for certain linguistic functions. This stroke devastated his ability to speak and write. In spite of this damage, however, he was still able to perform and critique music—abilities that were in other areas of the brain untouched by the ravages of his stroke. By putting together case histories like these from the literature with his own experiences as a neuropsychologist and his review of recent brain research, he was able to suggest that all of the original seven candidates met his first criteria. In other words, brain damage to specific areas of the brain had the potential to devastate particular intelligences while leaving the others alone. Here is a rough summary of specific areas of the brain that seem to be related to each intelligence (these indicate the most important structures involved but do not include minor structures or interactions with other areas of the brain):

Linguistic:	left temporal and frontal lobes (e.g., Broca's/Wernicke's areas)
Logical-Mathematical:	left parietal lobes (and the temporal and occipital association areas contiguous to them)
Spatial:	Posterior regions of the right hemisphere
Bodily-Kinesthetic:	Cerebellum, basal ganglia, motor cortex
Musical:	right temporal lobe
Interpersonal:	frontal lobes, temporal lobe (especially right hemisphere), limbic system
Intrapersonal:	frontal lobes, parietal lobes, limbic system

In determining that the naturalist qualifies under this criterion, Dr. Gardner points to examples in the literature of brain damage (in the left hemisphere) where individuals lose the ability to name instances of living things but retain the capacity to name non-living things, and to studies of face and paw recognition (which up to now had been considered part of spatial intelligence). Regarding existential intelligence, Dr. Gardner has indicated that the reason he has not definitely included this in his theory as a ninth intelligence is because of the yet unclear association of this intelligence to the brain. He does suggest some evidence in this direction by citing individuals who experience temporal-lobe epilepsy, which has among its symptoms hyperreligiosity and, in its incipient stages, even the experience of mystical rapture. Biographers have speculated that Fyodor Dostoevsky and Vincent van Gogh may have had temporal-lobe epilepsy and infused their work with spiritual elements that were derived from their disorder. There *are* some problems in asserting that religious feeling, mystical experiences, cosmic awareness, and other transpersonal moods stem from the brain. This type of bio-reductionism, all too common these days, diminishes the finest feelings of humanity to the firing of neurons and the crackling of synapses. Yet certainly one may conclude that the brain is a *conduit* for existential concerns without necessarily suggesting that it *causes* spiritual life or existential musings. In any case, Gardner's linking of humanity's existential strivings with the rich diversity of the brain is compelling and should stimulate discussion, especially as new findings in brain research emerge.

The existence of idiots savants, prodigies, and other exceptional individuals. Dr. Gardner suggests with this criterion that it is possible to study an intelligence in isolation by examining the lives of exceptional individuals who have developed an individual intelligence to a high level of accomplishment. We see this most commonly in the lives of any highly accomplished individual in a specific field, in the violin virtuoso, math whiz, talented writer, and so forth. But the most dramatic instances of this criterion are the savants—individuals who excel in one particular intelligence but who generally have significant difficulties with the others. Most people are familiar with the movie *Rain Man,* the Oscar–winning film about a man named Raymond (played by Dustin Hoffman and based on a true story) identified as autistic who had a phenomenal ability to calculate numbers despite having poor social skills, undeveloped language ability, and a diminished sense of self. In Raymond's case, logical-mathematical intelligence was highly developed even though his interpersonal, intrapersonal, and linguistic intelligences were severely underdeveloped. Dr. Gardner suggests that by studying people like Raymond, we can see that intelligences do exist autonomously from each other, how one specific intelligence can develop to an extraordinary level, while the other intelligences are left far behind. What follows are examples of types of savants in each of the intelligences:

Linguistic:

hyperlexics (e.g., low-IQ individuals who can read encyclopedias but without comprehension)

Logical-Mathematical:

mental calculators (e.g., low-IQ individuals who can memorize train tables, or tell what day of week your birthday will fall in the year 3500)

Spatial:

autistic individuals who have tremendous drawing ability (e.g., the book *Nadia* by Lorna Selfe chronicles the gifted artistic abilities of a five-year-old girl labeled autistic)

Bodily-Kinesthetic:

autistic individuals who can physically mimic objects (e.g., Joey, the "mechanical boy" studied by Bruno Bettelheim, who could pantomime being a machine with remarkable ability)

Musical:

certain individuals with Williams syndrome who have strong musical capacities (e.g., Gloria Lenhoff can sing opera in 26 different languages including Chinése, but has difficulty doing simple math)

Interpersonal: some individuals described as schizophrenic have an uncanny ability to pick up on nonverbal social cues, and may even possess a kind of extrasensory capacity of knowing when others are about to visit

Intrapersonal: individuals who have a highly developed sense of self but no way to communicate it to others (Gardner points out that, by definition, this type would be extremely difficult to identify)

With respect to the naturalist intelligence, one thinks of individuals like the Wild Boy of Aveyron, an eleven-year-old who was found naked and running wild in the woods in the south of France, and who had no socialization until he was found by a French doctor, Jean Marc Gaspard. Perhaps also Tempil Grandin, the autistic individual studied by Oliver Sacks who developed technologies for cattle management, represents a kind of naturalist savant. For existential intelligencé I am reminded of a book I read almost thirty years ago called *The Wayfarers: Meher Baba with the God-Intoxicated* by William Donkin (out of print), which spoke of individuals in India called "masts" who appeared outwardly to have severe mental disturbances, but who were regarded by the locals as being holy men ("God Intoxicated"), individuals who had essentially gone off on a spiritual quest and left their bodies and egos behind untended (they were frequently fed and cared for by the villagers or townspeople, sometimes in the hopes of getting a hot gambling tip!).

An identifiable core operation or set of operations. Dr. Gardner's background as a leading cognitive psychologist with an interest in how the mind processes information led him to stipulate that each of the intelligences in his theory should have specific mechanisms (core operations) for taking in information from the outer world and processing it or operating upon it, just as a computer operates upon an incoming set of data. The following are some of the critical core operations that Dr. Gardner identified for each intelligence.

Linguistic:	sensitivity to the sounds, structure, meanings, and functions of words and language
Logical-Mathematical:	sensitivity to, and capacity to discern, logical or numerical patterns; ability to handle long chains of reasoning
Spatial:	capacity to perceive the visual-spatial world accurately and to perform transformations on one's initial perceptions (i.e., to be able to manipulate the inner and outer visual-spatial worlds through art, visualization, and/or visual thinking)
Bodily-Kinesthetic:	ability to control one's body movements and to handle objects skillfully

Musical:	ability to produce and appreciate rhythm, pitch, and timbre; appreciation of the forms of musical expressiveness
Interpersonal:	capacity to discern and respond appropriately to the moods, temperaments, motivations, and desires of other people
Intrapersonal:	access to one's emotional life and the ability to discriminate among emotions; knowledge of one's own strengths and weaknesses
Naturalist:	the ability to recognize instances as members of a group (or species), to distinguish among members of species, to recognize the existence of other neighboring species, and to chart the relations, formally or informally, among the several species.
Existential:	the capacity to locate oneself with respect to the furthest reaches of the cosmos, and with respect to the significance of life, the meaning of death, the fate of the physical and psychological worlds, and such profound experiences as love or art

A distinctive developmental history, along with a definable set of expert "end-state" performances. Dr. Gardner made significant contributions to the field of developmental psychology (interestingly, the noted developmental psychoanalyst Erik Erikson was his freshman tutor at Harvard). He wrote a textbook on developmental psychology and pioneered important work in the development of young children's art and creativity. Stimulated by this background, Gardner sought to integrate developmental concepts into the theory of multiple intelligences by specifying that roles within each intelligence should have their own patterns of development, ranging from novice to expert. In the area of linguistic intelligence, for example, a very young child begins by babbling in front of a book or scribbling on a sheet of paper, and proceeds through specific stages of development until potentially reaching the high end-state of an accomplished writer. The following suggests some starting and ending places for each intelligence:

Linguistic:	from a toddler's pretend writing on a sheet of paper to Toni Morrison's *Beloved*
Logical-Mathematical:	from an infant's experimenting with making a mobile move in her crib to Einstein's theory of relativity
Spatial:	from a young child scrawling simple circular forms on a tablet to Leonardo da Vinci's *Mona Lisa*
Bodily-Kinesthetic:	from a child's first eye-hand coordination experiences to Mark McGwire's 1998 70 home run performance
Musical:	from a toddler's rhythmic banging on pots and pans to Bach's *Brandenburg Concertos*
Interpersonal:	from a baby's first eye contact with a stranger to Mother Theresa's work with the dying in Calcutta

Intrapersonal: from a young child's first awareness of himself as a separate person to Sigmund Freud's development of psychoanalysis

Naturalist: from the excitement of a young child's first encounter with a butterfly or raccoon to Charles Darwin's theory of evolution

Existential: from a child's first questions about what happens when we die to the Buddha's enlightenment under the bodhi tree and his subsequent teachings

Keep in mind that between the elementary beginnings and the end-states, one might be able to specify specific universal stages that all must go through (such as those indicated, for example, by Jean Piaget for logical-mathematical intelligence and Erik Erikson for intrapersonal intelligence), but that also there is room for tremendous individual variations, as some travelers reach dead ends, others go through periods of stagnation, while still others move into "explosions" of creativity or make steady incremental progress.

An evolutionary history. This intriguing criterion extends the idea of intelligences into the distant past, even before recorded history. Gardner suggests that in order for an intelligence to appear on the list, there must be evidence for it in the prehistoric life of humanity, and even in earlier stages of evolution, that is, in other species. He suggests that the intelligences extend back before civilization, sending their roots into the very core of living systems. Here are some indications of how each intelligence meets this criterion:

Linguistic:

early humanity: evidence of written notations have been found dating to 30,000 years ago; *other species:* apes have a rudimentary ability to name things.

Logical-Mathematical:

early humanity: number systems and calendars have been found in prehistoric settings; *other species:* bees calculate distances through their dancing behaviors.

Spatial:

early humanity: the well-known cave drawings in France and Spain; *other species:* territorial instinct of many species of mammals.

Bodily-Kinesthetic:

early humanity: evidence of prehistoric tool use (hands-on intelligence); *other species:* simple tool use discovered in primates, anteaters, and other species.

Musical:

early humanity: evidence of musical instruments extending back to the Stone Age; *other species:* bird song.

Interpersonal:

early humanity: evidence of early communal living groups; *other species:* maternal bonding observed in primates and other species.

Intrapersonal:

early humanity: self-consciousness evidenced in cave drawings, hunting skills (requiring planning, postponing of instinctual drives); *other species:* chimpanzees can locate themselves in a mirror, and express and symbolize basic feelings.

Naturalist: *early humanity:* the ability to identify poisonous and nonpoisonous plants, locate and avoid certain types of animals as sources of food, and in many other ways discriminate among different kinds of fauna and flora as a means of survival; *other species:* intricate systems for preying on their neighbors and avoiding becoming prey.

Existential: *early humanity:* evidence of prehistorical religious ceremonies such as those involved in burial or in hunting rituals (some early cave paintings show individuals who appear to be shamanic leaders using magic as a way of ensuring a good hunt); *other species:* elephants and other species appear to show certain types of ritualistic behaviors (and even evidence of grieving) after the death of one of their members.

Support from experimental psychological tasks. Gardner suggests that the intelligences can be distinguished through specific psychological experiments, including those having to do with memory, attention, perception, and transfer (or lack of transfer) in learning. For example, experiments might indicate that an individual has a great memory for faces but not for numbers or words, or that he pays particular attention to verbal stimuli but not to nonverbal (e.g., musical) stimuli. Further, some tasks might show that an individual's ability to learn mathematical concepts does not necessarily make her a better reader (e.g., logical-mathematical intelligence does not transfer to linguistic intelligence) or that her tennis-playing ability doesn't transfer to making her a better painter. Gardner's writings have devoted far less attention to this criterion, and there appears to be less clarity here than with the others. There does seem to be good evidence to support this criterion for at least some of the intelligences (or certain aspects of them). For example, gender research indicates that boys pay better attention to nonverbal stimuli, while girls show advantages with verbal cues. In the field of attention-deficit disorder, there is some evidence that children labeled ADD or ADHD show particular attention deficits in the logical-mathematical or linguistic areas but not necessarily in the bodily-kinesthetic or spatial areas. However, other evidence seems to contradict this criterion, including recent research suggesting that as young children learn music, their logical-mathematical and spatial abilities seem to improve as well. Dr. Gardner has attempted to explain this type of disparity by pointing to the *relative* autonomy of the intelligences and to the myriad interconnections that exist between each of the intelligences. It remains to be seen, though, whether or not this criterion will prove to be as solid an indicator of the theory of multiple intelligences as the others have been.

Support from psychometric findings. Dr. Gardner has been a severe critic of intelligence or IQ testing, yet in this area he ironically suggests that standardized measurements such as the IQ score can be used as a support for the existence of the intelligences. There does appear to be some support for the theory in the drastically different sub-test results that certain individuals receive on IQ and other standardized measures. For example, a person may show a high score on IQ sub-tests having to do with words (e.g., vocabulary), but a low score on those relating to numbers (e.g., arithmetic) or pictures and images (e.g., picture arrangement, object assembly). Anyone who has ever received widely disparate SAT scores on their math and verbal tests (I had a 100-point difference between the two myself) could argue persuasively for the relative autonomy of linguistic and logical-mathematical intelligences. One of the difficulties with this criterion, though, is the relative lack of tests in the neglected intelligences, especially bodily-kinesthetic, musical, and the personal intelligences. Furthermore, it's difficult to envision exactly what a standardized test for the existential intelligence might consist of. An item that might seem reasonable on such a test, such as "How often do you think about death?" could be used just as validly on a test for depression to indicate difficulty with intrapersonal intelligence. On the other hand, it seems possible to construct a test that involves discrimination of natural phenomena, just as there are tests for telling the difference between different types of three-dimensional objects (and there is some experimental support for the fact that an individual can be good at discriminating among living phenomena but poor at doing the same sort of thing with nonliving stimuli).

Susceptibility to encoding in a symbol system. The final criterion in Gardner's model opens up an astonishing perspective on human communication. He suggests that if you want to determine whether a person is intelligent or not, you should study how she *symbolizes*. The ability to symbolize, after all, is the key faculty that separates human beings from most of the other animals further down in the food chain! To be able to express a thought about something that is not immediately present to the senses (to bring back to the present or "re-present" something) through a sound, a gesture, or a mark on a piece of paper (like these that you're reading right now) is truly an extraordinary accomplishment when you really think about it. Through symbols we have a way of entering into the thoughts of people who were alive two thousand or more years ago. Dr. Gardner says that in order for an intelligence to qualify for his theory, it must be capable of being symbolized. A look at the different intelligences shows the wide variety of languages in which humanity has chosen to symbolize its internal world to others:

Linguistic:	written and spoken languages (e.g., English, Spanish, French, German, Italian, Russian, Greek, etc.)
Logical-Mathematical:	number systems, computer languages (e.g., Pascal, Basic, C++)
Spatial:	ideographic languages (e.g., picture aspects of Chinese, Japanese, hieroglyphics, etc., which also have phonetic components); line, form, shape, and color in art
Bodily-Kinesthetic:	languages of dance, movement, sports (e.g., baseball managers' hand signals)
Musical:	musical notations of different kinds
Interpersonal:	gestures, facial expressions, body postures, voice inflections, etc., that signify social cues (e.g., "I like you," "Back off!" "I'm impatient!")
Intrapersonal:	dream symbols indicating aspects of the self
Naturalist:	the totems of indigenous cultures which feature animal spirits to the sophisticated taxonomies of Aristotle and Linnaeus

Existential: the rich and diverse collections of
                        religious symbols (from cross and
                        crescent to star and serpent); the
                        compelling myths of world cul-
                        tures; the highly articulated sym-
                        bologies of mystics like Blake and
                        Swedenborg

Having reviewed the eight criteria used to support
the existence of multiple intelligences, we're now in a
much better position to determine whether or not any
more intelligences will be added to the model in the future. Thus far, many different types of additional intelligences have been suggested to Dr. Gardner, myself, and
others working in the MI field, including the following:
humor, creativity, cooking, spirituality, morality, sexuality,
intuition, olfactory capacities (sense of smell), extrasen
sory perception, memory, wisdom, mechanical ability,
common sense, and street smarts. If you feel that one of
these candidates deserves to be included in a theory of
multiple intelligences, or you have other candidates that
you believe qualify as intelligences, my advice would be
to go through each of the eight criteria discussed above,
and determine if it meets every one of them. For example,
if you feel humor deserves to be listed as an intelligence,
then attempt to discover if humor can be selectively impaired through brain damage, if it has unique ways of
being symbolized, if the role of the humorist, for example,
goes through specific developmental stages from novice
to expert, if there is evidence for it in early humanity and
other species, and so forth. In this way, it may be possible
to build a case for 10 kinds of smart, or 15 or 30 or more!

It is a testament to Howard Gardner's generous and
open spirit of inquiry that he has left room for the potential future expansion of his theory.

RESOURCES FOR DEVELOPING THE INTELLIGENCES

◆ BOOKS ──────────────────────

◆ LINGUISTIC INTELLIGENCE ──────────────

ADLER, MORTIMER JEROME. *How to Speak, How to Listen*. Collier Books, 1997.

────. *How to Read a Book*. Simon & Schuster, 1972.

APPELBAUM, JUDITH. *How to Get Happily Published*. 5th ed. HarperCollins, 1998.

AUGARDE, TONY. *The Oxford A to Z of Word Games*. Oxford Univ. Press, 1996.

BETTMANN, OTTO L. *The Delights of Reading: Quotes, Notes & Anecdotes*. Godine, 1993.

BURLEY-ALLEN, MADELYN. *Listening—The Forgotten Skill*. 2nd ed. Wiley, 1995.

────. *Managing Assertively: How to Improve Your People Skills*. 2nd ed. Wiley, 1995.

CASSELL, DANA, ed. *Writers at Work*. CNW Publishing, 1990.

The Chicago Manual of Style. 14th ed. Univ. of Chicago Press, 1993.

COLLINS, CHASE. *Tell Me a Story: Creating Bedtime Stories Your Children Will Dream On.* Houghton Mifflin, 1992.

COOPER, DONA. *American Film Institute's Guide to Writing Great Screenplays for Film and TV.* 2nd ed. Arco, 1997.

DILLARD, ANNIE. *The Writing Life.* HarperCollins, 1990.

ELBOW, PETER. *Writing Without Teachers.* 2nd ed. Oxford Univ. Press, 1998.

FADIMAN, CLIFTON. *The New Lifetime Reading Plan.* Harper-Collins, 1997.

FUNK, WILFRED. *30 Days to a More Powerful Vocabulary.* Pocket Books, 1993.

GALE, HAROLD. *Word Puzzles for Language Geniuses.* Times Books, 1993.

GLASS, LILLIAN. *Talk to Win: Six Steps to a Successful Vocal Image.* Perigee, 1988.

GOLDBERG, NATALIE. *Writing Down the Bones: Freeing the Writer Within.* Shambhala, 1986.

GORDON, KAREN ELIZABETH. *The New Well-Tempered Sentence: A Punctuation Handbook for the Innocent, the Eager, and the Doomed.* Ticknor & Fields, 1993.

KLAUSER, HENRIETTE ANNE. *Writing on Both Sides of the Brain: Breakthrough Techniques for People Who Write.* Harper San Francisco, 1987.

LEWIS, NORMAN. *Word Power Made Easy.* Pocket Books, 1995.

MOORE, ROBIN. *Awakening the Hidden Storyteller.* Shambhala, 1998, audiocassette.

NELL, VICTOR. *Lost in a Book: The Psychology of Reading for Pleasure.* Yale Univ. Press, 1988.

Poet's Market: 1,800 Places to Publish Your Poetry. Writers Digest Books, updated annually.

POYNTER, DAN. *The Self-Publishing Manual: How to Write, Print and Sell Your Own Book.* Para Publishing, 1997.

PRUES, DON, and CHANTELLE BENTLEY, eds. *Guide to Literary Agents: 500 Agents Who Sell What You Write.* Writers Digest Books, 1998.

QUINDLEN, ANNA. *How Reading Changed My Life.* Ballantine, 1998.

RAFFEL, BURTON. *How to Read a Poem.* New American Library, 1984.

RICO, GABRIELE LUSSER. *Writing the Natural Way: Using Right Brain Techniques to Release Your Expressive Powers.* Tarcher, 1983.

SEYMOUR-SMITH, MARTIN. *The 100 Most Influential Books Ever Written: The History of Thought from Ancient Times to Today.* Citadel, 1998.

STILLMAN, PETER. *Families Writing.* 2nd ed. Butterworth-Heinemann, 1998.

STONE, RICHARD. *The Healing Art of Storytelling: A Sacred Journey of Personal Discovery.* Hyperion, 1996.

STRUNK, WILLIAM, and E.B. WHITE. *Elements of Style.* 3rd ed. Allyn and Bacon, 1995.

THOMPSON, DOROTHEA. *Becoming a Writer.* Tarcher, 1981.

WALDHORN, ARTHUR. *Good Reading: A Guide for Serious Readers.* 23rd ed. Bowker, 1990.

WOHLMUTH, ED. *The Overnight Guide to Public Speaking.* Signet, 1993.

Writer's Encyclopedia. 3rd ed. Writers Digest Books, 1996.

Writer's Market: Where & How to Sell What You Write. Writers Digest Books, updated annually.

ZINSSER, WILLIAM KNOWLTON. *On Writing Well: The Informal Guide to Writing Nonfiction.* 6th ed. HarperCollins, 1998.

◆ LOGICAL-MATHEMATICAL INTELLIGENCE ──────────────

BRECHER, ERWIN. *The Ultimate Book of Puzzles, Mathematical Diversions, and Brainteasers*. St. Martin's Press, 1996.

BURNS, MARILYN. *I Hate Mathematics! Book*. Little, Brown, 1976.

DAVIS, PHILIP J. *The Mathematical Experience*. Mariner Books, 1999.

DEVLIN, KEITH J. *Life by the Numbers*. Wiley, 1998.

DEWDNEY, A.K. *200% of Nothing: An Eye-Opening Tour Through the Twists and Turns of Math Abuse and Innumeracy*. Wiley, 1996.

FLANSBURG, SCOTT. *Math Magic*. HarperPerennial, 1994.

FREEMAN, IRA M. *Physics Made Simple*. Doubleday, 1990.

GARDNER, MARTIN. *Entertaining Mathematical Puzzles*. Dover, 1986.

GULBERG, JAN, and PETER HILTON. *Mathematics: From the Birth of Numbers*. Norton, 1997.

HAMILTON, BEN. *Brainteasers and Mindbenders*. Fireside, 1997.

HAZEN, ROBERT M. *Science Matters: Achieving Scientific Literacy*. Anchor, 1991.

HEWITT, PAUL G. *Conceptual Physics*. Addison-Wesley, 1997.

HILTON, PETER. *Fear No More*. Addison-Wesley, 1983.

HOGBEN, LANCELOT. *Mathematics for the Million/How to Master the Magic of Numbers*. Norton, 1993.

HUFF, DARRELL. *How to Lie With Statistics*. Norton, 1993.

JACOBS, HAROLD R. *Mathematics: A Human Endeavor: A Book for Those Who Think They Don't Like the Subject*. 3rd ed. W. H. Freeman, 1994.

KLINE, MORRIS. *Mathematics for the Nonmathematician*. Dover, 1985.

KOGELMAN, STANLEY. *Mind over Math*. McGraw-Hill, 1979.

KUHN, THOMAS S. *The Structure of Scientific Revolutions*. 3rd ed. Univ. of Chicago Press, 1996.

LEIGHTON, RALPH. *'What Do You Care What Other People Thnk?': Further Adventures of a Curious Character*. Bantam Doubleday Dell, 1992.

LIEBERTHAL, EDWIN M. *The Complete Book of Fingermath*. Fingermath Intl., 1983.

MASCETTA, JOSEPH A. *Chemistry the Easy Way*. 3rd ed. Barrons, 1996.

PAULOS, JOHN ALLEN. *Innumeracy: Mathematical Illiteracy and Its Consequences*. Vintage, 1990.

PETERSON, IVARS. *Mathematical Tourist: New and Updated Snapshots of Modern Mathematics*. W. H. Freeman, 1998.

POLYA, GEORGE. *How to Solve It: A New Aspect of Mathematical Method*. Princeton Univ. Press, 1988.

ROTHSTEIN, ERICA, and STACEY E. FEINMAN. *The Dell Book of Classic Logic Problems*. Dell, 1994.

RUCKER, RUDY. *Mind Tools: The Five Levels of Mathematical Reality*. Houghton Mifflin, 1988.

STEWART, IAN. *The Magical Maze: Seeing the World Through Mathematical Eyes*. Wiley, 1998.

TOBIAS, SHEILA. *Overcoming Math Anxiety*. Rev. ed. Norton, 1995.

TREFIL, JAMES. *The Edge of the Unknown: 101 Things You Don't Know about Science and No One Else Does Either*. Houghton Mifflin, 1996.

ULAM, S.M. *Adventures of a Mathematician*. Univ. of California Press, 1991.

WELLS, D.G. *You Are a Mathematician: A Wise and Witty Introduction to the Joy of Numbers*. Wiley, 1997.

ZASLAVSKY, CLAUDIA. *Fear of Math: How to Get Over It and Get on With Your Life*. Rutgers Univ. Press, 1994.

◆ SPATIAL INTELLIGENCE ─────────────────────────

ACTON, MARY. *Learning to Look at Paintings*. Routledge, 1997.

ARNHEIM, RUDOLF. *Visual Thinking*. Univ. of California Press, 1989.

Artist's & Graphic Designer's Market. Writers Digest Books, updated annually.

BERESFORD, STEVEN M. *Improve Your Vision Without Glasses or Contact Lenses: A New Program of Therapeutic Eye Exercises*. Fireside, 1996.

BUZAN, TONY. *The Mind Map Book: How to Use Radiant Thinking to Maximize Your Brain's Untapped Potential*. Plume, 1996.

DEMILLE, RICHARD. *Put Your Mother on the Ceiling: Children's Imagination Games*. Viking, 1994.

DONDIS, DONIS A., and PETER A. DONDIS. *A Primer of Visual Literacy*. MIT Press, 1973.

EASTMAN KODAK. *How to Take Good Pictures*. Rev. ed. Ballantine, 1995.

EDWARDS, BETTY. *Drawing on the Right Side of the Brain: A Course in Enhancing Creativity and Artistic Confidence*. Tarcher, 1989.

———. *Drawing on the Artist Within: An Inspirational and Practical Guide to Increasing Your Creative Powers*. Fireside, 1987.

FIELD, JOANNA. *On Not Being Able to Paint*. Tarcher, 1983.

FINN, DAVID. *How to Look at Sculpture*. Abrams, 1989.

———. *How to Visit a Museum*. Abrams, 1985.

FRANCK, FREDERICK. *The Zen of Seeing: Seeing Drawing As Meditation*. Random House, 1973.

GALLAGHER, WINIFRED. *The Power of Place: How Our Surroundings Shape Our Thoughts, Emotions, and Actions*. HarperPerennial, 1994.

GAWAIN, SHAKTI. *Creative Visualization*. Bantam, 1983.

GELB, MICHAEL. *How to Think Like Leonardo da Vinci*. Delacorte, 1998.

GOODRICH, JANET. *Natural Vision Improvement*. Ten Speed Press, 1998.

GREGORY, RICHARD L. *Eye and Brain: The Psychology of Seeing*. 5th ed. Princeton Univ. Press, 1997.

HALL, EDWARD TWITCHELL. *The Hidden Dimension*. Anchor, 1990.

HANKS, KURT. *Draw!: A Visual Approach to Thinking, Learning, and Communicating*. Crisp Publications, 1990.

HEDGECOE, JOHN. *The Photographer's Handbook*. 3rd ed. Knopf, 1992.

HOFFMAN, DONALD DAVID. *Visual Intelligence: How We Create What We See*. Norton, 1998.

HURD, THATCHER, and JOHN CASSIDY. *Watercolor for the Artistically Undiscovered*. Klutz Press, 1992.

LONDON, PETER. *No More Secondhand Art: Awakening the Artist Within*. Shambhala, 1989.

LURIA, ALEXANDER. *The Mind of a Mnemonist: A Little Book about a Vast Memory*. Harvard Univ. Press, 1988.

MARGULIES, NANCY. *Mapping Inner Space: Learning and Teaching Mind Mapping*. Zephyr, 1991.

MAYER, RALPH. *The Artist's Handbook of Materials and Techniques*. 5th rev. ed. Viking, 1991.

MCKIM, ROBERT H. *Experiences in Visual Thinking*. 2nd ed. Brooks/Cole, 1980.

MONACO, JAMES. *How to Read a Film: The World of Movies, Media, and Multimedia Art, Technology, Language, History, Theory*. 3rd ed. Oxford Univ. Press, 1998.

NICOLAIDES, KIM. *The Natural Way to Draw: A Working Plan for Art Study*. Houghton Mifflin, 1990.

Photographer's Market: 2,000 Places to Sell Your Photographs. Writers Digest Books, updated annually.

SAMPLES, BOB. *The Metaphoric Mind: A Celebration of Creative Consciousness.* 2nd ed. Jalmar Press, 1993.

SHEPARD, ROGER N. *Mind Sights: Original Visual Illusions, Ambiguities, and Other Anomalies, with a Commentary on the Play of Mind in Perception and Art.* W.H. Freeman, 1990.

SIMON, SEYMOUR, and CONSTANCE FTERA. *The Optical Illusion Book.* W.H. Freeman, 1984.

WARNER, SALLY. *Encouraging the Artist in Yourself (Even If It's Been a Long, Long Time).* St. Martin's Press, 1991.

WENGER, WIN. *The Einstein Factor: A Proven Method for Increasing Your Intelligence.* Prima, 1996.

◆ BODILY-KINESTHETIC INTELLIGENCE

BENZWIE, TERESA. *A Moving Experience: Dance for Lovers of Children and the Child Within.* Zephyr, 1989.

BORYSENKO, JOAN. *Minding the Body, Mending the Mind.* Bantam, Doubleday, Dell, 1993.

BRENNAN, RICHARD. *The Alexander Technique Manual: A Step-by-Step Guide to Improve Breathing, Posture, and Well-Being.* Tuttle, 1996.

CASSIDY, JOHN. *Juggling for the Complete Klutz.* 4th ed. Klutz, Press, 1994.

CHENG, MAN-CHING. *Tai Chi Chuan: A Simplified Method of Calisthenics for Health.* North Atlantic Books, 1981.

CHOPRA, DEEPAK. *Ageless Body, Timeless Mind: The Quantum Alternative to Growing Old.* Crown, 1995.

COOPER, KENNETH H. *The Aerobics Program for Total Well-Being: Exercise, Diet, Emotional Balance.* Bantam Doubleday Dell, 1985.

DOUILLARD, JOHN. *Body, Mind, and Sport: The Mind-Body Guide to Lifelong Fitness and Your Personal Best.* Crown, 1995.

DOWNING, GEORGE. *The Massage Book.* Random House, 1972.

DYCHTWALD, KEN. *Bodymind.* Tarcher, 1986.

FELDENKRAIS, MOSHE. *Awareness Through Movement: Health Exercises for Personal Growth.* Harper San Francisco, 1991.

FLETCHER, COLIN. *The Complete Walker III: The Joys and Techniques of Hiking and Backpacking.* 3rd rev. ed. Random House, 1984.

GARFIELD, CHARLES A. *Peak Performance: Mental Training Techniques of the World's Greatest Athletes.* Warner, 1989.

GELB, MICHAEL J. *Body Learning: An Introduction to the Alexander Technique.* 2nd ed. Holt, 1996.

HANNA, THOMAS. *Somatics: Reawakening the Mind's Control of Movement, Flexibility, and Health.* Perseus Press, 1988.

HELLER, JOSEPH. *Bodywise.* Wingbow Press, 1991.

HOUSTON, JEAN. *The Possible Human: A Course in Enhancing Your Physical, Mental, and Creative Abilities.* Tarcher, 1997.

IYENGAR, B.K.S. *Light on Yoga: Yoga Dipika.* Rev. ed. Schocken, 1995.

KNASTER, MIRKA. *Discovering the Body's Wisdom.* Bantam, 1996.

KUNTZLEMAN, CHARLES T. *Complete Book of Walking.* Pocket Books, 1982.

LEONARD, GEORGE. *The Ultimate Athlete: Re-Visioning Sports, Physical Education and the Body.* Rev. ed. North Atlantic Books, 1990.

LIDELL, LUCINDA. *The Book of Massage: The Complete Step-by-Step Guide to Eastern and Western Techniques.* Simon & Schuster, 1984.

LOWEN, ALEXANDER. *Language of the Body.* Macmillan General Reference, 1977.

MILLMAN, DAN. *The Inner Athlete: Realizing Your Fullest Potential.* Stillpoint, 1994.

MURPHY, MICHAEL. *The Future of the Body: Explorations into the Further Evolution of Human Nature.* Tarcher, 1993.

New Complete Do-It-Yourself Manual. Rev. ed. Readers Digest, 1996.

ORLICK, TERRY. *The Second Cooperative Sports & Games Book.* Kendall/Hunt, 1995.

PATTERSON, MARILYN NIKIMA. *Every Body Can Learn: Engaging the Bodily-Kinesthetic Intelligence in the Everyday Classroom.* Zephyr, 1996.

ROTH, GABRIELLE. *Sweat Your Prayers: Movement as Spiritual Practice.* Tarcher, 1998.

STANISLAVSKI, CONSTANTINE. *An Actor Prepares.* Theatre Arts Books, 1989.

STEVENS, JOHN. *Aikido: The Way of Harmony.* Shambhala, 1984.

VISHNUDEVANANDA, SWAMI. *The Complete Illustrated Book of Yoga.* Crown, 1995.

WHITELAW, GINNY. *Bodylearning: How the Mind Learns from the Body.* Perigee, 1998.

WEINSTEIN, MATT, and JOEL GOODMAN. *Playfair: Everybody's Guide to Noncompetitive Play.* Impact Publishers, 1983.

◆ MUSICAL INTELLIGENCE ─────────────────────────

BAMBERGER, JEAN SHAPIRO. *The Mind Behind the Musical Ear: How Children Develop Musical Intelligence.* Harvard Univ. Press, 1991.

BERNSTEIN, SEYMOUR. *With Your Own Two Hands: Self-Discovery Through Music.* Hal Leonard Publishing, 1996.

BONNEY, HELEN L. *Music & Your Mind: Listening With a New Consciousness*. 2nd ed. Talman, 1998.

BRUSER, MADELINE, and YEHUDI MENUHIN. *The Art of Practicing: A Guide to Making Music from the Heart*. Bell Tower, 1997.

CAMPBELL, DON. *The Mozart Effect: Tapping the Power of Music to Heal the Body, Strengthen the Mind, and Unlock the Creative Spirit*. Avon, 1997.

CAMPBELL, DON, ed. *Music: Physician for Times to Come*. Quest, 1991.

COPLAND, AARON. *What to Listen for in Music*. Mentor, 1989.

DELIEGE, IRENE, and JOHN A. SLOBODA, eds. *Musical Beginnings: Origins and Development of Musical Competence*. Oxford Univ. Press, 1996.

DEWHURST-MADDOCK, OLIVIA. *The Book of Sound Therapy: Heal Yourself with Music and Voice*. Fireside, 1993.

GINDICK, JOHN. *Country and Blues Harmonica for the Musically Hopeless*. Klutz Press, 1984.

GREEN, BARRY. *The Inner Game of Music*. Doubleday, 1986.

HAAS, KARL. *Inside Music: How to Understand, Listen to, and Enjoy Good Music*. Anchor, 1991.

HEMMING, ROY. *Discovering Great Music: A New Listener's Guide to the Top Classical Composers and Their Best Recordings*. Newmarket Press, 1994.

HOLT, JOHN. *Never Too Late: My Musical Life Story*. Perseus Press, 1991.

JUDY, STEPHANIE. *Making Music for the Joy of It: Enhancing Creativity Skills and Musical Confidence*. Tarcher, 1990.

KAROLYI, OTTO. *Introducing Music*. Viking, 1991.

LINGERMAN, HAL A. *The Healing Energies of Music*. 2nd ed. Quest Books, 1995.

LUBOFF, PAT. *88 Songwriting Wrongs & How to Right Them: Concrete Ways to Improve Your Songwriting and*

Make Your Songs More Marketable. Writers Digest Books, 1992.

MACHOVER, WILMA, and MARIENNE USZLER. *Sound Choices: Guiding Your Child's Musical Experiences.* Oxford Univ. Press, 1996.

MATHIEU, W.A. *The Listening Book: Discovering Your Own Music.* Shambhala, 1991.

MAY, ELIZABETH, ed. *Musics of Many Cultures.* Univ. of California Press, 1983.

MCCOMB, CAROL. *Country & Blues Guitar for the Musically Hopeless.* Klutz Press, 1986.

MERRITT, STEPHANIE. *Mind, Music & Imagery: Unlocking the Treasures of Your Mind.* Aslan, 1996.

MILES, ELIZABETH. *Tune Your Brain: Using Music to Manage Your Mind, Body, and Mood.* Berkley, 1997.

MILLER, LEON K. *Musical Savants: Exceptional Skill in the Mentally Retarded.* Lawrence Erlbaum, 1989.

NEWMAN, FREDERICK R. *Mouthsounds: How to Whistle, Pop, Click, and Honk Your Way to Social Success.* Workman, 1980.

ORTIZ, JOHN M. *The Tao of Music: Sound Psychology.* Samuel Weiser, 1997.

PASSMAN, DONALD. *All You Need to Know about the Music Business.* Simon & Schuster, 1997.

RANDEL, DON MICHAEL. *Harvard Concise Dictionary of Music.* Harvard Univ. Press, 1978.

RISTAD, ELOISE. *A Soprano in Her Head: Right-Side-Up Reflections on Life and Other Performances.* Real People Press, 1982.

SHANET, HOWARD. *Learn to Read Music.* Simon & Schuster, 1977.

Songwriter's Market. Writers Digest Books, updated annually.

SUDNOW, DAVID. *Ways of the Hand: The Organization of Improvised Conduct.* Harvard Univ. Press, 1978.

WILSON, FRANK R. *Tone Deaf and All Thumbs?: An Invitation to Music-Making.* Vintage, 1988.

◆ INTERPERSONAL INTELLIGENCE ─────────────

AXTELL, ROGER E. *Gestures: The Do's and Taboos of Body Language Around the World.* Wiley, 1998.

BALDRIGE, LETITIA. *Letitia Baldrige's Complete Guide to the New Manners for the 90's.* Scribner, 1990.

BERNSTEIN, ALBERT J. *Dinosaur Brains: Dealing With All Those Impossible People at Work.* Ballantine, 1996.

BHAERMAN, STEVE. *Friends and Lovers: How to Meet the People You Want to Meet.* Writers Digest Books, 1989.

BOLTON, ROBERT. *People Skills.* Simon & Schuster, 1986.

BRAMSON, ROBERT N. *Coping With Difficult People.* Dell, 1988.

BROOKS, MICHAEL. *Instant Rapport.* Warner, 1990.

BUBER, MARTIN. *I and Thou.* Macmillan, 1974.

CARNEGIE, DALE, *How to Win Friends and Influence People.* Pocket Books, 1994.

COHEN, HERB. *You Can Negotiate Anything.* Bantam, 1989.

COOPER, ROBERT A., and AYMAN SAWAF. *Executive EQ: Emotional Intelligence in Leadership and Organizations.* Putnam, 1997.

COVEY, STEPHEN R. *The 7 Habits of Highly Effective People: Powerful Lessons in Personal Change.* Fireside, 1990.

DIMITRIUS, JO-ELLEN, and MARK MEZZARELLA. *Reading People: How to Understand People and Predict Their Behavior Anytime, Anyplace.* Random House, 1998.

FISHER, ROGER. *Getting to Yes: Negotiating Agreement Without Giving In.* Penguin, 1991.

FROMM, ERICH. *The Art of Loving.* HarperCollins, 1989.

GILBERT, ROBERTA. *Extraordinary Relationships: A New Way*

of Thinking about Human Interactions. Chronimed, 1992.

GOFFMAN, ERVING. *The Presentation of Self in Everyday Life.* Anchor, 1959.

GORDON, THOMAS. *Leader Effectiveness Training, L.E.T.: The No-Lose Way to Release the Productive Potential of People.* Bantam Doubleday Dell, 1986.

HALL, EDWARD T. *The Silent Language.* Anchor, 1973.

HENDRICKS, GAY, and KATHLYN T. HENDRICKS. *Centering and the Art of Intimacy Handbook: A New Psychology of Close Relationships.* Fireside, 1993.

HENDRIX, HARVILLE. *Getting the Love You Want: A Guide for Couples.* HarperPerennial, 1992.

JOHNSON, ROBERT A. *We: Understanding the Psychology of Romantic Love.* Harper San Francisco, 1985.

KEMPTHORNE, CHARLES. *For All Time: A Complete Guide to Writing Your Family History.* Heinemann, 1996.

KOHN, ALFIE. *No Contest: The Case Against Competition.* Rev. ed. Houghton Mifflin, 1992.

MCGOLDRICK, MONICA. *Genograms in Family Assessment.* Norton, 1986.

MOORE, CHRISTOPHER W. *The Mediation Process: Practical Strategies for Resolving Conflict.* Jossey-Bass, 1996.

NIERENBERG, GERALD I. *How to Read a Person Like a Book.* Pocket Books, 1982.

POST, EMILY. *Emily Post's Etiquette.* 16th ed. HarperCollins, 1997.

RAM DASS. *How Can I Help: Stories and Reflections on Service.* Knopf, 1985.

SATIR, VIRGINIA M. *New Peoplemaking.* 2nd ed. Science & Behavior Books, 1988.

SMITH, MANUEL J. *When I Say No I Feel Guilty.* Bantam, 1985.

URY, WILLIAM L. *Getting Past No: Negotiating Your Way*

from Confrontation to Cooperation. Bantam, Doubleday, Dell, 1993.

WELWOOD, JOHN. *Love and Awakening: Discovering the Sacred Path of Intimate Relationship.* HarperCollins,
1997.

ZIMBARDO, PHILIP G. *Shyness: What It Is, What to Do about
It.* Perseus Press, 1990.

◆ INTRAPERSONAL INTELLIGENCE

ADAMS, KATHLEEN. *Journal to the Self: 22 Paths to Personal
Growth.* Warner, 1990.

ANTHONY, ROBERT. *The Ultimate Secrets of Total Self-Confidence.* Berkley, 1984.

BRANDEN, NATHANIEL. *Honoring the Self: The Psychology of
Confidence and Respect.* Bantam, 1985.

————. *The Six Pillars of Self-Esteem.* Bantam, 1995.

BRIGGS, DOROTHY CORKVILLE. *Celebrate Your Self: Enhancing
Your Self-Esteem.* Doubleday, 1986.

BYRD, RICHARD E. *Alone: The Classic Polar Adventure.* Ko-
dansha, 1995.

CAPACCHIONE, LUCIA. *The Creative Journal: The Art of Finding Yourself.* Newcastle, 1989.

CATFORD, LORNA, and MICHAEL RAY. *The Path of the Everyday
Hero: Drawing on the Power of Myth to Meet Life's
Most Important Challenges.* Tarcher, 1991.

FERRUCCI, PIERO. *What We May Be: Techniques for Psychological and Spiritual Growth Through Psychosynthesis.* Tarcher, 1983.

FIELD, JOANNA. *A Life of One's Own.* Tarcher, 1981.

GARFIELD, ARTHUR. *Peak Performers: The New Heroes of
American Business.* Avon, 1991.

GENDLIN, EUGENE T. *Focusing.* Bantam, 1982.

GOLDSMITH, JOEL S. *The Art of Meditation*. Harper San Francisco, 1990.

GOLEMAN, DANIEL. *Emotional Intelligence: Why It Can Matter More than IQ*. Bantam, 1997.

————. *Working with Emotional Intelligence*. Bantam, 1996.

GROSS, RONALD. *The Independent Scholar's Handbook*. Ten Speed Press, 1993.

HELMSTETTER, SHAD. *Choices*. Pocket Books, 1990.

HORNEY, KAREN. *Self-Analysis*. Norton, 1994.

JAMES, MURIEL. *Born to Win: Transactional Analysis With Gestalt Experiments*. 25th anniv. ed. Perseus Press, 1996.

JOHNSON, ROBERT A. *Inner Work: Using Dreams and Active Imagination for Personal Growth*. Harper San Francisco, 1989.

JOHNSON, SPENCER. *One Minute for Myself: How to Manage Your Most Valuable Asset*. Avon, 1987.

KATZ, MARK. *On Playing a Poor Hand Well: Insights from the Lives of Those Who Have Overcome Childhood Risks and Adversities*. Norton, 1997.

KEEL, PHILLIP. *All About Me*. Bantam, Doubleday, Dell, 1998.

KEGAN, ROBERT. *The Evolving Self*. Harvard Univ. Press, 1983.

LABERGE, STEPHEN. *Lucid Dreaming*. Ballantine, 1998.

LAKEIN, ALAN. *How to Get Control of Your Time and Your Life*. New American Library, 1996.

LEONARD, GEORGE. *Mastery: The Keys to Success and Long-Term Fullfillment*. Plume, 1992.

LEVINE, STEPHEN. *A Gradual Awakening*. Anchor, 1989.

MALLON, THOMAS. *A Book of One's Own: People and Their Diaries*. Hungry Mind, 1995.

MARSHALL, CARL. *The Book of Myself: A Do-It-Yourself Autobiography in 201 Questions*. Hyperion, 1997.

MASTERSON, JAMES F. *The Search for the Real Self: Unmasking the Personality Disorders of Our Age.* Free Press, 1990.

MILLER, ALICE. *Thou Shalt Not Be Aware.* Meridian, 1991.

NEWMAN, MILDRED. *How to Be Your Own Best Friend.* Ballantine, 1990.

OLDHAM, JOHN M. *The New Personality Self-Portrait: Why You Think, Work, Love and Act the Way You Do.* Bantam, 1995.

ORSBORN, CAROL. *The Art of Resilience: 100 Paths to Wisdom and Strength in an Uncertain World.* Crown, 1997.

PEAL, NORMAN VINCENT. *The Power of Positive Thinking.* Ballantine, 1996.

PEARSON, CAROL S. *The Hero Within: Six Archetypes We Live By.* 3rd ed. Harper San Francisco, 1998.

PROGOFF, IRA. *At a Journal Workshop: Writing to Access the Power of the Unconscious and Evoke Creative Ability (Inner Workbook).* Rev. ed. Tarcher, 1992.

————. *Life-Study: Experiencing Creative Lives by the Intensive Journal Method.* Dialogue House Library, 1988.

PROTO, LOUIS. *Be Your Own Best Friend: How to Achieve Greater Self-Esteem, Health, and Happiness.* Berkley, 1994.

RAINER, TRISTINE. *The New Diary: How to Use a Journal for Self-Guidance and Expanded Creativity.* Tarcher, 1979.

ROGERS, CARL R. *On Becoming a Person: A Therapist's View of Psychotherapy.* Houghton Mifflin, 1995.

SEGAL, JEANNE S. *Raising Your Emotional Intelligence: A Practical Guide.* Holt, 1997.

SINETAR, MARSHA. *Do What You Love, the Money Will Follow: Discovering Your Right Livelihood.* Dell, 1989.

STEINER, CLAUDE. *Achieving Emotional Literacy: A Personal Program to Increase Your Emotional Intelligence.* Avon, 1997.

STORR, ANTHONY. *Solitude: A Return to the Self.* Ballantine, 1989.

TAYLOR, DANIEL. *The Healing Power of Stories: Creating Yourself Through the Stories of Your Life.* Doubleday, 1996.

VISCOTT, DAVID. *Emotional Resilience: Simple Truths for Dealing with the Unfinished Business of Your Past.* Crown, 1997.

WAKEFIELD, DAN. *The Story of Your Life: Writing a Spiritual Autobiography.* Beacon Press, 1990.

WEISINGER, HENDRIE DAVIS. *Emotional Intelligence at Work: The Untapped Edge for Success.* Jossey-Bass, 1997.

◆ NATURALIST INTELLIGENCE ──────────────

DAVID ABRAM, *The Spell of the Sensuous—Perception and Language in a More-than-Human World.* Pantheon Books, 1996.

GOODALL, JANE. *My Life with the Chimpanzees.* Minstrel Press, 1996.

MCMURRAY, LINDA. *George Washington Carver: Scientist and Symbol.* Oxford Univ. Press, 1982.

THEODORE ROSZAK, MARY GOMES & ALLEN KANNER, eds. *Ecopsychology—Restoring the Earth, Healing the Mind.* Sierra Club Books, 1995.

WILSON, EDWARD O. *Naturalist.* Island Press, 1994.

YI-FU, TUAN. *Topophilia: A Study of Environmental Perception, Attitudes, and Values.* Columbia Univ. Press, 1990.

◆ EXISTENTIAL INTELLIGENCE ──────────────

CAMPBELL, JOSEPH. *The Hero with a Thousand Faces.* Princeton Univ. Press, 1990.

——— *Myths to Live By.* Arkana, 1993.

FRANKL VIKTOR E. *Man's Search for Meaning.* Rev. ed. Washington Square Press, 1998.

GOLEMAN, DANIEL. *The Meditative Mind: Varieties of Meditative Experience.* Tarcher, 1996.

JAMES, WILLIAM. *The Varieties of Religious Experience.* Macmillan, 1997.

JUNG, CARL. *Man and His Symbols.* Laureleaf, 1997.

KRISHNAMURTI, JIDDU. *The Awakening of Intelligence.* Harper San Francisco, 1987.

LESHAN, LAWRENCE. *How to Meditate: A Guide to Self-Discovery.* Bantam, 1984.

OFENER, ROSE. *Journal to the Soul: The Art of Sacred Journal Keeping.* Gibbs Smith, 1996.

◆ MULTIPLE INTELLIGENCES ———————————

ARMSTRONG, THOMAS. *In Their Own Way: Discovering and Encouraging Your Child's Personal Learning Style.* Tarcher, 1987.

———. *Multiple Intelligences in the Classroom.* Association for Supervision and Curriculum Development, 1995.

BOWER, BERT, JIM LOBDELL, and LEE SWENSEN. *History Alive! Engaging All Learners in the Diverse Classroom.* Addison-Wesley, 1994.

CAMPBELL, BRUCE. *The Multiple Intelligences Handbook.* Zephyr, 1994.

CAMPBELL, LINDA, BRUCE CAMPBELL, and DEE DICKINSON. *Teaching and Learning Through Multiple Intelligences.* Allyn and Bacon, 1995.

CHAPMAN, CAROLYN. *If the Shoe Fits: How to Develop Multiple Intelligences in the Classroom.* Skylight, 1993.

————, and LYNN FREEMAN. *Multiple Intelligences Centers and Projects*. Skylight, 1997.

FOGARTY, ROBIN, ed. *Multiple Intelligences: A Collection*. Skylight, 1996.

————, and JUDY STOEHR. *Integrating the Curriculum with Multiple Intelligences*. Skylight, 1995.

GARDNER, HOWARD. *Frames of Mind: The Theory of Multiple Intelligences*. Basic Books, 1983.

————. *Multiple Intelligences: The Theory in Practice*. Basic Books, 1993.

————. *Creating Minds: An Anatomy of Creativity Seen Through the Eyes of Freud, Einstein, Picasso, Stravinsky, Eliot, Graham, and Gandhi*. Basic Books, 1994.

————. *Intelligence Reframed: Multiple Intelligences for the 21st Century*. Basic Books, 1999.

HAGGERTY, BRIAN. *Nurturing Intelligences*. Addison-Wesley, 1994.

LAZEAR, DAVID. *Multiple Intelligence Approaches to Assessment*. Zephyr, 1994.

————. *Seven Pathways of Learning: Teaching Students and Parents about Multiple Intelligences*. Zephyr, 1994.

————. *Seven Ways of Knowing: Teaching for Multiple Intelligences*. Skylight, 1991.

————. *Seven Ways of Teaching: The Artistry of Teaching for Multiple Intelligences*. Skylight, 1991.

NELSON, KRISTIN. *Developing Students' Multiple Intelligences*. Scholastic, 1998.

NEW CITY SCHOOL. *Celebrating Multiple Intelligences*. Order from New City School, 5209 Waterman Ave., St. Louis, MO 63108.

O'CONNOR, ANNA, and SHEILA CALLAHAN-YOUNG. *Seven Windows to a Child's World: 100 Ideas for the Multiple Intelligences Classroom*. Skylight, 1994.

TORFF, BRUCE, ed. *Multiple Intelligences and Assessment: A Collection of Articles.* Skylight, 1997.

"Teaching for Multiple Intelligences." Special issue of *Educational Leadership,* September 1997 Available through the Association for Supervision and Curriculum Development, 1-800-933-2723.

WAHL, MARK. *Math for Humans: Teaching Math Through 7 Intelligences.* LivnLern Press, 1997.

◆ ORGANIZATIONS AND INTERNET SITES ──────

◆ MULTIPLE INTELLIGENCES ───────────────────

Association for Supervision and Curriculum Development, 1703 North Beauregard Street, Alexandria, VA 22311-1711; 703-578-9600 or 800-933-ASCD; fax 704-575-5400; www.ascd.org. Publishes my book *Multiple Intelligences in the Classroom* and also other materials on multiple intelligences, including *Multiple Intelligences* CD-ROM and *Multiple Intelligences* video series.

Harvard Project Zero, Harvard Graduate School of Education, 323 Longfellow Hall, Appian Way, Cambridge, MA 02138; 617-495-4342; fax 617-495-9709; www.pz.harvard.edu. The research and organizational umbrella under which Dr. Howard Gardner created and is developing the theory of multiple intelligences. If you write them and make a specific request, they will send you a list of schools using multiple intelligences around the country, and a catalog listing their various publications.

National Professional Resources, 25 South Regent Street, Port Chester, NY 10573, 914-937-8879. Producer of several videos on multiple intelligences, including Howard Gardner, *How Are Kids Smart?*, Jo Gusman, *MI and the Second Language Learner,* and Thomas

Armstrong, *Multiple Intelligences: Discovering the Giftedness in All.*

New Horizons for Learning, P.O. Box 15329, Seattle, WA 98115; 206-547-7936; www.newhorizons.org. An online learning community that includes much information about multiple intelligences and other new learning approaches.

Skylight Publications, 2626 S. Clearbrook Drive, Arlington Heights, IL 60005-5310; www.iriskylight.com. A division of Simon and Schuster, it is a publisher and distributor of many multiple intelligences resources.

University of California, Education Extension. Multiple Intelligences Teacher Certification Program, 1200 University Avenue, Riverside, CA 92507-4596; 909-787-4361, ext. 1663; e-mail: steele@ucx.ucr.edu. Runs two week-long summer institutes on multiple intelligences and a variety of other courses during the school year that lead to the only teachers' certificate in multiple intelligences in the world.

Zephyr Press, P.O. Box 66006, Tucson, AZ 85728; 602-322-5090; www.zephyrpress.com. Publisher and distributor of many multiple intelligences resources.

◆ LINGUISTIC INTELLIGENCE ───────────────────

Amazon.com, www.amazon.com. The world's largest bookstore.

Books on Tape, Inc., P.O. Box 7900, Newport Beach, CA 92658; 800-626-3333; fax 949-548-6574; e-mail: botcs @booksontape.com; http://www.booksontape.com/.

Great Books Foundation, 35 East Wacker Drive, Suite 2300, Chicago, IL 60601-2298; 800-222-5870; fax 312-407-0334; http://greatbooks.com/.

HarperAudio—Caedmon, http://www.harperaudio.com. Quality audio recordings of great books.

InkSpot, www.inkspot.com. Writer's resources.

LitWeb, http://streams.com/litweb. Writers can contribute to an interactive journal, write on specific topics, and read classifieds related to the writing profession.

Living Poets Society, www.linda.com/. Offers poets of any age and background the opportunity to share their work and publish it electronically.

Mad Libs, http://hel.uns.tju.edu/madlib/. Fill in interactive form with parts of speech to create wacky stories.

National Speakers Association, 1500 South Priest Drive, Tempe, AZ 85281; 602-968-2552, 602-968-0911; e-mail: nsasmain@aol.com; http://www.nsaspeaker.org.

Newsword, http://www.polar7.com/cc/. Archive of crossword puzzles.

Scrabble Home Page—Official, http://www.scrabble.com/home.html. Play on-line against a computer.

Toastmasters International, P.O. Box 9052, Mission Viejo, CA 92690; 949-858-8255; fax 949-858-1207; e-mail: tminfo@toastmasters.org.

◆ LOGICAL-MATHEMATICAL INTELLIGENCE —————————

Amateur Science, http://www.eskimo.com/~bilb/amasci.-html. Promotes science literacy by bringing together experts and amateurs in science.

American Association for the Advancement of Science, 1200 New York Avenue NW, Washington, DC 20005; 202-326-6400; http://www.aaas.org.

Edmund Scientific Company, 101 East Gloucester Pike, Barrington, NJ 08007-1380; 609-573-6250, 609-573-6295; http://www.edmundscientific.com/.

Family Math Program, EQUALS, Lawrence Hall of Science,

University of California, Berkeley, CA 94720; e-mail: equals@uclink.berkeley.edu; http://equals.lhs.berkeley.edu/fm.sites.html.

MathMania, http://csr.uvic.ca/!mmania. Work on unsolved problems in mathematics.

Math, http://forum.swarthmore.cdu. Wealth of information about math topics from Swarthmore College.

Mathematical Association of America, 1529 18th Street NW, Washington, DC 20036-1385; 800-741-9415, 202-387-5200; fax 202-265-2384; http://www.maa.org/.

Mathematics Archives, http://archives.math.utk.edu. Wide range of math resources, links, software, and more.

Museum of Science and Industry, http://www.msichicago.org. Visit Chicago's famed Museum of Science and Industry through virtual exhibits.

Popular Science Online, http://www.popsci.com. Covers the latest in automotive industry, computers, electronics, and home technology.

Science Online, http://sciencemag.org. E-zine developed by the American Association for the Advancement of Science.

Scientific American, http://www.sciam.com. Post questions to scientists, read articles from the print magazine, link to other sites.

◆ BODILY-KINESTHETIC INTELLIGENCE ─────────────

Amateur Athletic Union, P.O. Box 10000, Lake Buena Vista, FL 32830-1000; 800-228-4872, 407-934-7200.

American Running and Fitness Association, 4405 East West Highway, Suite 405, Bethesda, MD 20814; 301-913-9517, 800-776-ARFA; fax 301-913-9520; e-mail: arfarun@aol.com; http://www.arfa.org.

Fit-Net, http:///www.fit-net.com. Provides information

about local health clubs, personal trainers, contests, training camps, and other fitness sites.

Fitness Zone, http://www.fitnesszone.com. On-line information about fitness equipment.

Juggling.org. http:///www.juggling.org. Based at Indiana University, provides info on festivals, local organizations, juggling software, and products.

Martial Arts Network, http://www.martial-art-network. com. Includes chat rooms, bulletin boards, calendars, shopping mall, and information about martial arts styles of the world.

National Outdoor Leadership School, 288 Main Street, Lander, WY 82520-3140; 307-332-6973; fax 307-332-1220; e-mail: admissions@nols.edu; http://www. nols. edu/NOLS.html.

Sports Medicine Online, http://sports-med.com. Information on injury prevention, treatment, conditioning, and more.

Outward Bound USA, Route 9D, R2 Box 280, Garrison, NY 10524-9757; 800-243-8520, 914-424-4000.

◆ MUSICAL INTELLIGENCE ─────────────────────

AudioNet CD Jukebox, http:///ww2.audionet.com/jukebox. Hundreds of CDs are available on-line through this Internet broadcast site.

CDNow, http://cdnow.com. Huge Internet music store. Locate CDs by artist, title, or genre.

Library of Musical Links, http://www.wco.com/~jrush/ music. Alphabetized lists of music-related Internet links in several categories including music genres and styles, band and artist home pages, and musical instruments.

National Academy of Songwriters, 6255 Sunset Boulevard,

Suite 1023, Hollywood, CA 90028; 800-826-7287, 323-463-7178; fax 323-463-2146; http://www.nassong.org/.

Suzuki Association of the Americas, P.O. Box 17310, Boulder, CO 80308; 303-444-0948; fax 303-444-0984; e-mail: Suzuki@rmi.net; http://www.suzukiassociation.org/.

◆ SPATIAL INTELLIGENCE ─────────────────────────

American Institute of Graphic Arts, http://www.dol.com/AIGA. Includes gallery and information about local chapters, events, and programs around the country.

Artist's Resource, http://www.number9.com. Includes databases of artists and art services, list of gallery openings, and information on displaying your art work on the site.

Cinemania, http://cinemania.msn.com/Cinemania/Home.asp. Reviews latest film releases, interviews, polls. Supplements Microsoft's film-review software program Cinemania.

Design Architecture, http://cornishproductions.com. Includes interviews with famous architects, archive of architectural inks, and bulletin board.

Kodak, http://kodak.com. The home page for the Eastman Kodak Company leads to loads of information for both the amateur and professional photographer.

Photographic Society of America, Inc., 3000 United Founders Boulevard, Suite 103, Oklahoma City, OK 73112-3940; e-mail: hq@psaphoto.org; http://www.psaphoto.org/.

◆ INTERPERSONAL INTELLIGENCE ─────────────

American Association for Marriage and Family Therapy, http://www.aamft.org. Information on topics related to adoption, alcoholism, divorce, finding a therapist, and marriage wellness.

Gordon Training International, http://www.webcom.com/ gordon. Resources, training, and information on communication, conflict resolution, and leadership development.

The National Conference for Community and Justice, http://www.nccj.org. Organization for fighting bias, bigotry, and racism in America.

Peace Corps, 1111 20th Street NW, Washington, DC 20526; 800-424-8580; http://www.peacecorps.gov/.

◆ INTRAPERSONAL INTELLIGENCE ─────────────

American Humanist Association, 7 Harwood Drive, P.O. Box 1188, Amherst, NY 14226-7188; 800-743-6646, 716-839-5080; fax 716-839-5079; e-mail: humanism @juno.com; http://humanist.net/.

Association for Humanistic Psychology, 45 Franklin Street, Suite 315, San Francisco, CA 94102; 415-864-8850; e-mail: ahpoffice@aol.com; http://www.ahpweb.org/.

Association for the Study of Dreams, P.O. Box 1600, Vienna, VA 22183; 703-242-0062; fax 703-242-8888; e-mail: asdreams@aol.com; http://www.ASDreams.org.

Esalen Institute, Highway 1, Big Sur, CA 93920-9616; 831-667-3000; fax 831-667-2724; http://www.esalen.org/.

Focusing Institute, 34 East Lane, Spring Valley, NY 10977; 914-362-5222; e-mail: info@focusing.org; http://www. focusing.org/.

Naropa Institute, 2130 Arapahoe Avenue, Boulder, CO

80302; 303-444-0202; fax 303-444-0410; e-mail: admissions@naropa.edu; http://www.naropa.edu/.

National Association for Self-Esteem, http://www.selfesteemnase.org. Information about books, videos, speakers, and events related to self-esteem development.

◆ NATURALIST INTELLIGENCE ─────────────────────

National Audubon Society, 700 Broadway, New York, NY 10003; 212-979-3000; fax 202-979-3188; e-mail: webmaster@list.audubon.org; http://www.audubon.org/.

National Geographic Society, 1145 17th Street, N.W., Washington, DC 20036-4688; 1-800-NGS-LINE; National Geographic Online: http://www.nationalgeographic.com/.

The Nature Company On-Line Customer Service, P.O. Box 6432, Florence, KY 41022-6432; 800-477-8828; e-mail: DCOL Service@discovery;.com; http://www.natureco.com/index.html.

Sierra Club, 85 Second Street, Second Floor, San Francisco, CA 94105-3441; 415-944-5500; fax 415-977-5799; http://www.sierraclub.org/.

◆ EXISTENTIAL INTELLIGENCE ─────────────────────

Association for Research and Enlightenment, P.O. Box 595, Virginia Beach, VA 23451; 800-333-4499, 757-428-3588; http://www.are-cayce.com/.

Association for Transpersonal Psychology, P.O. Box 3049, Stanford, CA 94309; 650-327-2066; http://www.igc.org/atp/.

Foundation for Mind Research, P.O. Box 3300, Pomona,

NY 10970; 914-354-3288; http://www.jeanhouston.
org/foundation.html.

Insight Meditation Society, 1230 Pleasant Street, Barre, MA
01005; 978-355-4378; http://www.dharma.org/ims.
htm.

Institute of Noetic Sciences, 475 Gate Five Road, Suite
300, Sausalito, CA 94965; 415-331-5650; fax: 415-331-
5673; e-mail: Webmaster@noetic.org; http://www.
noetic.org/.

◆ COMPUTER SOFTWARE ───────────────

I used to think that computers were designed for the
logical-mathematical person. This misunderstanding
emerged, I suppose, from my stereotypical image of the
"computer nerd" whose PC or mainframe existed at the
hub of a super-rational universe. The truth, of course, is
that a computer can help each of the seven intelligences,
depending on the kind of software program driving it.
The following is a rundown of some of the high-tech
possibilities for each intelligence. Many of these programs,
especially those that are multimedia-oriented programs
that integrate images, words, sounds, and action, involve
several intelligences. I've generally placed them in the intelligence category that seems to be dominant in each
case. Also, since most of the programs are self-paced, they
are geared to intrapersonal intelligence, although a number of them also provide opportunities for interaction with
others. In most cases I've left off any reference to level,
upgrade, or version since these will have undoubtedly
changed by the time you read this book. The programs
listed here are not necessarily the most highly rated of
each type; they are illustrative only. Check with your local
computer software outlet, consumer guides, or Internet

sites for a list of recommended programs, as well as for specific hardware requirements for each program.

◆ LINGUISTIC —————————————————————————

Word processing: Microsoft Word, Corel WordPerfect

Encyclopedias: Encyclopedia Britannica CD, Microsoft Encarta, Compton's Interactive Encyclopedia (The Learning Company), Grolier Multimedia Encyclopedia (Grolier Interactive)

Other reference guides: Microsoft Bookshelf

Foreign language instruction and translation software: Easy Translator (Transparent Language), Learn to Speak Spanish (The Learning Company), Italian for Everyone (The Learning Company)

Typing tutors: Mavis Beacon Teaches Typing (Mindscape)

Web site creation software: Front Page (Microsoft)

Dictation software: Via Voice (IBM), Kurzweil Voice Pad (Alpha Software)

◆ LOGICAL-MATHEMATICAL —————————————————

Database management: Microsoft Access, My Data Base (My Software Company), Lotus Organizer

Desktop publishing: The Print Shop (Broderbund), Publish It (Macmillan), Print Master Deluxe (Mindscape), Home Publishing (Microsoft)

Financial management programs: Quicken Deluxe (Intuit), Microsoft Money, Business Plan Pro (Palo Alto Software), Peachtree Accounting

Science reference guides: Encyclopedia of Science (DK Interactive), The Universe: From Quarks to the Cosmos (Scientific American Library)

Science study tools: RedShift: The Ultimate Hands-On Planetarium (Pirana)
Logical game software: Chessmaster 5500 (Mindscape)
Math skills tutorials: Math Library (The Learning Company)
Spreadsheets: Lotus Spreadsheet
Computer programming tutors: Turbo Basic

◆ SPATIAL ————————————————————————

Graphic image processing: Print Artist (Sierra Home), Picture It! (Microsoft)
Art history guides: History Through Art (Zane Home Library)
Home and landscape design software: Floor Plan 3D (IMSI), Bob Vila's Home Design (Compton's Home Library), Complete LandDesigner (Sierra), 3D Home Architect (Broderbund)
Maps and atlases: Eyewitness World Atlas (DK Multimedia)
Computer-aided design (CAD) programs: Quick CAD (Autodesk), Key CAD (Creative Office)
Graphic image (clip-art) libraries: Master Clips (IMSI), One Million Images (Corel), Imagine It! (Macmillan)
Photo-processing software: Adobe Photo Deluxe, Photo-Paint (Corel), Photo Suite (MGI), Picture Publisher (Micrographx)
Video-processing software: Video Wave (MGI), Lumiere Video Studio (IMSI)
Draw and paint programs: Dazzle Draw
Spatial problem-solving games and puzzles: Tetris, Living Jigsaws

◆ BODILY-KINESTHETIC ————————————————

Human anatomy and health reference guides: A.D.A.M. Deluxe: All-in-One Anatomy Program and Family

Health Guide (Mindscape/ADAM Software), Body-
Works (The Learning Company)

Physical fitness software: Active Trainer (LaserMedia)

High-action simulation software: Flight Simulator
(Microsoft)

Action play and arcade games: various titles involving Star
Wars, Star Trek, military, detective, police, and automotive themes

Sports software: Golf Pro (Sierra Sports), NCAA Football
(EA Sports), Baseball Pro (Sierra Sports), Indy Car
Racing (Papyrus), World Cup (EA Sports)

Hands-on construction kits that interface with computers:
Lego to Logo

Virtual-reality system software: Dactyl Nightmare

Tools that plug into computers: Science Toolkit

◆ MUSICAL ──────────────────────────────────────

Musical recording and mixing software: Music Studio
(Magix Entertainment), Mixman Studio (Mixman),
Midisoft Studio Recording Session (Midisoft)

Musical notation programs: Desktop Sheet Music (Midisoft)

Musical instrument instruction software: Interactive Guitar
(Playpro), Teach Me Piano (Voyetra), Guitar 101
(Fender)

Tone-recognition and melody-memory enhancers: Arnold

Singing software (transforms voice input into synthesizer
sounds): Vocalizer

Music literature tutors: Exploratorium

◆ INTERPERSONAL ────────────────────────────────

Mailing list programs: My Mail List and Address Book (My
Software Company)

Geneology programs: Create Family Trees Quick & Easy (Individual), Family Tree Maker (Broderbund), Generations (Sierra), Ultimate Family Tree (Paladium Interactive)

Electronic phone books: 88 Million Households Phone Book (CD USA), Select Phone (Pro CD), Streets USA (CD USA)

Board games: electronic versions of popular board games such as Monopoly, Scrabble, Risk, Chess, etc., which themselves involve diverse intelligences—see Games section

Role-play, strategy, and war games: Age of Empires (Microsoft), Civilization (Micro Prose Strategy), Dune (Westwood), Sim City (Electronic Arts)

◆ INTRAPERSONAL ───────────────────────────────

Career search software: What Color Is Your Parachute? (Bumblebee Technologies), Career Finder (Info USA)

Fashion software: Cosmopolitan Virtual Makeover (SegaSoft)

Self-understanding software: Emotional IQ Test (Virtual Entertainment), Personality Test (Virtual Entertainment)

Fantasy software: Riven, Myst (Broderbund/Red Orb)

◆ GAMES ──────────────────────────────────────

Playing commercially made games is a particularly enjoyable way to develop the seven intelligences. The following can be found in most toy stores and in the toy and game departments of many department and discount stores (or try Internet sites such as www.faoschwartz.com

and www.toys.com). Many of the games I've put under the logical-mathematical category also help develop spatial intelligence (e.g., chess, checkers, Othello, Connect Four). Most of the games help develop interpersonal intelligence through the process of give-and-take, rule negotiation, and other forms of social interaction during the game (including bluffing!). Except for generic games like chess, I've usually included the brand name and manufacturer, as well as an age range, so that you can involve other members of your family in the development of their multiple intelligences through games.

◆ LINGUISTIC

Scrabble (Milton Bradley—age 8+)
Blurt (Patch—10+)
Boggle (Parker Brothers—8+)
Outburst: The Game of Verbal Explosions (Parker Brothers)
Mastermind: Crack the Word Code! (Pressman—6+)
Mad Gab (Patch—10+)
Password (England Games)
Scattergories (Milton Bradley—12+)
Trivial Pursuit (Parker Brothers)
Upwords (Milton Bradley—10+)
Balderdash (Parker Brothers—10+)

◆ LOGICAL-MATHEMATICAL

Poker
Keeno
Backgammon
Bingo

Dominoes
Chess
Checkers
Chinese Checkers
Clue (Parker Brothers—9+)
Connect Four: The Vertical Checkers Game (Milton
    Bradley—7+)
Guess Who (Milton Bradley—6+)
Monopoly (Parker Brothers—8+)
Mastermind (Pressman—8+)
Othello (Pressman—8+)
Payday (Parker Brothers—8+)
Parcheesi (Milton Bradley—7+)
Quarto (Pressman—8+)
Racko (Parker Brothers—8+)
Sequence (Jax—7+)
Triominoes (Pressman—8+)
30 Second Mysteries (University Games—12+)
Where in the USA Is Carmen San Diego (University
    Games—8+)
Where in Time Is Carmen San Diego (University
    Games—8+)
Yahtzee (Milton Bradley—8+)

◆ SPATIAL ───

Tic-Tac-Toe
Pin the Tail on the Donkey
Battleship (Milton Bradley—7+)
Pictionary (Milton Bradley—12+)
Myst (University Games—10+)
Stratego (Winning Moves—10+)

◆ MUSICAL ────────────────────────────────

Encore: The Memory Game of Lyrics and Laughs
NoteAbility: The Name-the-Song Game
Song Burst: The Complete-the-Lyric Game
Simon (Milton Bradley)
Pocket Simon (Milton Bradley)
Henry: Match the Sounds Memory Game (Tiger Electronic
    Games—5+)

◆ BODILY-KINESTHETIC ──────────────────────

Jacks
Tiddly-Winks
Pick-up Sticks
Guesstures: The Game of Split-Second Charades (Milton
    Bradley—12+)
Jenga (Milton Bradley—8+)
Ker-Plunk (Tyco—5+)
Twister: The Game That Ties You Up in Knots (Milton
    Bradley—6+)

◆ INTERPERSONAL ───────────────────────────

Family Feud (Endless Games—8+)
Game of the Year (University Games—8+)
Ouija (Parker Brothers—8+)
Life Stories
Scruples

◆ INTRAPERSONAL ─────────────────────────────────

Careers (Pressman—8+)
Life (Milton Bradley—9+)
Risk (Parker Brothers—10+)
Judge n' Jury (Winning Moves—12+)
Therapy: The Game
True Colors
The Ungame

INDEX

TO CONTACT THE AUTHOR

For those who'd like additional information about Dr. Armstrong's work regarding multiple intelligences (including information on books, videos, presentations, web links, and other resources), please visit his website at www.thomasarmstrong.com. You can also send e-mail to him directly at thomas@thomasarmstrong.com or write him at P.O. Box 548, Cloverdale, CA 95425.

PLUME

Self-Improvement

SMART SPEAKING *60-Second Strategies for More Than 100 Speaking Problems and Fears* **by Laurie Schloff and Marcia Yudkin.** A fast, easy, problem-solving guide to communicating effectively in a multitude of situations. 0-452-26777-3 $12.95

PERSUADING ON PAPER *The Complete Guide to Writing Copy That Pulls in Business* **by Marcia Yudkin.** Learn to write copy that improves your image, attracts more business, and increases profits.
0-452-27313-7 $12.95

THE OVERWHELMED PERSON'S GUIDE TO TIME MANAGEMENT by Ronni Eisenberg with Kate Kelly. The ultimate guide to giving yourself more time for everything. 0-452-27682-9 $12.95

TOUGHNESS TRAINING FOR LIFE *A Revolutionary Program for Maximizing Health, Happiness, and Productivity* **by James E. Loehr, Ed.D.** This empowering guide shows you how to master stress and blend strength with resiliency to achieve peak performance in all aspects of life.
0-452-27243-2 $12.95

Prices slightly higher in Canada.